# BUCK McNAIR
# CANADIAN SPITFIRE ACE

# BUCK McNAIR

## CANADIAN SPITFIRE ACE

Norman Franks

The story of Group Captain R W McNair
DSO, DFC & 2 Bars, Ld'H, CdG, RCAF

GRUB STREET · LONDON

Published by
Grub Street
The Basement
10 Chivalry Road
London SW11 1HT

**British Library Cataloguing in Publication Data**
Franks, Norman K. R. (Norman Leslie Robert), 1940-
 Buck McNair: Canadian Spitfire Ace: the story of Group
 Captain R. W. McNair DSO, DFC & 2 Bars, Ld'H, CdG, RCAF
 1. McNair, Robert 2. Canada. Royal Canadian Air Force –
 History 3. Air pilots – Canada
 I. Title
 358.4'0092

**ISBN 1 902304 74 8**

Edited by Amy Myers

Typeset by Pearl Graphics, Hemel Hempstead

Printed and bound in Great Britain by
Biddles Ltd, Guildford and King's Lynn

Buck had the true 'royal jelly' of leadership. I would have followed that
guy to hell and back and so would most who knew him well. He was a rare
and gallant man, able to draw the best out of all who served with him.

The Honourable Douglas R Matheson QC
former Flight Lieutenant RCAF

CONTENTS

# ACKNOWLEDGEMENTS

This story could not have been told without the generous help of Barbara McNair. It has been a pleasure listening to her recollections and memories of her husband Robert and I am naturally indebted to her. I only hope what has emerged does justice to his memory.

I have also been helped by Robert's son Bruce, an eminent judge in Hong Kong. He has searched the internet on my behalf, and it was he and his late brother Keith who discovered the original notes taken by Ivers Kelly at the end of the war. He had wanted to write of Robert's war experiences. Circumstances made that impossible, but the boys traced him before his death and secured their father's memories and permission to use them. Ken McNair, Robert's brother, I am also indebted to.

At the very beginning I was glad to have on my side a very great gentleman, Rod Smith DFC, a fighter pilot of distinction, who saw considerable action over France, and over Malta during World War Two. Our telephone conversations from his home in Vancouver have been helpful, interesting, warming and encouraging. His taped thoughts about his friend Buck were gratefully received.

Several of Buck McNair's wartime comrades have been interested enough to write and give their recollections of the man and the air fighter. In no particular order I have to thank the following: John Sherlock DFC, (Calgary), George Aitken (Edmonton), Karl Linton DFC (Halifax, NS), The Hon Douglas Matheson QC (Edmonton), R G 'Bob' Middlemiss DFC (Barrie, Ont), Art Sager DFC (Aix en Provence, France), Don Laubman DFC (Alberta), Hugh Godefroy DSO DFC MD (including permission to quote from his book *Lucky Thirteen*), Gordon Lapp DFC BSc MD, (BC), John Stock (Mississauga, Ontario), William 'Tex' Ash MBE (London, England), Baron Michael Donnet CVO DFC CdG FRAeS, and post-war, Serge Morin (Montreal) and Moses Rothman.

Others, friends and acquaintances, also have my thanks. Mrs Jill Lucas for access to her husband's photo album and for permission to quote from *Malta, The Thorn in Rommel's Side*, Chris Goss, Brian Cull, Ken Nelson (Whitby, Ontario), Mary Beard, Robbins Elliott (Wolfville, NS), Ray Mills and Larry Milberry.

# An Appreciation

BY

Lieutenant-General Baron Michael Donnet
CVO DFC CdG (Belg) FRAeS

I first met Robert McNair in November 1941 when, as a member of 411 Royal Canadian Air Force Squadron, he arrived at RAF Hornchurch. His unit was to be one of the squadrons of the Wing. At that time I was a member of 64, another of the three squadrons in the Wing.

I noticed Buck, who appeared an outstanding character with authority, a real leader, outspoken but at the same time ready to listen before putting out his own views. We became good friends and we were able to talk together about many subjects of different nature. He had an open mind, but was able to stand firm on those important points he felt essential. More than once we were out together in our spare time and he always showed the same enthusiasm and the same high spirit. He would enliven any gathering.

When more intensive air operations began, Buck was always at the head of his team and his leadership inspired those under his command. He always had a protective eye for each of them. He led them in flight with success. As a fighter pilot he was outstanding.

Buck and I met again many times during the war years even though we were no longer members of the same Wing. We always enjoyed seeing each other and we had so many tales to exchange between us. His views were those of a wise man.

For nearly thirty years we saw each other from time to time. At one stage he was with No.4 ATAF, while I was chief of staff of No.2 ATAF, both with headquarters in Germany. Finally we were together in London, both of us as members of our respective Embassy. Beside out official functions, we enjoyed our friendship, which had started so long before, and which had remained strong over all those years.

Buck's last fight was an example of courage and determination as it had been in front of the enemy. He accepted the challenge and stood firm, until he felt beaten by the illness. We miss Buck, a great warrior, a born leader, a man with a kind heart, who did not spare any effort for those under his command, an outspoken man with character but also full of kindness. We miss him but will never forget him.

FOR KEITH MCNAIR
1949–1998

# CHAPTER ONE

# THE BOY FROM NOVA SCOTIA

## Goodbye to All That

Telegrams can often bring bad news. The one that arrived for Wing Commander Buck McNair just as his Devon honeymoon was coming to an end could have heralded many things: a promotion, another job, or even a recall to duty. The invasion of Europe was in the offing – this could mean he was needed back with his Spitfire fighter wing. It might just conceivably be about that medical examination by Cam McArthur, the Wing MO.

Opening the envelope, he read the contents, which told him he was to report to No.127 Wing Headquarters upon his return. It was not what he had expected. No recall, no promotion, and if this was a new job, it wasn't what he wanted. He was a fighter pilot, and he wanted to be around for the invasion that could not be that far away.

He had flown his last operational sortie on the last day but one of March 1944. Then came the wedding to his fiancée, Barbara Still, whom he called 'Pip', on Easter Sunday. He had been granted ten days' leave, and that telegram had spoiled the end of it. He was pretty certain what it was all about but he kept the truth from his new bride until he knew for certain. Perhaps he could yet still wangle something before things went too far.

Returning to Surrey, Buck McNair went to see Air Commodore Livingstone, a fellow Canadian in the Royal Air Force and a senior eye surgeon. He confirmed what Buck already knew, that his left eye was all but useless. The thrombosis in it had all but dried up but it left poor and blurred vision, something akin to looking through a myriad of tiny dots. He was immediately sent off to a RCAF hospital for a couple of weeks, but there was no getting away from it. His operational days were over. He had come a long way.

When he finally sat in front of a Group Captain he'd known for a long time, the man confirmed it kindly but bluntly. He had done more than his share. Time to let others take up the torch.

'You know that George Keefer has taken over the Wing?'

'Yes,' said McNair. It was one of the first things Buck had asked about. 'George will do a good job.'

'We've got one or two things planned for you,' continued the Group Captain, and no doubt your new wife will be happy you're out of it.' McNair smiled, knowing that until it was set in concrete he probably wouldn't tell

1

her. He was no doubt hoping he could get in a few Ops when the invasion came, but he was kidding himself. He knew only too well his eyes were giving him increasing problems, especially the left one. He was becoming a danger to others not just to himself. Men relied on his tactical thinking and the ability to judge instantly a situation, and that judgement would be marred if he couldn't see immediately any problems that developed in the air. War in a fighter aeroplane was instant, immediate, needing quick reactions; there was no room for hesitation for whatever reason.

He had flown almost 200 major operational sorties since his return from Malta two years earlier. Of these the last sixty had been whilst leading No.126 Canadian Wing, in charge of Spitfire Squadrons – 401, 411 and 412. Thirty-five young men relied on him each wing show. His experience could no longer get him by. The road had come to an end.

*   *   *

**The Start of All That**

That road had started several thousand miles away, in the small town of Springfield, in Annapolis County, Nova Scotia, Canada. He was the middle boy of three, born 15 May 1919, just six months after the end of the Great War of 1914-18 and given the names Robert Wendell. His parents were Kenneth Frank McNair and Hilda May McNair, née Grimm. Kenneth McNair had been overseas in France during World War One. It had not been pleasant. He'd been gassed on one occasion, and his time in the trenches had been long.

Buck had an elder brother, Franklyn – Frank – and another brother, Ken, would come along later. Springfield was a quiet town, virtually a village, of about 1,000 souls, virtually all descendants of early pioneers, many distantly related to each other. Indeed there had been few newcomers to the area for several generations. The family name had originally been spelt McNayr. His great-grandfather had been a pioneer settler of the district and had come from Boyd, Scotland. This great-grandfather lived in this rural area at a time that saw the start of mail service deliveries to houses and farmsteads off the beaten track. One member of the family began delivering mail, warning people of his approach with the use of a horn, which young Robert McNair knew was still in the possesion of the family when he was young.

Boyd McNayr came into the world in 1778 and married Rachel Beals in 1802. Of two sons by this marriage, John and Israel, the latter had, having married Elizabeth Roop in 1829, produced another Boyd McNayr in 1830. From this union came Emma (who married Edgar Mullock, and later John Mullock, and had two sons, Fred and Vernon) and Oscar in 1858; the latter married Alice Mullock in 1882.

Robert's father was the youngest of their three sons (Percy, Lorne and Kenneth *McNair*), there were no daughters, and one of the boys had moved to the USA to farm. Robert's father, born in 1891, and another uncle had both gone into the Canadian Pacific Railway, where Kenneth become a conductor. No one in the town was rich, but then no one was destitute either. The town/village was self-sustaining with independent citizens mostly of British ancestry. It was situated in a fertile valley where fruit was the main crop, while during the harsh winter months the men worked at pulp lumbering. Wood was hauled in by oxen and horses to a huge mill. This was later to burn down, but there were a number of smaller mills which continued to operate.

The area was pretty rich in game too and like many other Canadians across the whole country, huntin', shootin' and fishin' were a way of life. Their religion was mostly 'chapel'; baptist and presbyterian churches predominated. If any strangers did arrive in the valley they were usually men of the clergy. There were few newcomers, but one new family was the Grimms. Mister Grimm senior, came from German stock, a merchant shipper, who had retired to Springfield, settled and purchased a small shop, running it as a sort of general store. The man's father had earlier married an English woman whose maiden name had been Milne, and the union produced eleven children, one of whom Robert's father was destined to marry at the time of the Great War, Hilda May Grimm, who was seven years younger than Kenneth.

More of Robert's early life was spent with the Grimm family than with the McNairs. This led to him becoming the product of both Scottish and German influences, not only from genetics but in personal contact, which made him both determined and stubborn.

The three McNair brothers swam a good deal, mostly nude, in the lake, which was about 1-1½ miles long by a mile wide. This usually took place by the saw mill, and the bottom of the lake was covered with water-logged sawdust. It gave the bottom a fine, spongy feel. They could also use the lake in winter, but for ice skating! Robert and Ken were also ardent fishermen, although Frank was not so taken.

Robert's early schooling took place in a one-room schoolhouse in Lake Pleasant, two or three miles from Springfield, but when he was about nine, the family moved to North Battleford, Saskatchewan, on the North Saskatchewan River, although they only remained there about a year. It was quite a distance across the vast Canadian land mass. Here Robert attended school before a further move saw the family go to Rocky Mountain House, Alberta, where they remained for less than a year.

Out west there wasn't much swimming, although his father once carried him on his back whilst swimming across the North Saskatchewan River. Robert played hockey and loved rugby. Once, whilst playing for Prince Albert C.I., he had the ball and was running toward the end. As he was tackled, he was grabbed so tightly his whole outfit was ripped off, but he continued running with just the ball. Determined and stubborn!

Moving once more this time a little further west, to Edmonton, Alberta, they stayed put for three or four years, Robert's school now being Kenora Public School, in the west end of the city. Among Robert's school chums were two brothers, Bob and Doug Matheson. Bob was more Robert's age, but Doug remembers Robert. He would come to their house, but being 18 months junior, Doug was considered to be strictly 'out of it'. As it turned out, Doug was later to fly in the same fighter squadron as Robert.

The family left Edmonton, returning east again, when Robert's father was ill. McNair senior had been paying taxes on his father's farm at Lake Pleasant but it had become vacant so the family took up residence there. This only lasted two years and they then returned west, to Prince Albert, Saskatchewan, where Robert attended the local high school.

Robert's father bought the boys a car, a Ford Model A. Robert was too young to have a licence but this didn't preclude him from driving it in order to chase the half-dozen milchcows up from the fields for milking. On one occasion, mother asked him to drive into town to buy oil for the lamps, seeing him off with her usual: 'Come back at once!' However, in town Robert met his cousin Johnny Grimm and they decided to go off for a drive. It got dark and began sleeting as they were parked on a hill and as he then pulled away he skidded, hitting something which inflicted some minor damage to one wheel and the fender. When he finally got home he had some explaining to do to his mother.

Reaching the age of 15, Robert decided to go into the logging business, but needed oxen 'power' to haul timber out of the woods. His cousin Maynard Grimm, who had an experimental farm near Springfield, gave him two calf steers, Robert undertaking to break them in as a pair of oxen. That winter he made a bobsleigh, and having passed the stage of having to lead the animals, could now ride the sleigh by being pulled by the two steers.

He was regularly seen out shopping, driving them into town pulling him on the sleigh. It did not, of course, raise that much interest, but a few who saw him thought the animals 'cute'. They were certainly powerful, slow and friendly.

Came the time it was decided that the family should head west and rejoin McNair senior, Robert helped 'Uncle' Maynard to slaughter the two steers, and three cows. There seemed to be little sentiment. Robert held onto the oxen while Maynard brought down a great sledge-hammer blow onto their foreheads. The stunned animals collapsed and this gave them the opportunity to cut their throats, then skin them. Robert himself was given the task of stunning one of the cows, after being carefully instructed to hit it low between the eyes.

It was now that Robert first became actively interested in aeroplanes (airplanes in North America). As teenagers, all three boys helped out with a floatplane which operated from the North Saskatchewan River and another one at Yellowknife, on the northern shore of Great Slave Lake, North West Territories. Robert's brother Ken recalls this time:

> 'Our Father worked for the C.N. Railway. In the early thirties our Mother and we three boys went back to Springfield, Nova Scotia and lived on the family homestead for around three years. Meanwhile, Dad continued working for the railway as a conductor.
>
> 'When we returned, we settled in Prince Albert, Sask. We had quite a large house, so Mother decided to take in two boarders; one was Al Parker, a bush pilot, the other Mickey Sutherland, who worked for Canadian Airways. Mickey got Bob and myself interested in building a Ham radio. Later on Bob got a job at Canadian Airways as a radio operator. Frank went to work for them too, as a mechanic. I eventually joined the army as a signalman.
>
> 'Whilst working for Canadian Airways at Lac La Ronge, war

broke out, so Bob decided he wanted to join up and become a
pilot. So he plain up and walked to Prince Albert to enlist.'

\* \* \*

## A Taste of the Air

Brother Frank's job with Canadian Airways was as a sort of assistant helper,
but with the arrival of Mickey Sutherland, Robert felt he really had an 'in' at
the base and could easily get much closer to the aircraft than simply standing
looking over the fence. He had previously helped in mooring the floatplanes
at Prince Albert, someone throwing out a rope which he would catch, then
help to moor the machine to the jetty decking. Now he was able to help refuel
the aircraft with gasoline and oil.

Mickey Sutherland liked the youngsters around him. He was a
conscientious, hard working sort of guy who took life seriously yet enjoyed
good clean fun. He liked to keep fit, working out with bar-bells and using a
sun lamp. He later married, Eileen, from Edmonton, a charming girl. By the
time war came they were living in Winnipeg and had a child.

Mickey, of course, had a private pilot's licence, although his eyes were not
good, so he served his three-year apprenticeship as an aero engineer just so
he could be near aeroplanes. This work, in a sense, was by way of
compensation for not being able to fly as he would have wished.

In an alcove in his bedroom, Mickey built an amateur radio set and
receiver – Station VE4YB. Robert became interested in this, and learnt the
international morse code. Mickey built an oscillator for hearing morse
signals, which Robert took to, having decided now to get a job with Canadian
Airways as a radio operator. He thought that with money earned in this way
he could afford flying lessons.

Most of the time school proved distasteful to young Robert McNair. If
there was the slightest excuse to be absent he took it, skipping off to the river
base to help out with any sort of work with the aircraft. Meantime he
continued with his studies about aero engineering, morse code, etc, with a
view to obtaining, one day, his engineering ticket.

Not surprisingly he got to know the various pilots pretty well and it was
not long before he was being offered a seat during test flights. The two he
mostly flew with were Walter Gilbert, superintendent at the base, and Bill
Windrum. The latter had been a pilot with the Royal Flying Corps in WW1
(Captain) and later succeeded Gilbert as superintendent.

Robert's first flight was with Walter Gilbert. He spotted the young McNair
kid standing nearby, no doubt looking doleful. Suddenly Gilbert slid back the
window of the cockpit and yelled for Robert to 'hop in'. He didn't need a
second bidding, although he later said he found it: '. . . quite dull, although
it was nice to be in the air'.

Later he went up with Bill Windrum, and Robert asked if he might take the
controls. Bill trimmed the aircraft for straight and level flight, and the
youngster took over and flew in on a straight course at about 3-4,000 feet.
This obviously whetted his appetite, and on a later flight, he asked Bill if he
might try a few manoeuvres. Bill agreed, so Robert got to move the stick
about. Despite some basic knowledge, Robert had not fully appreciated that

unless the stick was returned to its normal position, the aircraft would turn over and go into a spin.

The aircraft this day was a Noorduyn Norseman, a machine built by the Noorduyn Aviation Co, in Montreal, the first production variant being built in 1936. It was a rugged high-wing, single-engined aeroplane that could be used with wheels, skis or floats. It could also carry a number of passengers and/or cargo. On this flight it carried a number of 10-gallon petrol drums standing loose down the back of the cabin, and as Robert held the stick over to one side, the drums began moving about. Alarmed, Bill yelled and reached at Robert, who quickly centralised the stick and brought the machine onto an even keel. Bill then explained how things should be done, but allowed Robert to continue with a few more turns which he managed successfully. As Robert said later: 'It was a good lesson for me in aileron control.'

Bill continued to let Robert fly the Norseman. He showed him how to take off and land back on the water – there were miles and miles of runway! – until he could get off and land back again without difficulty. He would also be given a couple of dollars for the occasional trip up north, more than likely flying a trapper up to a northern lake area, in order to help refuel the machine for the flight back. The trapper's canoe would be lashed to the aircraft's floats, the Norseman having special fittings for such eventualities. Robert got himself a summer job, when he was 18, with the Department of Natural Resources for the Province of Saskatchewan, as a fire-watcher, keeping a watchful eye for any signs of forest fires from various forestry outposts.

Otherwise he was kept busy with the flying business. Transportation was an important part of life in the province. Mail 'up country' only went by air, taken to trappers in the north, outposts and trading stations. From Prince Albert flights were made to Waskesiu, in the lake district, a summer resort 70 miles to the north. It was an area also made famous by the naturalist known as Grey Owl, whose extraordinary life has recently been the subject of a major movie. For years he had pretended to be a native Indian but in reality came from England. Further north was a base at Goldfields, on Lake Athabaska.

North again brought them to Yellowknife, and they even went as far north-west as Aklavik on the north of the Mackenzie at the delta in the Arctic Sea (almost Yukon Territory), although most traffic for this place went via Edmonton. Robert began his radio operator work with Canadian Airways at the Goldfields base. He had passed the necessary 14-words per minute test, actually developed to 40-words, and learnt to type (with two fingers!). Flights became few and far between now, but the occasional test flight might have a spare seat for him. He spent a month or so at Goldfields, then went to Yellowknife, where pilot Jack Crosby took him on a few flights.

Then the guy who was the radio operator at Prince Albert went sick and Robert had to return there to take over the radio traffic work. When this other chap recovered, he went north, Robert remaining at PA. Then in the winter of 1938/9, Robert went to Victoria and Vancouver, looking for a job. He secured one in a lumber camp up near the British Columbian coast, but returned shortly afterwards as a relief operator for Canadian Airways. It was while back up north several months later that Robert heard the address by Neville

Chamberlain, the British Prime Minister, on the radio, that a state of war now existed with Germany.

Robert was now 20 years, three and a half months old. There was no hesitation about what he had to do. He immediately typed out an application to the Royal Canadian Air Force in Ottawa, and within a few weeks, no doubt due to his knowledge of radio and his experience with aeroplanes, came an offer from the RCAF of a provisional commission in the service. However, the company couldn't replace him at a moment's notice. Robert also felt he could not embarrass his friends in Canadian Airways – amongst whom were Wilfred 'Wop' May DFC and Con Farrell, both distinguished airmen from WW1 – so he lost out on this initial chance. Wop May had been involved in the action which resulted in the death of Baron von Richthofen, the German air ace, in April 1918.

When finally he was able to be released, he contacted the RCAF again, only this time he was informed he had lost his chance of a provisional commission, and if he joined now he would have to start at the bottom, as an Aircraftman Second Class (AC2), the lowest grade. Robert didn't care how he started, so long as he started, but the RCAF was slow. Everyone was clamouring to join and with the initial influx of volunteers it took time to clear everyone and get them on the training road. In desperation Robert even applied to the French Air Force at their office in Ottawa, but they were sorry, they were not taking recruits. He would just have to wait his turn.

CHAPTER TWO

# THE GREAT ADVENTURE BEGINS

AC2 Robert W McNair reported to Manning Depot, RCAF, Toronto, on 28 June 1940, just a month past his 21st birthday. Once assembled the embryo aviators received a welcoming address by a young penguin (non-flying) officer, who, despite his lack of flying brevet, made a strong impression on them. He spoke of the glorious traditions of the air force, of the wonderful future about to be opened out before them, the flying heroes of the Great War, etc, etc. At the time, Robert recalled later, they were all impressed and imbued with ardent fervour. In later years he changed his opinion somewhat, feeling rather that they had all been taken in.

They were kitted out, but strangly there was a shortage of headgear – at least, Robert couldn't get one to fit. He found that one belonging to a sergeant fitted him very well and he occasionally managed to get hold of it. At least without one, he was not obliged to 'throw up' a salute if an officer appeared. As his career progressed, he probably yearned for those early days when he did not have to salute certain superiors, but by the same token, the young airman in him undoubtedly felt he would like to try his hand at saluting, which is why he borrowed the sergeant's hat. His rather jaundiced view of some senior officers had yet to manifest itself.

He remained at the Depot Pool for just on a week, but was then shipped off to the Initial Training School at Hunt Club, Avenue Road, Toronto, on 5 July. This was the home of No.1 ITW. He was to remain here for exactly three months to the day. If there was any thought of instant association with aeroplanes he was mistaken. Ground school instilled many things into young would-be aviators, square-bashing, theory of flight, morse and some navigational work, but no aeroplanes.

The first job was to sort the newcomers into aircrew trades, that is, whether they were to become pilots, observers or air gunners. Tests in a Link Trainer helped to determine who might become pilots. In this Robert held some advantage with his previous flying experience, and it was no surprise that he was immediately accepted for pilot training.

After those three months he and some of the others who had survived thus far, and been selected for pilot training, were sent west to Windsor, Ontario, where Canada met the United States at Detroit, Michigan. It was a good land mark location, with the huge Lake Erie to the south, and the smaller Lake St Clair to the north. At the far end of Lake Erie, the mighty Niagara falls crashed into the beginnings of Lake Ontario. At Windsor, the home of No.7 Elementary Flying Training School (EFTS) they at last got their hands on an aeroplane. He also met Pete Linney, who had been fire-watching with him in the summer of '38. Pete wanted to fly Wellington bombers, but Robert wanted Spitfires. Each trainee could put down three choices of aeroplane they would like to fly if they got through their flying courses. Pete put *all three* down as Wellingtons; Robert did the same, but wrote, *Spitfire, Spitfire, Spitfire!*

Nine days after arriving, AC2 McNair was shown over a Fleet Finch II two-seat biplane trainer, and along with a few others, was given over to the gentle hands of Sergeant Stewart. Built by the Fleet Aircraft Co Ltd, at Fort Erie, Ontario, Canada, an original order was made for 400 of these Finch II aircraft for primary training with the Commonwealth Air Training Plan, and delivered in 1940. Robert's first flight came on 14 October, a 35-minute familiarisation flight in Finch No.4531, noted in his new green-coloured RCAF flying log-book (officially known as a Form R-95 (RAF Form 414 – the services love Forms) as a 'passenger'. More flights followed over the next four days, so that by the end of the first week he had had five flights and could log an impressive four hours ten minutes of air time.

Week two saw him ticking off more items of instruction that he had to either master or at least be competent in. There can be no doubt that his previous flying experience assisted his advancement, for on 26 October he was handed over to another instructor, Sergeant Vassry. After a 25-minute check-flight, Robert was told to go off on his own. This was the moment: first solo. First he had to sign in his log book to the effect that he understood the cockpit controls, fuel and oil systems of the Finch. That meant that if he crashed, his instructors were 'off the hook'! Robert went off and flew a circuit of 20 minutes duration, then landed. He noted that it was a struggle, but he had got down in one piece (Finch 4515), so had mastered the first hurdle. And he had done so in just on six hours of dual instruction.

Now the work started in earnest. Before the month was out he had flown solo and on half a dozen further occasions with his instructor, and hadn't broken anything. Sergeant Stewart was still taking him through the various tasks and tests, then the flight commander, Flight Lieutenant G Hiltz, flew with him on the 20-hour test, for 30 minutes, which he passed without mishap. However, overconfidence could now be an enemy, and if added to bravado and stupidity, could prove fatal.

**A Slap on the Wrist**
He and Pete Linney, who was also progressing nicely, knew the golden rules of the school: no flying solo outside a radius of 20 miles, no flying above cloud, and most importantly, no dog-fighting with other students. However, Pete and Robert decided they were above such things, after all, they had a massive 20+ hours under their belts, and were no doubt feeling invincible. They made an appointment to meet above the clouds at some distance from the airfield and dog fight. (So, not bad, boys – all three no-no's in one hit. Way to go!) Each would climb into the sun so as to be in position to bounce the other at the rendezvous. It seems, therefore, that Linney was feeling more like a fighter pilot than a bomber pilot on this occasion.

They did this a couple of times but on the third day a third aircraft appeared and seemed anxious to join in, so they both bounced him and the unknown pilot quickly beat a hasty retreat. The two 'aces' had triumphed. That is, until they landed. No sooner had the two aircraft rolled to a stop than they were hauled before an instructor who put them both on a charge. They would be up before Flight Lieutenant Hiltz for breaking flying regulations. As luck would have it the third aeroplane was being flown by an instructor.

Two days later they found themselves in the flight commander's office. Both pleaded not guilty, and Hiltz thought the matter over, his eyes boring into the two men before him. If they continued to plead thus, he said finally, he would have to send a full report to that enigmatic 'higher authority', but, he continued, if they pleaded guilty, he would be able to settle the matter himself. The two innocents mulled this over and were persuaded by Hiltz's manner that he was a good type so both reversed their earlier pleas and entered new ones of guilty. Now with a twinkle in his eye, Hiltz awarded his punishment, confined to camp for two days from the time they had been put under arrest, which had been two days earlier. And with a 'don't do it again!' ringing in their ears, they were dismissed.

**Progress and a Move**
Throughout November training went on apace. One important qualifying flight was the cross-country to London, Ontario, and back. Robert, and another pal, Owen Pickle, arranged to go together on the 19th, after an identical flight in the morning with Sergeant Stewart. However, Rob and Owen became so embroiled in a dog-fight (so Robert had learnt his lesson then!) over the airfield south of London, that they didn't notice it and when they'd finished, continued on eastwards. Before long they were running out of juice, got mixed up in some cloud and had become hopelessly lost.

As Robert's fuel gauge began to register zero, he headed down towards a large field. At the last moment he spotted some strands of barbed-wire along the nearby roadside and just managed to scrape over them, but now he could see the field had been recently ploughed. Almost hovering on a stall, he just made it to a grass area and put the machine down without damaging it. As he sat in the now silent cockpit, he felt both relief and some pride.

Robert climbed down from the cockpit and noticed what he took to be a farmer or at least a farmhand, close by. He called the man over, told him to guard the aeroplane, and then, despite a surprised look on the man's face, Robert strode off to find a telephone. He found a nearby house, but the elderly couple did not have a telephone, However, they could provide some tea and cakes for this 'hero in flying boots, helmet and flight suit'. When finally he asked the couple where he might find a telephone, they directed him towards the Ontario Reformatory up the road! Robert then realised why the 'farmhand' had looked so surprised – he was a prison inmate! He now realised too the reason for the barbed-wire. Few things got past McNair for too long!

He finally got to a telephone, called the long suffering Flight Lieutenant Hiltz, to tell him: 'I'm in jail at Guelph!' One can imagine the poor man's disarray, as it transpired that he had only just put down the phone after speaking to Owen 'Pic' Pickle, calling from Toronto. That location was supposed to be too far away to be reached in a Finch, without refuelling!

Hiltz appeared far from amused and Robert noted, with some disdain, that he wasn't being congratulated on not bending the aeroplane, despite the spot in which he had put down. One reason Hiltz was not offering congratulations, of course, was that he was too busy giving both men 'hell' upon their return, because people on the airfield at London had reported them dog-fighting, and there was no escape this time either, for their aircraft numbers' had been taken. One has to wonder if Flight Lieutenant Hiltz rued his earlier leniency. But at least it showed the two boys had spirit.

**On to Kingston**

Fortunately for Flight Lieutenant Hiltz, McNair left Windsor a couple of days later, this time posted to No.31 SFTS at Kingston, Ontario. He now had $57^1/_2$ flying hours on the Finch II, but at Kingston McNair found they had Fairey Battle aeroplanes and North American Harvards. The Battle was an obsolete three-seat, low-wing, single-engined monoplane bomber. It was still only December 1940, and these aircraft had, just six or seven months earlier, been the RAF's main bombing aircraft during the Battle of France. They had been found seriously wanting, and shot out of the sky by German fighters and ground fire with unceremonious ease. Now they had been quickly relegated to training machines, both in the RAF and RCAF. The Harvard was a noisy two-seat, single-engined low-winged monoplane, but at least it was built for training.

Robert McNair and his companions from Windsor, arrived at 3 pm on the afternoon of 1 December – a cold day – with a blizzard blowing. They were collected in an open truck from the railway station which didn't endear them to the RAF personnel who ran the school, as the drivers had to leave their warm stoves to pick them up. They arrived perished.

The pupils found the base a foul place, and became amused hearing English voices saying, 'bloody this' and 'bloody that' all the time. They also had to exist on RAF rations, just as if they were in Britain, so to the Canadians this did not offer up very palatable food so they would go into town each night and buy their one decent meal of the day, also buying more food to take back to camp, keeping it in their lockers. Cold macaroni was one breakfast choice, and if that wasn't eaten up, it would return as an equally cold savoury or dessert at the next meal.

No.31 Service Flying Training School had only been operating since September. Its function was to progress newly trained pilots onto service-type machines, although the Battle was hardly a machine pilots would find – or want to find – in service now. However, the difference between them and the Finch II was that it and the Harvard had a cockpit canopy, an undercarriage that needed to be raised and lowered, and they were monoplanes. The first thing Robert had to do was to again sign his life away – in writing – to say that he understood three things: the petrol, oil, water and ignition systems of the Battle, then that he had received instruction in and understood the action needed in the event of a fire in the air, and finally, now that he had a retractable undercarriage, that he 'fully' understood the hydraulic and emergency systems of the aircraft. Once the instructors and the camp CO felt they were covered in the event of a crash, Robert could begin. If now the first thing to touch the ground was the Battle's belly, having forgotten to lower the wheels, it was his fault, not theirs!

Robert was now put into the tender hands of Flying Officer Smyth, and his first flight with him, in a Battle, came on 13 December, a full 30-minute test and air experience flight. Next day came two more flights with Smyth, followed on day-three with his first solo landing. He noted this in his log-book as: 'Softly as in a morning sunrise – well almost!'

Inspecting the Battles in these first days, the pilots spotted that some had Polish crests painted on them, and students found too, little holes in them and imaginatively felt they were old bullet holes. There was some kind of vicarious thrill flying machines they thought might have seen some action. However, the truth was a little less glamorous. Some of these Battle Trainers had indeed been with squadrons in England, the Polish-marked ones having been with 300 and 301 Squadrons, the first two Polish squadrons within the RAF, during the summer of 1940. But they only used them to train, prior to the units taking on Wellingtons. They were certainly not used operationally so the holes must have been made through accidents. But it was nice to dream!

Robert progressed and then on the 18th he had to have a check-flight with the flight commander, Flying Officer Hamlin, followed then by his first solo on the type. Again, he made a note in his log book, this time reading: 'Look out Jerry (you rat) here I come.' Had Jerry known, they might have heeded these words.

As December slid towards Christmas, flight entries in his log increased, both with Smyth and solo. Then just before Christmas, Smyth was posted – Robert wrote: 'Smyth posted – am I mad? – No!' Perhaps he didn't like him!

The students had a break over Christmas, and Robert didn't fly again until the 30th, which, seeing his notation for this flight entry, was just as well: 'Still have big head from Xmas.' One then wonders if this affected two fellow students this same day, who were both killed low flying in Harvards! Robert's third flight that day had also been detailed as 'low flying'. His new instructor became Sergeant Baker.

Baker took him up in a Harvard for the first time on New Year's Day, following two Battle sorties. This author does not understand Robert McNair's noted comment but it is recorded here for those who might: 'Only a Frenchman should fly these things.' [Hope it isn't rude!] Flight Lieutenant Sloan, the 'A' Flight commander, took him on a flight commander's test in a Battle on the 2nd, then he began some flights with Pilot Officer Ross in between his solo trips. Ross took him on a short night flight on the 11th, and from Robert's comment indicates that Ross forgot to lower the wheels: 'Where was the undercarriage? Do as I say, not as I do!' Robert was to record:

> 'The procedure was that in dual-equipped planes the instructor would have the student place his hand on the stick gently and follow the movements made by him on his own stick in the second cockpit. "Do exactly as I do," the instructor said. The next procedure was for the student to do it with the instructor

not touching the controls. "Do exactly as I do," the instructor kept repeating. But the instructor had forgotten to lower the wheels – it came in on its belly. He and I puzzled for hours over joint reports which would not put either of us "in the fire".'

By and large, his flying took similar lines to that at Windsor, for now came the cross-country tests. A dual flight with Pilot Officer Holloway on the 15th was followed by a solo trip a few days later. However, he must have had a hard landing on the 16th, commenting: 'Never knew an aircraft could bounce so high – phew!'

Shades of dog-fighting returned on the 19th during a cross-country, scheduled for base-Tichbourne-Napanee-base in a Battle. After 55 minutes he returned, noting: 'Never did reach Tichbourne, but had a good time with a Harvard.' (Not dog-fighting again, surely!) On the 24th he noted a scrap with Bobby Kipp – in a Battle! But the day afterwards he completed a test with the Chief Flying Instructor, Squadron Leader R Pattison.

Wing Commander D McC Gordon, OC 31 SFTS, assessed McNair 'Above Average' at the end of January 1941, and his flying hours had topped the 100 mark. There was still a lot of work to do, but it was not all plain sailing. On 4 February he made a cross-country flight, taking fellow student LAC Whitney for a ride. However, Whitney was sick, but he was obviously not put off by the experience for Whitney went off with him again the next day, but this time Whitney was the pilot, Robert the passenger. A couple of days later Robert had his first visit to the USA – he got lost during a sortie and ended up above America!

Hours began to build in the flight log. Experience was the key. Robert was known to have a good eye in the air too, especially on one reconnaissance flight. He noted in his log: 'Nothing special to report – except a blonde on the corner of Princess and Main.' He was also flying dive-bombing sorties and making flights at night, and by the end of the month, his flying hours had raced ahead to 156 hours.

Flight Sergeant Moffat took him up in a Yale biplane trainer on 14 March, for an hour long aerobatic sortie, the first taste of real dog-fight practice. Robert found the Yale much easier than the Battle. Towards the end of March No.2 (RCAF) Course at Kingston came to an end, Robert passing out with an 'Average' assessment on all four categories, as a single-engined pilot, pilot-navigator, in bombing and in air gunnery.


**Wings, a Commission, and a Ship**
Robert had his pilot's 'wings' although a short time before it nearly all ended in tears – literally. Another student named Louis Conshon threw an apple at him during a free-for-all in the billets. The apple caught Robert squarely in the eye, which became so swollen it looked as if the socket had been reversed. He had to walk about for several days with a patch over it and as he could not see overly well with the other eye he nearly landed 50 feet up on one flight. The eye was discoloured for days.

Sixteen students on the course filled in applications for a commission.

Bobby Kipp[1] and Robert were both told to apply and of them all only five received them, including Bobby and Robert. On the day Robert strode down to HQ to put in his application he did not wear a tie or collar, just a scarf around his neck, a khaki jacket and blue trousers. His instructor told him that if he received a commission he would have to smarten himself up, Robert promising he would. But he also confided in him that he did not recommend people for commissions unless he was sure they would get them.

Obviously Robert wasn't as sure as the instructor for feeling he needed a better fitting uniform having paid a Kingston tailor $32 for a made-to-measure sergeant's uniform. He then had to sell it once he found himself commissioned as a pilot officer. He only learned of this after he had left for embarkation leave, had already visited home, and had reported to Debart, Nova Scotia. This was their embarkation point, where 700 aircrew were crowded into hangars awaiting ships to England. Accommodation was of the poorest kind.

Robert also learnt that some youngsters at ITS in Toronto, deciding they wanted better fitting uniforms, had them made from officer's material in town. The tailors did not tell them this would be unacceptable in the service, so they had wasted their money.

The pilots left Kingston on 25 March, Robert going home to North Battleford. During this leave he visited Mickey Sutherland and his wife in Winnipeg, where Mickey was working as an engineer with Trans-Canadian Airways. Mickey was very proud of his protegé, although naturally a little envious. Once Robert was ordered to report to Debart, he visited some relatives in Maritimes on the way.

Finally a ship was available. They boarded the SS *California*, a ship converted into an armed merchant cruiser. Within a day they had sailed, heading out into the Atlantic for England – and the war.

---

[1] Bobby Kipp (Robert Allan Kipp), from Kamloops, BC, was retained as an instructor at Yorkton until 1943, something that would have crucified McNair. However, Bobby eventually managed to get onto operations in England as a Mosquito intruder pilot, winning the DSO and DFC, achieving almost a dozen victories, and several more destroyed on the ground. Sadly he was killed in a flying accident in a Vampire at St Hubert in July 1949.

CHAPTER THREE

# ENGLAND

Among the new friends he met aboard ship was another trainee pilot, Pilot Officer R I A Smith, from Regina, who was ten months younger than Robert. Rod Smith would also have a successful war with the RCAF, and although they did not fly together after 1941, their careers covered similar ground, both fighting over Malta and Europe. Rod recalls this first meeting:

'I first met Buck on an armed merchant cruiser, the *California*. We departed from Halifax in mid-April 1941, both having got our "wings". We were the sort of main defence for the large six-knot convoy and we were some thirteen pilot officers on board, including Buck, Laddie Lucas, Babe Whitamore and Daddo-Langlois. We had all graduated from Uplands.

'The *California* was an old liner of 20,000 tons which had eight 6″-guns, and in the hold it carried empty steel barrels so it would stay afloat for a long time if it were damaged or holed. We had very good weather and on our second day out – not having met Buck before – someone took me to his cabin. Buck was sitting on his bed – a handsome guy, very engaging and confident with a devil-may-care attitude – and I instantly took a liking to him.

'We got talking about our experiences and he told me he had trained on Battles at SFTS, Kingston, on the north shore of Lake Ontario, which had two cockpits for pupil and instructor. I'd never seen one of these before close-up, although once flying over Kingston I'd spotted one on the ground there.

'Buck told me he had pranged one on its nose and once even landed wheels-up, but the instructor was technically in command so was responsible, although Buck said he felt a bit sheepish about it! He also told me that when they were nearing the end of the course, one of the Naval Officer instructors had said to him: "Would you like a commission, McNair?" Buck was rather casual, he said, in his dress, so he replied: "Sure, if you're dishing them out, I'd like one." So the Naval guy said: "Well, you'll have to keep yourself spruced up a bit!"

'We were on this convoy for about ten days and then one

beautiful morning we turned due north and ran up speed – something like eight knots – and began to zig-zag. A little later in the day the Commander told me we were going to Iceland. The next morning we were off Reykjavik, with its coloured roofs and mountains behind. We turned into a fjord just north of the town where there were several British ships, plus two Irish mail-boats, one being the *Royal Ulsterman*. To our great surprise we saw HMS *Hood* lying there. One of the officers told us it was the finest ship ever built. She was certainly a good-looking ship. [One month later the Hood was sunk in action against the *Bismarck*.]

'We trans-shipped to the *Royal Ulsterman* and she was a neat little vessel, with cabins again for we officers, two double bunks in each, although the poor sergeant-pilots were down in the hold, where the propeller shaft went out, and a single light-bulb hanging from the ceiling. Both mail-ships sailed escorted by several destroyers and next morning we were within sight of the Butt of Lewis, then down through The Minch. On 1 May, another beautiful morning, we entered the Clyde Estuary where we anchored. A lighter took us ashore, then we were put on a train and went through Glasgow and on to Edinburgh before turning south. Next morning we arrived at Uxbridge.

'RAF Uxbridge was a super depot, the first RAF station many of us had been on. Buck and I shared a large bedroom there then they gave us some tests for night vision and a few other medical things, then we had to fill in the list of aircraft we wanted to go on. Of course, I put down "single-engined day fighter" or perhaps "twin-engined night fighter", but I knew I had to have the word "fighter" in there somewhere. We had three choices and Buck put down something similar to me.

'They then gave us ID cards, so Buck and I set off for London. We took the underground and decided to get out at Piccadilly Circus. Once out we looked down Lower Regent Street, then got into the Haymarket, and needing a raincoat, we went into Burberry's, having read in various aeroplane magazines all about this famous brand, and once fitted out, we headed for the Canadian Officers' Club just off Trafalgar Square – Cockspur Street – where we could get lunch.

'Mrs Alice Massey, the wife of Vincent Massey, the High Commissioner in UK – and had been since about 1936 – was there, a charming woman. Later, on various leaves, we would often drop in there for lunch. After lunch I wanted to look up a cousin of mine who was at the Admiralty, and Buck – typical Buck – had picked up some gal at the club and went off with her.

'The next time we travelled into London, we decided that as our uniforms which we had got in Halifax were not up to much, we'd get new ones; we needed two anyway. There were about six of us, Buck, myself, two Australians and a couple of others, so off we went to Gieves.

'Finally we got our postings and most of us were going to No.58 Operational Training Unit (OTU) at Grangemouth, on the Firth of Forth, Scotland. We began to wonder what sort of school this was, but meantime we were able to make one final trip into town. Once there, Buck and I went into one of those RAF Information Centres, finding a sergeant sitting at a desk. We said we had been posted to 58 OTU and could he tell us what sort of OTU it was. He looked astounded and asked for our ID cards, then spoke to a flight sergeant, who must have agreed we were not spies, and told us: "Army Co-op". We groaned and felt very downcast.

'Saturday was our last day there and there was an air raid on, and oh, boy, was it exciting. The following day, sometime before noon, we took a bus to King's Cross Station and going through London we could see piles of rubble and bricks all around. We got to our train and headed north, and next morning we were put off at a little station, to wait for another train to take us closer to Grangemouth. As we were doing this we saw a Spitfire overhead and as we looked up we said something like, "lucky bastard", then a little while later a pair of Spitfires flew over, then a group of three. The thought came to us that perhaps there was a Spitfire station nearby. A bus finally arrived and we asked the driver what aircraft 58 OTU had, and he said Spitfires; it was a great relief.'

Robert McNair also recalled the journey to England, smoke screens being laid several times by the convoy escort ships, and finally Iceland, and seeing the *Hood*. His memory of the mail-ship was less glamorous than Rod Smith's – 'the aircrew were thrown like cattle aboard a small fast ship, which went full out for Glasgow.'

He also noted that the trip to London was: '. . . awful, no food, long and tedious'. Once they had arrived at Grangemouth, they saw a Spitfire for the first time and all were highly impressed. One was on blocks to allow students to sit in the cockpit and be shown how to retract and lower the wheels.

The CO of the OTU was a veteran air fighter, Squadron Leader M H Brown DFC & Bar, (known as Hilly) who had fought in France and during the Battle of Britain with No.1 Squadron RAF. He had around 18 victories so would have impressed the new intake of pupils. He was also a Canadian, from Manitoba. Two of the instructors were Flight Lieutenant A R 'Paul' Edge, who had also seen some action the previous year, and Flight Lieutenant Fischer. One flight commander was Flight Lieutenant A D J Lovell DFC, another experienced fighter pilot who had seen much action during the Battle too, with 41 Squadron. He would survive the war by just a few months before a fatal crash ended his life. By that time Tony Lovell had the DSO and Bar, DFC and Bar, and American DFC.

They had arrived at Grangemouth on 12 May, and the huge London raid had been on the 10th – the final massive night raid upon the British capital during the period known as the Blitz. Robert's first flight for several weeks came on the 15th, a dual control sortie in a Miles Master two-seat trainer. His instructor was a New Zealander, Flying Officer M C Kinder. Maurice Kinder had seen action in the later stages of the Battle of Britain and been wounded. Next day he flew solo in a Master, was then checked out by Flight Lieutenant E S Hogg, who had also been in the Battle of Britain, then the next day was sent off on his first flight in a Spitfire.

Spitfire I No. X4777 had also been with an operational squadron briefly at the end of 1940 and Robert flew it for 80 minutes of local flying. He made only one comment in his log book – 'Glasgow Balloons' – which suggests he either saw them, or got too near to them for comfort! For the rest of the month his time was spent building up hours and experience on the Spitfire, with occasional test flights in the Master with an instructor. One of these was Flying Officer J R Ritchie, yet another Battle of Britain man. No doubt some of their words fell on to the receptive ears of the young Buck McNair. We do know he spoke frequently to Hilly Brown, taking in all that was talked about.

The first half of June 1941 was an intense learning period on the Spitfire. Robert was immensely impressed with the sleek, trim, manoeuvrable fighter, as all fighter pilots were. As his flying hours increased he began leading others about in the sky. He would fly along Scottish valleys, round mountains, and zoom up over them as the valley came to an end. In fact he got so advanced on Spit time he had to be told to slow down. He would then fly Masters, so long as he could keep in the air.

Paul Edge would give the students a navigation test. Shown a pinpoint on a map the pupil would have to find his way there and upon returning would have to tell him what he had seen. As it was, in fact, Paul's own house, it was easy to check that they had found it, for Paul's wife would be in the garden waving up at them. Robert had already noted that Paul's wife was a very lovely 19-year-old, so no doubt he easily recognised her on the occasion he was told to find the spot – 9 June.

On the 16th, on one of four flights that day, he recorded that he had 'kissed a mountain top!' He was detailed to do some cloud flying and aerobatics, and on coming out of cloud over the Scottish highlands, he found himself just ten feet below a mountain peak. It was slap, bang in front of him and he only just pulled up in time.

By 20 June, the day he flew his last sortie at 58 OTU, his flying hours had increased to 193, of which 40 were on Spitfires. Near the end of the course the pupils were asked where they would like to go. Robert asked Hilly Brown's advice. Brown said that a number of RCAF squadrons were being formed which were probably going to get Spitfire V machines soon, and suggested Robert try for one of them. Hilly also advised him that once he arrived on a new squadron, he should not associate with small groups, not be stand-offish, but not to try and assert himself or to talk about himself. He should stand back for the most part and listen to what was going on with a view to learning. It was good, sound advice. Hilly Brown himself was posted not long afterwards, going as a wing commander to the island fortress of Malta. Sadly he was killed on a sortie over Sicily soon after his arrival.

Of this period, Rod Smith has recorded:

'Buck was in A Flight with Paul Edge as his flight commander, whom he liked very much – invited him home to dinner as a matter of fact. I was in B Flight under a guy named Jones. We had already asked if the Spitfire was easy to fly and nobody would ever say yes; they would generally qualify a bit. Buck went off before me, disappeared off to the west, very low cloud, 1,500 feet with hills all around. Then when he landed, I went off. Take-off was smooth. I was perfectly OK, got up, closed the hood, got the engine back to 2,400 rpm, and levelled off – IAS 245 mph. The Master usually cruised at 165.

'When Buck first landed he over ran the runway a bit. There was a great big dirt pile there but fortunately he got by and didn't go up on his nose. When I landed I thought I'd do a circuit, with a touchdown, and then go round again. I didn't know you shouldn't do that in a Spitfire as the early mark of Spitfire heated up a bit. Anyway, I landed, took off again, only to find my air pressure failed so I had to land without flaps or brakes. I too hit this dirt pile dead centre and at a faster speed than Buck, and left my undercarriage legs behind and so on, and nearly went over on my nose. Buck told me he was afraid I was going to go over on my back and catch fire; I was afraid of the same thing. I got hell for that!!

'Once we started dog-fights we got a bit more confidence. That's the best way when you forget all about the instruments and everything is just try to get on the other guy's tail and keep on it. Buck and I used to go down to the Flights early after breakfast, before all the others. We made a nuisance of ourselves but if anything needed taxying over to the maintenance hangar, we'd do it, Spitfire or Master, and they'd let us do it. At least they knew we were keen, and it was all experience.

'At the end of the course I had 46 hours on the Spitfire – the top. Buck had about 40 and the lowest on the course had around 25. That's just because he didn't try and fill in the gaps and make a nuisance of himself.

'Buck's flight commander changed to Tony Lovell during the course. He was a handsome guy and had been in the Battle of Britain, got several Huns and a DFC, but I don't think he took much of a shine to Buck. About the same time we got a new Squadron Leader Flying, a chap named West, and Squadron Leader Hilly Brown was with us, a hell of a fine guy. Brown was certainly looked up to by everyone. Very much a leader with a good sense of humour. Tony Lovell was a bit more like the school prefect.

After a while Hilly said to us that he hadn't flown Spitfires much, being a Hurricane pilot, and wanted us two (Buck and me) to fly formation with him. So I was No.2 on Hilly's right, Buck as No.3 on his left. Of course, we tried to get in as close as we could to impress him. It was amazing how quickly we students learnt to do all these things. We were up with Hilly for over an hour and as we came in over the hangar, he waved and we broke away either side. After landing he said, "Well boys, you did very well. Smithy, you were flying a little too close for your experience!"

'When I was instructing at an OTU a little over a year and a half later, I recall using that exact same phrase to a student of mine, and I admit I was scared but didn't want to appear so!

'At the end of our six weeks' course, the postings came through and we heard where we were going, hoping it was 11 Group. We just had to get into squadrons in 11 Group where all the fighting was going on. Low and behold, Buck was posted to 411 Squadron – we'd never heard of it – and I was posted to 412. It turned out they were two brand new Canadian squadrons at Digby. They didn't even have any Spitfires when we arrived!

'Buck and I caught a night train from Edinburgh, taking some beer with us, and we had a carriage to ourselves. Buck had been asked to take an envelope, addressed to his new CO, marked "Confidential". Buck guessed inside were the confidential reports of the guys being sent to 411. Well, we got drinking as we headed south, and we had both seen our assessments in Canada during our early training and at SFS. My assessment had been: "Smooth and accurate Pilot, flies with confidence." Buck's had said something like: "Flies with a touch of dash." I thought that summed up Buck McNair!

'Buck was worrying about what Tony Lovell might have put down about him so he, to my surprise, decided to break the seal and open the envelope, which he did crudely. Sure enough, there were the reports on the guys going to 411 and finding his own, he read it. "That bastard Lovell," he said. Tony had written: "McNair is a good pilot but wants everyone to know it," which was most unfair to Buck. Actually he did want everyone to know it but he wasn't the only one. But it was a bit mean of Lovell to put it down in writing.

'Buck then got a little bit morose and wondered what chance he was going to have on the squadron with a report like that? I said I was sure he'd be alright.'

At some stage in the journey, they must have been joined in the carriage by a girl, to whom Buck introduced himself. She got off at Lincoln, having been given Buck's new telephone number. She telephoned him the next day and every day thereafter but Buck soon stopped answering it. Buck McNair had other interests. His war was about to begin.

CHAPTER FOUR

# No. 411 Squadron RCAF

As Buck McNair arrived at RAF Digby to join his first operational squadron, he found there was no commanding officer, and almost no squadron. The CO actually turned up the next day, Squadron Leader P B Pitcher, who hailed from Montreal. Paul Pitcher had studied law at McGill University and in 1935 had joined the RCAF Auxiliary in his home town. With the war he had been sent to England and flown with No.1 RCAF Squadron during the Battle of Britain, then had taken command of the unit in December as it became 401 Squadron RCAF.

The RCAF were rapidly expanding their war effort. The British Commonwealth Air Training Plan (BCATP) was well under way by this time although new Canadian pilots were tending to be sent to RAF squadrons. Therefore, in January 1941, it was agreed to establish 25 RCAF squadrons to add to the three already in Europe, and the Canadian training schools would fill them with new pilots.

No.412 Squadron, to which Rod Smith had been posted, was forming at the same time and place, under the command of Squadron Leader C W Trevena, but he too had yet to arrive. Trevena had been a pre-war pilot and had also been with 1 RCAF Squadron during the Battle of Britain. Rod Smith:

> 'My CO had just been on the fringes of the Battle of Britain, Buck's CO, Paul Pitcher, had been in it, both with 1 RCAF Squadron. After about three or four weeks I was made deputy flight commander because of my seniority (I'd got my wings on 8 March) and wasn't pleased over much. I'd much rather have gone to 92 Squadron or some outfit like that, where they had experienced flight commanders and deputy flight commanders, but that was Canadian politics; everyone in Canadian squadrons had to be Canadian, experienced or not.
>
> 'Buck, however, was not made a deputy flight commander in 411. Don Blakeslee was in 411 too and he wasn't made a deputy flight commander either, which surprised me; he really had something. At Digby we finally got some Spitfire Is and a couple of weeks later some Spitfire IIs.'

**Formation**

No.411 Squadron officially formed on 16 June 1941 but was very much an embryo unit. Buck did not arrive until the 23rd, about the same time 18 Spitfire Mark IAs began to be flown in. Also arriving with him were Sergeants H P Sharum, T D Holden and R M Booth from Grangemouth OTU. Three days later Sergeant J J B Howard arrived from 401 RCAF Squadron and two days later Flying Officers K A Boomer and R C Weston, again from 401, both designated as flight commanders. Ken Boomer took over A Flight in which Buck was a member, Ralph Weston, B Flight. The Squadron became known as the 'Grizzly Bears' due to the bear insignia on its crest, but was also referred to as the 'Roaring' Squadron.

More guys turned up on the 30th. Pilot Officers D M Blakeslee, W F Ash, J E T Asselin; Sergeants C B Ramsey, J W Sills, C I Nutbrown, D J Brown, G A Chamberlain and L G Edwards, all from 57 OTU, Hawarden. During July, yet more postings materialised. From Grangemouth came Pilot Officer T C Cryderman and Sergeants W G Pavely, J H Long, W F Kenwood, and Sergeant J H Price, J H Whalen, W J Curtis from Hawarden, followed by Sergeants E E Green, J A Maclauchlan, J D Macfarlane and R M Murray from 53 OTU at Heston.

Before the month was out, Whalen, Ramsey and Price had been posted to 129 Squadron, and Murray had been killed in a crash flying Spitifre P7755. On 30 July the CO and Sergeant Brown flew the Squadron's first operational sorties, a convoy patrol.

William Ash, in fact, was an American, from Dallas, Texas. As soon as the war started he headed north for Canada to join the RCAF. Inevitably he was generally known, not as Bill, but 'Tex'. He recalls:

'The squadron had just been formed and few of us had much experience on Spitfires, and except for the CO, no operational experience at all. What things were like in those days was that the amount of training one got at OTU was pretty little really. We'd only done about 10-12 hours on Spitfires when we arrived and one of the things I remember was that once ops began, for the most part we were doing sweeps. The whole idea was to escort a few bombers in order to entice the Germans to put up fighters against us. For most of us, if we could keep up with the bombers and stay out of each other's way, that was fine.'

\*   \*   \*

Tex Ash heralded a friendly face for Buck as they had both trained at Hamilton. On the 24th Buck took up a 411 Spitfire for the first time to fly a sector recco – a flight to gain knowledge of the surrounding area, and to note landmarks which would come in useful if landing back in poor weather. Spitfire X4913 did not treat him kindly. Once airborne the air speed indicator packed up which gave him problems coming in to land. Unfortunately the CO was watching him and Buck's lousy landing did not impress.

Over the next couple of days more flights gave him more confidence and Tex Ash and he flew in the squadron's Tiger Moth to nearby Cranwell and back on a joy ride. The Squadron pilots continued to 'work up' throughout July, formation flying, cloud flying, practise interceptions and some air to air firing. This latter was to help pilots hone their skills at air gunnery firing at a drogue pulled along by another training aircraft. Buck's first score was eight hits out of 80 rounds fired, which impressed nobody, certainly not him. Not the least of their requirements was to build up flying hours. Hours meant experience, and experience would be needed most once operations began.

At the start of August some Spitfire IIs started to arrive, but practice flights of all kinds continued to occupy everyone. The odd Scramble came along. Buck raced to his Spitfire for the first time on 22 August, but it ended up with just a stooge over the Wash area at 15,000 feet with nothing sighted. Another Scramble came five days later, but this time he found an aircraft – an RAF Blenheim!

Night and dusk flying became part of the syllabus. On the 28th Buck flew three dusk landings which compelled him to note in his log book: 'How to keep from growing old!!' By the end of the month his flying hours totalled 289.15.

Another part of daily ritual was the air tests following routine or non-routine work on the Spitfires. All pilots did their share of these, whether it was their usual aircraft or not. On 2 September Buck took up a machine which had been given a new engine, which he thought 'a honey' but was less impressed after a few minutes, finding that the ailerons were not working and the hydraulic lines had been crossed. But he got down without damaging the Spitfire or himself. He made no recorded comment on what he may have said to the mechanics.

A blur of excitement filled the air on the 7th, as the Squadron flew down to West Malling in Kent from where its first Sweep was to be flown. However, the weather proved a far more effective enemy and the operation was 'washed out'. A Scramble the next day netted them an RAF Wellington bomber.

Up until this time the RAF had had a fixation about formation flying. From pre-war days it had favoured four sections of three aircraft for squadron formations, each sub-section having a leader and two wingmen tucked in close. This had been fine in the peaceful skies over England before the war, especially nosing up through cloud. It could then be reasonably expected that each three-man section would break through into the sunlight rather than have everyone spread out over the landscape each trying to locate one another.

The German fighter pilots had found during the Spanish Civil War that flying in pairs, within a sub-section of two pairs, was a much easier combat formation. Once combat was joined, each basic pair of one leader and one wingman protecting him was much easier to handle. With the RAF three-man vic, it took most of the wingmen's time and effort just to stay close to the leader, so effectively only one pair of eyes was looking out for hostile aircraft. If he did not see an attacker in time, or at all, at least one of the three aircraft would soon be falling away on fire, if not all three.

During the Battles of France and then Britain, fighter pilots had discovered how dangerous the vic formation was and at squadron level many had changed it to three sub-sections of four. This was not immediately made universal, nor was any official change heralded by Fighter Command HQ. Slowly the message got around via the grapevine until it did become official policy in the summer of 1941 that fours would be the basic fighter element. Each 'four' would comprise of two leaders and two wingmen, and if a fight developed this would break down into two fighting pairs. The leader would do the shooting, the wingman would protect the other's tail.

In early September 411 Squadron was advised of the new formation tactic, and it started to practise with the four-man sub-sections. This quickly became established and known as the 'finger-four' formation, as it looked rather like the finger (nails) of an outstretched hand. The middle two fingers were the two leaders, the index and little fingers being the wingmen. The leader would be lowest, the second section leader next highest, the two wingmen slightly higher still. This way all four pairs of eyes could scan areas of sky around them, without too much emphasis on formation keeping, as the four Spitfires would be spread out a little, not be tucked in tight as the old vic had been.

### Bale-Out!

The 11th September 1941 saw a very strange event for 411 Squadron. Although it took a while for the story to be told in truth, the basic tale can, even at this distance, only be judged as amazingly childish, even unprofessional, if not downright stupid on Buck's part.

That evening, Tex Ash and Buck McNair took off in the Magister (L8270) for a flip round the countryside. What appears in the official squadron diary is that not long afterwards, Ash landed again, but with the other cockpit devoid of Buck McNair, Ash reported that his passenger had fallen out. Luckily, the 'story' goes, McNair had managed to parachute down safely and without personal injury.

McNair's story had been that he had actually fallen asleep, the pin of his safety harness had then become loose and as Ash had made a sharp banking turn, it had ejected him out into space, where, waking up with a start, he had had the presence of mind to pull his parachute rip-cord thereby saving himself.

Looking at Buck's flying log entry, two things become apparent. First his words: 'Fell out and had to use parachute.' All well and good, but what about him falling asleep? The flight time is noted as just ten minutes of passenger flying. So we have to believe this man who ate, slept and dreamt flying, was so easily able to 'drop off' into slumber after just a few minutes, during which time they had gained height, while his seat harness pin had not only become loose, but must have come out altogether. Of course, for official purposes one could not even hint that anything less accidental had occurred which is why his logbook comment was recorded as above, for other, senior, eyes to read.

Any serious aviator will always comment, generally when talking about parachutists, that no sensible person jumps from an aeroplane unless forced to do so. But this is exactly what Buck had done this summer evening. Life at Digby had started to become a little dreary and dull with all the training. Down south 11 Group were taking the fight to the enemy almost daily, and the summer was fast drawing to a close. At this moment, T E 'Felix'

Cryderman, a professional parachutist in civil life, appeared at Digby. Don Blakeslee, Tex Ash and Buck, decided to have a go at this. They elicited all the do's and don'ts from Cryderman, then started to look for a suitable opportunity to put everything into practice. After all, as Buck insisted, one day they might have to do it for real and should know how to do it properly. Prophetic words as it turned out.

This particular lovely summer's evening, Tex and Buck were off duty after a period at Readiness. Don was flying around somewhere, and Buck thought that this windless evening should not be wasted. Keeping his thoughts to himself he persuaded Tex that they should take the Magister up for a ride round: 'You get in front,' suggested Buck, 'I'll get in the back.' Off they went and soon they were around 2,000 feet above the airfield, on the windward side of it. Without a word, Buck began to prepare to jump out but in that same moment, Tex turned round, saw what was about to happen and knowing that this could cause trouble tried to tell him not to do it. By then he could see he was not going to succeed, so tried to forestall his friend jumping out by diving. This is how Tex Ash remembers the event:

> 'I can remember very well I was not keen. After we'd been up for a bit Buck told me of his intention to bale out. After all, he argued, our lives might depend at some stage on using parachutes, so we'd better find out how they worked. He decided he was going to have to go. I knew that this was strictly against the rules and tried to talk him out of it. Then I thought that if I put the nose down and lost height it would be impossible for him to jump. So I did that but he had already undone his harness and when I put the nose down, that was his chance to go out.'

After a few seconds, Buck pulled the ripcord, the parachute opened, and he descended slowly to the ground below. Spitfires were starting to return to the airfield too and when Don Blakeslee saw someone dangling in a parachute, he said to himself, 'I bet anyone that's either McNair or Ash.'

Buck, however, wasn't directly over the airfield because he and Tex had tangled for so long over the controls, and he was going to land several miles away. Coming up below him was the A15 from Sleaford to Lincoln and he was heading directly for dozens of telephone wires strung on poles along the highway. Buck crossed his legs, pulled on the shrouds to miss the wires, remembering what Cryderman had advised, and came down just ten feet from the road.

A farmer working nearby heard Buck yelling and ran at him with a pitchfork, thinking he must be a German but the man was quickly appraised of the situation. Buck gathered up the precious parachute as quickly as he could, not wanting to get it dirty. People from a nearby farm began to arrive and it was then he realised he no longer had the rip-cord handle in his hand. Not to bring this back was a mortal sin, often taken as a sign of panic – at least regarded as such. He knew he had it most of the way down, so implored the farm folk to look around and search for it, telling them it was a highly secret piece of equipment that must not, under any circumstances, fall into enemy hands. Impressed by all this, everyone began to look for it feverishly and eventually someone located the valued object.

Not long afterwards, Ralph Weston, the B Flight commander, arrived with an ambulance and several pilots in tow. Buck knew he had injured an ankle slightly but was damned if he was going to show it. Despite it hurting like mad, he strode manfully to the vehicle – just for the ride.

Unfortunately, the AOC of 13 Group, Air Vice-Marshal R E Saul DFC, was visiting Digby that night and would undoubtedly want a full report on the jump he would soon hear about. 'Get together on your story,' Squadron Leader Pitcher advised Buck and Tex. The two then decided that Buck had been thrown from the cockpit because the split-pin holding the seat straps had become loose and fallen out. They went to the Magister, 'fixed' the pin so it would fit loosely, but not so loosely it would get an airman into trouble. The official explanation for the report was that Buck's flying helmet had also worked loose, that he had put up his hand to adjust it and his glove probably caught the loose pin and yanked it out.

Whether the AOC 'bought' the story or not is unrecorded, but he must have thought it all a strange collection of circumstances best left alone as nobody had been hurt. By way of penalty, Pitcher prohibited either Buck or Tex Ash from flying in the Magister as passengers. Buck had got away with it. He had wanted to know what it felt like to parachute from an aircraft and now he knew. As events unfolded, the experience probably did him a lot of good. It is understood a request for a Caterpillar badge from the Irvin parachute company was not accepted, as Tex remembers:

> 'Buck decided he was due for a Caterpillar badge, but the Irvin Company were furious, saying he could only get one if he had jumped to save his life. That's when Buck made the remark: "Have you ever seen Tex Ash land an aircraft?", which I thought an excellent joke and thoroughly enjoyable as a matter of fact. That was another thing about Buck, he had a good sense of humour. I always considered him one of my good friends in 411 and was delighted to hear later on about how well he had done. Our CO, Paul Pitcher, was an excellent chap, and we all knew he would never have allowed any censure against Buck for this moment of high spirits.'

Rod Smith also recalls this incident:

> 'One day Buck went up with Tex Ash and Buck came down by parachute near the aerodrome. He had some cock-and-bull story about his safety pin coming loose, but everyone, knowing Buck, knew he'd baled out for fun, but he got away with it. They probably admired him, and so did I.'

**Operations**
The time was soon approaching for the squadron to test all its training for real. On 20 September the squadron flew down to RAF West Malling, Kent, where it would refuel and be ready for a wing show under the leadership of

another Canadian veteran, Wing Commander H P 'Cowboy' Blatchford DFC. Unhappily for Buck he was not part of it. However, it proved uneventful. Together with 266 and 401 Squadrons, 411 went into France at Cap Gris Nez, circled at 25-30,000 feet and came out over Le Touquet, then patrolled along the Channel till the bombers they were supporting came out. Only one Messerschmitt 109 fighter was seen, and it did not come near.

The next day the squadron flew south again, this time to Manston in company with 412 Squadron. The problem going south, especially in poorish weather, was that pilots had to circuit the London balloon barrage amongst others. This provided a not uneventful flight down. Just south of base, two Oxford twin-engined trainers suddenly flew through the Spitfire formation and later, Wing Commander Blatchford led the whole Wing through a balloon barrage over two convoys in the Thames estuary! Both events were a little disconcerting to say the least.

Refuelling the Spitfires at Manston, the Wing flew out and into France that afternoon; 411 and 412 were below 266 which provided them with top cover. It flew again over Cap Gris Nez, then along and out at Gravelines, but although small groups of Me109s could be seen hovering some distance away, none felt like attacking. Pilots on this, Buck's first real operation were:

| Pilot | Spitfire | Pilot | Spitfire |
|---|---|---|---|
| S/L P B Pitcher | P7694 | F/L R C Weston | P7603 |
| P/O W F Ash | P7679 | P/O D M Blakeslee | P8657 |
| F/L K A Boomer | P7595 | F/S J W Sills | P8136 |
| Sgt G A Chamberlain | P7915 | P/O T E Cryderman | P7985 |
| P/O R W McNair | P7694 | Sgt T D Holden | P8076 |
| Sgt J Long | P7914 | Sgt D J Brown | P7966 |

Buck noted the 'Battle of the Balloons' in his log, and after the uneventful Sweep, also wrote: 'No hits, no runs, no errors.' in time-honoured baseball parlance. On his next operation, things would be a little different.

### First Combat Claim
Flight Lieutenant Ken Boomer led the squadron south to Manston again on the 27th, along with 412, meeting up with the CO there. This time the Wing was to be led by Squadron Leader T P de la P Beresford, CO of 266 Squadron, his pilots again flying as top cover. This time the pilot roster from 411 Squadron read:

| Pilot | Spitfire | Pilot | Spitfire |
|---|---|---|---|
| S/L P B Pitcher | P8371 | F/L R C Weston | P7603 |
| P/O W F Ash | P7679 | P/O D M Blakeslee | P8657 |
| F/L K A Boomer | P7595 | P/O R W McNair | P8263 |
| Sgt J D Macfarlane | P8172 | Sgt J Long | P7914 |
| Sgt W J Curtis | P7915 | Sgt J W Sills | P8136 |
| Sgt E E Green | P7966 | Sgt T D Holden | P8076 |

It was another afternoon Sweep, this time heading for Montreuil. The squadron took off from Manston at 1400 hours and over France, after patrolling for almost half an hour, with just a few Me109Fs seen at a distance, the Wing then ran into a considerable force of Me109 fighters from above and this time they engaged. Suddenly it was everyone's party, only sections being able to keep together. Two came down behind Ken Boomer but he managed to shake them off, firing at one. Buck McNair saw a 109 and chased it down, damaging it. Sergeant Macfarlane's aircraft was hit by AA fire over the coast and after gliding some way he was forced to bale out. The breeze took him over the English coast by Beachy Head and he landed safely – and dry. He had a few shrapnel pieces in one leg, otherwise he was OK.

As the fight began, Buck and the squadron was turning at about 18,000 feet and there was a lot of milling about, with aircraft heading towards each other. He recalled:

'I thought, this is stupid, I'm going to get out of this; there'll be a collision any second. I climbed up to get out of the milling and saw a couple of 'planes I was sure were enemy, positioning themselves in the sun. I lost sight of them, so I got over on the other side towards the sun, then I saw them half a mile away diving down towards where I was at their level, and I could see they were heading for some of our chaps below. They had not seen me detached from the group.

'I started towards them but they spotted me as I closed to 2,000 yards and was getting into position. They veered back into France and although I lost one, I followed the other. When I was about 1,000 yards from it, this Me109 went into a 30-degree dive towards Amiens. I pulled the plug for emergency power and went full out. We were going with a hell of a speed, but I wasn't gaining. Just beyond Abbeville I took a squirt with machine guns but nothing happened.

'At 10,000 feet the 109 levelled out, then I gained on him. The pilot probably thought he had lost me so had throttled back. I closed to 800 yards, but couldn't get closer. I fired four bursts, expending all my ammunition. The third hit it on the starboard wing and I saw pieces of metal coming off. I was watching and watching to see him blow up, but nothing happened. I'd forgotten all about any other aircraft – I was just thinking about him – just thinking of getting him. I saw Amiens below me and suddenly had the wind-up; I was frightened.

'In 1941 it was suicidal to be in the condition and place I was – no ammunition and well inside France all alone. It was one warning Hilly Brown, the CFI at Grangemouth had emphasized: "Never get separated from your squadron," I remembered him telling me. As soon as you find yourself without any friends near you, don't search for them. Turn about and go for home as fast as you can. If you're by yourself, you've had it.

'By "had it" he meant anyone alone would be shot down and probably killed. As I turned around and headed for England I

kept thinking of what Hilly Brown had said. I was at 10,000 feet
and went in a slight dive that brought me out at about 5,000 feet
at the enemy coast going as fast as I could.'

Buck was credited with one Me109 'damaged', which of course, was the
first claim by 411 Squadron. Rod Smith recalls another episode around this
period:

'About this time both squadrons were sent down south on some
exercise but I was left behind to look after 412 and Buck was
left to take care of 411. As I said to him, a noble knight must be
left to guard the gate!

'We were the only two pilots left of the two squadrons and we
were asked to fly over a factory near Lincoln, beating it up to
give the light-AA gunners some practice. So I led us and it was
then I noticed Buck was edging real close – just inches away –
on my right wing. He was testing my nerve and I could imagine
his smile under his oxygen mask. I kept rock steady and finally
we arrived at our destination. The factory had a roof with a large
chimney at each end and we could see the gap between them
was not much wider than the wingspan of a Spitfire.

'Buck got in line-astern behind me and we went down and
made several passes, flying as low as possible but going
between those chimneys, which was a bit dicey. Buck was still
line-astern of me, that is, below my tail-wheel, and looked
determined to stick there and not be shaken off. So I thought I'd
show him he couldn't stay under there and dropped down to
scrape over the roof. It was kind of dangerous for him but I
thought I could never look him in the face again unless I was
making him break off from there and sure enough he did. I
steeled myself to the task, although afterwards I realised it had
almost been a case of his life or my self respect!

'He was a bit sheepish when we landed but I had to better him
or I wouldn't have been able to face him in the future. But it all
came out alright.'

**Spitfire Vs**
Most RAF squadrons had been flying the Spitfire Mark V during the summer,
although others, including 411, were still struggling on with the old IIA. At
the start of October 1941 the squadron began to receive its first Spitfire V and
the pilots quickly appreciated the increased power and the two 20 mm
cannon, each carrying 60 rounds. The eight machine guns had been reduced
to four, two in each wing, but the punch of the cannon more than
compensated for this. As Buck remarked once:

'The Squadron was flying the Spitfire IIA, which was not so
good as the Me109. We couldn't cope with them at this time in
speed or in height, or in diving. All we could beat them with

was by turning. We could out-turn them any time so we had to
be cautious; we had to develop tactics that would meet the
enemy's superior aircraft.'

The German fighter aircraft had carried cannons since the beginning of the
war and now the RAF fighters were fast catching up. For 411 Squadron,
things were beginning to look up.

CHAPTER FIVE

# WAR OVER NORTHERN FRANCE

**Shot Down**
Getting used to the new Mark V Spitfire did not take long. The squadron
would still have liked to be down in 11 Group but that would come in time.
Meanwhile, the odd Scramble and some sea sweeps out over the North Sea
kept its operational hand in. Then on 13 October the squadron was ordered
down to West Malling again for an Offensive Sweep over France in support
of Circus 108A. It was a day the Luftwaffe reacted in force.

Take-off was slated for 1250 pm after a hurried snack lunch, and for some
reason only ten pilots are listed as taking part in the show, although 12 are
recorded in other documents, most probably the two flight commanders,
Boomer and Weston, flew too:

| Pilot | Spitfire | Pilot | Spitfire |
|---|---|---|---|
| S/L P B Pitcher | P7595 | Sgt G A Chamberlain | P7915 |
| P/O W F Ash | AD264 | Sgt J D Macfarlane | W3639 |
| P/O R W McNair | P7679 | Sgt E E Green | P7694 |
| Sgt J Long | AD117 | Sgt T D Holden | P8076 |
| Sgt W J Curtis | P7926 | Sgt R M Booth | P8136 |

The Spitfire serial numbers indicate that only three pilots, Ash, Macfarlane
and Long, had Spitfire Vs, the others were still flying Spitfire IIA types.
Known section leaders on this show were Pitcher (Red Section), Buck
McNair (Yellow) and Holden (Black). They would fly the Mark IIA
machines rather than the new Vs so that, as leaders, the better performance
of the Mark V would not give their wingmen the added problem of trying to
keep up with them.

This time the Wing would be led by Wing Commander P G Jameson DFC,
who ordinarily led the Wittering Wing, so Cowboy Blatchford must have
been on leave. Pat Jameson, famous for being one of the few RAF survivors
from the sinking of HMS *Glorious* in 1940 off Norway, was a New
Zealander. 46 Squadron's epic flight and landing on the carrier from its
airfield in Norway as they retreated, deserved a better fate but the carrier was
discovered by the German battle-cruisers *Scharnhorst* and *Gneisenau* on
8 June.

The Wing's task was one of Withdrawal Cover, that is covering the

31

withdrawal of a Circus operation over northern France. Jameson would lead 266 Squadron, flying at 20,000 feet, 412 Squadron would be at 26,000 and 411 at 27,000 feet – top cover. The Wing crossed the English coast east of Dungeness in sections of four and patrolled over the Channel for 20 minutes.

Sergeant Holden, flying a quarter of a mile behind and 500 feet below the others, observed two Me109 diving at him and turned to engage, but the German pilots immediately dived away. Crossing the Channel again Holden observed a splash and dived to take a look but saw another aircraft circling the spot so returned to base.

As the signal to return home came, McNair was two miles off Boulogne and having somehow lost his wingman, found himself alone. Again, just what he had been warned never to be. He then heard over the radio that scattered forces of Me109s were over Boulogne and instead of heading away north, flew instead towards Boulogne – and the bandits. He was at 18,000 feet and spotted several aircraft below him. He dived to 5,000 feet, then climbed above an aircraft before diving once more, singling out a Me109, and opening fire from 250 yards astern.

The 109 pilot took evasive action with a sharp left-hand turn, then dived. Buck followed and closed to 60 yards, thumbing a three-second burst before pulling away to starboard. He watched as the 109 fell away and dived into the sea, without the pilot being seen to bale out.

He now headed for home after climbing and giving a fix over the radio in case the enemy pilot had got out, but soon after this a 109 came at him out of the sun from his port side. Its first burst hit Buck's engine, and although he took violent evasive action by skidding and side-slipping, the 109 pilot stayed on his tail, firing and registering hits. The cockpit filled with smoke and then the 109 overshot him by 50 yards and Buck saw it just ten feet above. Buck pulled up and fired a short burst, seeing the hood of the 109 come off.

Flames were now flickering back into the cockpit and Buck stuck his nose down. As the engine started cutting out he slid back his own hood, undid his straps and dived over the side from a height of 400 feet. His parachute had hardly opened as he plunged into the cold Channel. However, he had been spotted and within 15 minutes was rescued by Air Sea Rescue launch No.24. He was put ashore at Dover at 1515. McNair later recorded:

> 'A few uneventful trips followed the show on 27 September, and we flew some withdrawal support missions. Fighters would meet the bombers as they were coming out of France, occasionally have an encounter with the enemy, but Spitfire fighters could not be highly aggressive. Their task was to protect the bombers from attack, so if there were any Germans off to the side and not bothering anyone, they were left alone. We were not supposed to be drawn away from our charges.
>
> 'Often the Digby Wing would refuel down south before a show. West Malling was a favourite with the Digby boys; we liked the food there, and the WAAFs seemed particularly nice too.
>
> 'On 13 October the Wing was on a routine Sweep near Le

Touquet and we heard the Controller say there were 20+
hostiles climbing near Boulogne. The CO apparently didn't
hear and continued on course. At the time we were high up over
the coast and we could have dived down out of the sun, attacked
anything we found, then continued in our dives down past them,
over the coast and home.

'I was leading Yellow Section – four aircraft – with Jack Long
as my Number Two; Jack was later killed in the Middle East.
Jack and I had kidded each other before taking off, that as we
were fed up with little happening of late, we would go off
together after any Huns and try to get at least one if there were
any in the sky. I also kidded Jack that I wouldn't break off. After
the Controller repeated that Huns were climbing, I called my
Section to follow me and peeled off into a dive.

'I was doing well over 300 mph, but I had the 'plane under
control. I didn't look behind me as I'd just been up there after
another dive and knew nobody was there. However, I had lost
the others and I spent all my time aiming at a 109 I found. I
started firing at 8-900 yards and held the Spitfire steady on
target. I gave it a great long burst and could see strikes all over
it. Pieces and chunks were coming off his engine.

'The 109 pilot turned the opposite way and as I passed it in
my dive, I turned and watched it go into the sea a couple of
miles off Boulogne. As I watched I also saw a Spitfire come
down and go into the water, then saw a parachute open at about
2,000 feet, which I assumed was the Spit's pilot. I circled the
pilot to give a Mayday radio fix for him but Control said I was
too low. I climbed to 600 or 700 feet, continued a circle and
gave another signal. I could see the pilot in the water, and the
green dye around him. Control asked me to go even higher for
a more accurate fix on his position.

'I was beginning to get twitchy about the Huns. I was nearly
out of ammunition and I was again alone near to the French
coast. I kept thinking that I had been pretty lucky the time
before and I didn't want to ride my luck too much. I climbed to
1,000 feet and told Control: "For God's sake hurry up; I've got
to get out of here!" Then the Huns arrived.

'A smart one came out of the sun at me before I could see him.
He hit my engine and blew off the cowling. I got right down on
the water and tried to out-turn him, but had to be careful as I
didn't want to do a high-speed stall right above the sea. I could
hear and feel his heavy cannon shells hitting my aircraft, and
every once in a while the rattle of machine gun bullets hitting
the machine too. The smell of cordite was getting ever stronger
in the cockpit.

'I was also getting annoyed as hell. I thought the Spit could
out-turn the 109 but I was getting hit all the time. If I couldn't
out-turn him, what could I do? Suddenly the aircraft became
very hot. I hadn't realised it before because I was sweating so

much. I wasn't afraid yet, but I was beginning to worry. The
bloody thing was full of holes and as I looked at the glycol and
oil gauges, I could see the temperatures were right off the clock
and I had no oil pressure, which meant the engine would seize
any second. I thought – Oh Hell!

'I suddenly saw the Hun was not behind me, so I went full out
in a straight line, but the enemy pilot dived at me from the port
side, but overshot me. I was going much slower than he
anticipated, but I had felt his bullets hitting the plane, but could
also see splashes in the water ahead of me as most of his burst
overshot. I was still going full out and purposely left my turn
late as he continued to overshoot me.

'By this time smoke and stuff was pouring from my machine
and the Hun must have thought I was through. He got careless;
he expected me to flip any minute into the water during my turn.
The 109 pulled around in front of me and was within close
range. I pulled up the nose of the Spit and squirted. His hood
came off and swept past me.

'Then my aircraft burst into flames. I pulled back on the stick
to get up as high as I could with what speed I had left in order
to bale out. The chances of getting out in a ditching under these
circumstances are very poor indeed. I struggled up to 400 feet
or so in a steep climb, then it started to stall. I was very calm
about removing the oxygen mask during my climb, but as soon
as I stalled I didn't bother any more. I had the canopy off my
cockpit, the side door open and I jumped.

'I realised I didn't have much height. Even as I jumped I
pushed the aircraft away with one hand and pulled the rip-cord
with the other right away. The Spitfire cut an arc in front of me
as I went into the water. In going down it just looked like I was
going in off a high-diving board as a kid. I knew the parachute
wasn't opening and I wondered whether I could get rid of it and
just dive. But it was already too late to try that and just as I
touched the water the parachute snapped open above me.

'I had maps of the Dutch coast, maps I didn't want to lose
because they'd been so scarce and hard to get. They'd been in
my flying boot and I looked for them in the water but they'd
come out and sunk. I got my dinghy out, climbed in and used
the paddle to bale the water out of it, then felt myself for broken
bones. I found I was alright, so started paddling towards
England, setting a course by the sun.

'I'd been too busy looking after myself to wonder what had
happened to the German. I was sure he was in the drink too, but
I didn't think about him until the launch arrived. They were on
their way to the spot from my Mayday call for the other Spit
pilot I'd seen. They had been watching the German and me
through glasses, seen both aircraft dicing around, then suddenly
there were no aircraft at all.

'When I was in my dinghy I could hear the motor launch

coming towards me, but I couldn't see it. I thought it probably was a German boat since I was so close to the French coast. I was very, very happy to see it was one of ours when it did come into view.

'They lowered a rope net to help me in, but I told them not to bother, that I could get up myself. But then found I couldn't get up, I was too exhausted and tired from the dog-fight and my immersion. I nearly fell back again, but they grabbed and helped me into the boat. They gave me dry clothes and some whisky and I told them as they started to head for England that there was another chap nearer the shore, probably two miles away as far as I could guess. I explained I had not sent the Mayday for myself but for this other guy. We could see the French coast quite plainly, and we searched and searched but couldn't find him. Another boat nearby then signalled that it had picked him up. He was an Australian Spitfire pilot. The two boats then started a friendly race for Dover Harbour, but the other boat burned out one of its engines so that ended that.'

However, despite his words, it is far from a cut and dried situation. The RAF were inclined to over-claim in many of these confused combats, and the exuberance of youth did little to help future historians. The two German fighter Gruppen left on the Channel front at this time were JG2 and JG26. JG2 generally looked after the area from the Seine estuary to Cherbourg, while JG26 covered the area north to Holland. On occasions they overlapped as they appear to have done on this day.

Despite the RAF claiming more than 20 German fighters shot down and losing more than a dozen, the unhappy fact is that only one Me109 was actually lost, and that was shot down by a Blenheim. Other than this JG26 had two 109s damaged, JG2 just one, and only one of these was thought to be combat-related.

There is little doubt that Buck saw an aircraft go into the sea after he had fired at a 109, but it is often the case that a pilot loses sight of an opponent whilst manoeuvring and by the time he can once more take stock of the situation, his opponent has disappeared; seeing a splash on the sea, he puts two and two together, and gets it wrong. What Buck saw go into the water was without doubt, a Spitfire, shot down by another 109 in the area.

That he claimed the cockpit hood of his target shattered, is probably correct, although whether it was the full canopy or just a panel or two is not known. Certainly this sort of damage would not have been reported above Geschwader level, and would have been easy to repair, so it would not be recorded on the German Quartermaster returns. But who was the pilot who shot McNair down?

Claims by JG26 were not really off Boulogne, one being as far across the Channel as 10 km east of Dungeness, another further south along the French coast, off Berck-sur-Mer. However, Hauptmann Johannes Schmid, CO of 8/JG26, made two claims (victories 41 and 42) but the locations are not known. JG2 had made its initial interception after Arques was bombed and continued west, out to sea, so had the chance of making claims off Boulogne.

The Stab (staff) Staffel of JG2 claimed six Spitfires. Major Walter Oesau gained his kill 15 km south-west of Boulogne, while Oberleutnant Erich Leie shot down two in three minutes (victories 27 and 28 – locations unknown). He and Oberleutnant Rudolf Pflanz and Günther Seeger then downed three more 10 km west of Etaples. Anyway, JG2 looks favourite to have got McNair, but we'll never know for certain.

* * *

An ambulance awaited Buck at the dock, and he needed it as he had imbibed a bit too readily with the whisky. He was given some dry clothes and some food, then a car arrived from RAF Hawkinge and drove him there. An intelligence officer came into the Hawkinge mess bar and told him all about the day's activities. Later he listened to the 9 o'clock CBC broadcast about the air battles that day.

Meantime, Buck telephoned his CO, who wasn't sounding too happy. Apparently 412 Squadron was having a great party at Digby in celebration of the first German aircraft destroyed by either squadron. When Buck told him that he had destroyed one too, plus another probably destroyed, Paul Pitcher could hardly wait to get away from the telephone so he could tell the rest of 411, and to tell 412 as well!

By the time Buck got back to Digby the next day, the CO was ready to bawl him out. 'You broke the rules by breaking away. You're not supposed to do that. I won't let you lead a Section again until you show me you realise that!' And so on.

Buck, of course, knew only too well that in breaking away from the squadron he had been asking for trouble. But he also felt that he would not have been shot down if he had not hung around to give the Mayday for the other pilot. He was annoyed that he was blamed for being shot down because he had been helping another pilot. But he also knew it was fair treatment.

The good news, however, was that the Squadron had been having a sweepstake for the first pilot to shoot down a German, everyone contributing 50 cents each fortnight into the pool. Buck had won it and had a nice holiday in London with the prize money.

The Australian pilot that Buck had helped rescue had been Sergeant J R H Elphick of No.452 Squadron RAAF, one of two pilots it had lost, the other not surviving. He had also been seen in the water by two other pilots of his squadron so between them all, the NCO, from New South Wales, had more than his share of guardian angels over him. Elphick would survive the war as a flight lieutenant.

It was not usual at this time for pilots to always fly totally the same Spitfire day after day, although Buck McNair usually had aircraft 'H' or 'W'. On 13 October he had been flying aircraft 'F' (P7679) that another American from Texas in the RCAF, Bill Acheson, often flew. Acheson had only just finished painting a large apple on the side of the cockpit, and now it was at the bottom of the Channel. Acheson later became a prisoner of war.

The Germans had certainly reacted this day and the RAF did over-claim somewhat. An important feature, however, was that a new fighter had been seen over France in recent days. They were thought initially to be captured

Hawk fighters the French had used in 1940 but it now transpired the Luftwaffe had a new radial-engined single-seat fighter: the Focke Wulf 190. It was a vast improvement on the Me109E and 109F fighters but what is more, it was superior to the RAF's Spitfire V machines. Tex Ash remembers:

> 'I found Buck had an eagerly aggressive attitude and the first real action was taken by him. Not long after we'd really got started, Buck went off on his own after some 109s, claimed one, but was hit by another, although he got a shot off at that one too. He baled out and finally got the Caterpillar he'd tried for when he jumped from the Magister!
>
> 'The interesting thing about Buck was that one could tell even at that time that if he survived he was likely to do very well. Yet he was never aggressive in a way that put others at risk in order to roll up his own score, unlike some, like Wally McLeod.[1] Wally was so obsessive about it and was terribly keen on a kind of egoism in building his own score. Buck never had this really. I always found Buck a delightful person to be around.
>
> 'After I was shot down[2] I was not to see him for a long time, not in fact until he was air attaché in London. We had two or three very good meetings remembering old times.'

* * *

Back at Digby, with the weather beginning to turn colder, it was a return to the usual routine, with sea sweeps from there and from RAF Coltishall. The cold was not lost on Buck McNair, especially on the 21st, when he noted in his log book: 'Need a stove in the kite to keep from freezing.' The following day his pal Don Blakeslee was posted to 401 Squadron down at Biggin Hill in 11 Group. Don was an American from Ohio, who had joined the RCAF and trained at Windsor, Ontario, when Buck was there. He would see much success with 401 and later with the American Eagle Squadrons, operating with 133. After he finally transferred to the USAAF in late 1942, he rose to command the US 4th Fighter Group, 8th Air Force. He developed into one of the great fighter leaders of WW2, taking his Mustang fighters right to Berlin for the first time in March 1944.

On the first day of November 1941 Buck managed to get his hands on a Hurricane again (having first flown one back in early September), another 401 Squadron aircraft. He hadn't been impressed then and he still hadn't changed his mind. A week later, on the 7th, Flight Lieutenant Boomer was on a dusk patrol and intercepted a Ju88. Attacking it, his gunfire smashed the German's port engine, which caught fire, and the machine crashed into the

---

[1] Squadron Leader H W McLeod DSO DFC & Bar, killed in action 27 September 1944 with a score of 21 destroyed.

[2] Tex Ash was shot down by JG26 on 24 March 1942. After evading capture for three months he was finally betrayed and became a prisoner. He made several escapes from camps, and at one time was on the escape committee at Stalag Luft III; he was made a MBE after the war.

sea off the Norfolk coast near Sheringham. Victory number two for the squadron.

On the 8th, it was back to West Malling for a Sweep with 412 and 616 Squadrons. The Luftwaffe fighters reacted vigorously once again, Buck noting in his log book: 'Jack-pot for Hermann's boys. We lost 15!'

The operation was Circus 110 and it was led by Wing Commander D R Scott AFC, who had not, apparently, flown on a combat mission let alone led one. He was among the casualties, being heard to call over the radio: 'I guess I'm too old for this, boys.' He was 33 and was buried by the Germans at Dunkirk. Worse for the Digby crowd was that 412 was bounced and had three pilots killed, one of whom was the same Owen Pickles who had been on that cross-country stunt with Buck back at Windsor, Ontario. Most of the casualties were caused by Jagdgeschwader 26, the same bunch that had been so successful the day Buck was shot down in October.

A couple of days later Buck rode his luck again during a Sea Sweep. He got so low over the water he actually hit the sea, but there was not much damage and he managed to get back to base. Then during a dusk patrol he ran into the balloons over the Humber but again luck was with him. However, on the 12th news came of a possible move to the south. This came about with the arrival of the C-in-C of Fighter Command, Air Chief Marshal Sholto Douglas, and the AOC, Air Vice-Marshal Saul, on a visit to Digby, taking tea with 411 Squadron. They confided the possibility to Pitcher and the Station Commander, Group Captain Campbell.

More excitement the next day with a visit to the Station by His Majesty King George VI, which included him having lunch in the officers' mess. Everyone was impressed and upon his departure all the mess windows suddenly shot open and everyone jumped out into the pouring rain so they could wave him off as he drove by in his car. By then it had been confirmed that the squadron was heading for RAF Hornchurch on the 19th.

Perhaps the excitement proved too much for Bill Ash, for on the 16th he was returning by air to Digby in a Havoc (a twin-engined Boston turned into a night fighter and intruder). This landed at another aerodrome first and the pilot undershot and turned the aircraft over onto its back. Ash was alright and managed to get another lift in a lorry but this too ran into difficulty on the journey and also turned over. Ash finally made it but he was somewhat shaken.

## RAF Hornchurch

As luck would have it the weather stalled the move south and it was not until the 22nd that it was sufficiently clear for the pilots to fly out. Buck's last sortie from Digby was a routine convoy patrol on the 17th, for one hour, 40 minutes.

Buck was not posted to B Flight, but the summer 'shooting' season had come to an end and operations over France had all but finished. So while they were now in the 11 Group fighting area, the month ended and December began with only a number of boring convoy patrols off the Thames estuary. The Hornchurch Wing consisted of 411, 313 Czech Squadron, with 64 and 603 joining in. The Station Commander was Group Captain Harry Broadhurst DSO DFC AFC, a fighter who often led the Hornchurch Wing too. Buck would come under this formidable leader later in the war.

Ever since RAF Fighter Command had begun to take the offensive at the end of 1940, Rhubarb sorties had been encouraged during poor weather days. These sorties, flown generally by two or four aircraft in pairs, would take advantage of low cloud to zip across into France at low level intent on shooting up anything Germanic. Anything and everything was fair game, and while they proved exciting, caused a nuisance to the dreaded Hun, and sometimes some damage, they were extremely dangerous – and costly in aircraft and pilots. However, before they were more or less stopped later in the war, most hot-blooded fighter pilots worth their salt were pretty happy to indulge themselves when circumstances permitted.

Buck McNair and 411 Squadron, now within easy flight distance of the French coast, and having to contend with the winter weather, mounted some Rhubarb sorties of their own in December. The CO took three pilots with him on the 7th – Ash, McNair and Green – but the weather improved too much over the other side so they could only stooge around off the French coast and nothing happened. Buck noted his excitement by writing down: 'Lots of Fun?' in his logbook.

Next day came the squadron's first Ramrod. These sortie code-names covered a variety of operations. A Circus was the name for fighters escorting a few bombers, the object being to entice enemy fighters up in order to destroy them. A Sweep was either a pure fighter sweep with a number of squadrons, or wings, again in the hope of shooting down hostile fighters, although in both cases the Germans did not alway play unless they had a distinct advantage in position and numbers. So the Ramrod became a few bombers, again with large escorts, going for a target of importance, rather than a Circus just bombing something to stir up the hornets. These encouraged the Luftwaffe to react – sometimes. A Roadstead was an operation for a few bombers to attack shipping in the Channel or a port, again escorted by fighters.

This first Ramrod for 411, comprised of Hurricane fighter-bombers going for a specific target, was escorted by both the Hornchurch and Biggin Hill Wings. As the Hurricanes attacked, a large force of Me109s and FW190s was encountered which cost 411 two pilots killed: Flying Officer J R Coleman from St Johns, and Sergeant D A Court from Toronto. JG26 had scored again.

A few days later the CO was posted back to Canada. If what Buck related is true, it seems that one of the squadron pilots had overshot the runway and hit an army gun-post, and the army had had a few words. Then Paul Pitcher crashed into the same gun position and this heralded his departure. On the 16th the squadron lost two more pilots from an operation launched from RAF Manston. Apparently the leader of the operation took the squadron over Calais instead of Dover returning from a convoy patrol – some miss! It was pounced on by a gaggle of Me109s that shot down Pilot Officer S D Chamberlain and Sergeant T D Holden.

Buck was to relate what actually happened. Sergeant Chamberlain had led the sortie with three other pilots following. Instead of climbing for altitude and pin-pointing himself by some landmark, he and his trio kept close to sea level whilst looking for the ships. They covered a good deal of the North Sea, but couldn't find the ships anywhere. In doing this they had missed the south-east coast of England and crossed into France. Then the German fighters came at them.

Instead of turning towards them, the four turned away. Tommy Holden and Chamberlain were shot down. Chamberlain never knew of his commission, which came through the next day, and Holden was to have been married that week to a WAAF up at Digby.

It was noted that the Squadron motto was 'Hostile to the Enemy' and perhaps after recent days, it might be changed to 'Hostile to Ourselves'! It was JG26 again, Hauptmann Joachim Müncheberg, commanding JG26's II Gruppe, who claimed both – his 61st and 62nd kills. And he was flying a FW190A-2, not a Me109F, and although 411's diary noted the operation as a convoy patrol, it was in fact a G.O. Operation, escorting minesweepers.

### Stan Turner Arrives

The day following this action, Squadron Leader P S Turner DFC and Bar arrived to take command of the squadron. Stan Turner had been in action in France, and then in the Battle of Britain, flying alongside the legendary Douglas Bader, CO of 242 Squadron. He was a natural choice, being a Canadian. At least, a near Canadian. He had been born in Devon but had emigrated to Canada with his family as a child and had grown up in Toronto.

According to Buck, life in 411 Squadron had been fairly free and easy until Stan Turner took over. He had definite ideas how pilots should fly and he demanded his squadron follow them. He thought 411 had been spoiled for several months and Buck and some of the others decided he was a nasty old man (he was 28). But inside a week they had completely reversed their opinion and were sure he was the best squadron leader in Fighter Command. Buck commented:

> 'He was really hot. He did a lot of things that were not in the book. He showed initiative. He would take the squadron out in the middle of the English Channel and fly various formations back and forth. Control didn't like us to go beyond the English coast – it was asking for trouble.'

One day Turner suggested that he and Buck should go as a pair to the French coast as escort to a single Blenheim, going along as bait to scare up some Huns. The plan was that if the Huns rose to the bait, the rest of the Wing would tear in and surprise the enemy, hopefully shooting down a few.

As Buck was putting on his flying boots and getting ready to go, the other pilots started kidding him, and asking if his insurance premiums were paid up, or if he had any juicy telephone numbers he might leave them.

As they started out and were climbing, Buck found he could not keep up. His engine would be OK one minute, then it would lose power and he would drop back, so that his flying became a succession of spurts and drags. He was starting to get embarrassed, wondering what sort of clot Turner would think him. Then he wondered if he should break radio silence and tell the CO his engine was playing up and he'd have to abort, but then, would Turner think he had the wind-up? It would also mean cancelling the bait plan.

Buck finally decided to keep quiet and try to keep station as best he could. He didn't know that the operation had been scrubbed, and that as they neared the rendezvous with the Blenheim, Turner continued on as though everything was going according to plan; all the while, Buck was struggling to maintain some sort of position.

They flew in long line abreast from Calais to Boulogne, Buck twitching for fear his engine would stop altogether at any second. They returned without incident to Hornchurch where Buck later discovered that water had got into his fuel tank, causing his motor to miss. He told Turner of his problem, his erratic engine and his thoughts over the Channel about calling up to abort. Turner laughed, but told him next time to turn back if his engine was missing, and not to be a clot.

Turner led his first Op over France on the 18th, but word had long since arrived about the Japanese attack on the US fleet and base at Pearl Harbour. It seemed now that everyone was keen to be posted overseas to fight the Japanese. More than likely the slow pace of life, even now they were in 11 Group, was starting to make people get itchy feet.

Convoy patrols and escorts over minesweepers in the Channel did little to lift spirits as Christmas passed and the New Year of 1942 began. There was a good deal of wet snow about and life was extremely dull. And of course, the Canadians were a long way from home.

Buck was coming in to land at Manston on 8 January after a minesweeper patrol. He saw a large fire blazing on the airfield. Charlie Semple of Toronto, then a sergeant pilot in 411, but two years later a squadron leader in command of it, had overshot on landing. His Spitfire crashed into a Hurricane in one of the bays, and the impact had fired a bullet into the Hurricane fighter there, scoring a hit in the petrol tank which set it on fire. Charlie broke a leg but was dragged out OK.

Ken Boomer and three others made the first Rhubarb of 1942 on 14 January, shooting up barges and a ship, then strafing some troops on a beach. A canal lock and a gun emplacement also received some attention. It seems that the squadron was putting together an Air Firing Team and on the 16th it was announced that Pilot Officers McNair, McLeod and Eakins, along with Sergeant Mowbray, had been chosen for the 11 Group Air Firing Competition.

Next morning, Ralph Weston and Buck went on a Rhubarb, crossing the French coast four miles east of Dunkirk. Buck shot up canal barges, some soldiers and a goods train, while his flight commander strafed a canal bridge and a bofors-type gun. Three Me109s were seen but evaded, then Buck's Spitfire was hit by AA fire in the port wing and in the radiator, but he managed to get it home. Spitfire 'K' (AD268) was a new Spitfire and this was its first and last flight. It was repaired and returned to strength but was lost in March – shot down by JG26. Rod Smith remembers Buck flying up to see him in January 1942:

> 'In late January Buck came up and stayed with me at Wellingore, and he was full of Stan Turner and what a difference he had made to the squadron. Buck was on leave and

wanted to go on a flight in a bomber over Germany one night!
He'd tried various bomber stations around Lincoln but just
couldn't arrange it with anyone. I was amazed he even wanted
to go, where he'd just be a passenger in a bomber.'

Buck was certainly keen to get into action, but soon he would have all the
action he could cope with – and more.

CHAPTER SIX

# TO MALTA

At the beginning of February 1942, Squadron Leader Stan Turner received a posting overseas, and this heralded another rush of squadron pilots wanting to go overseas too, if not to the Far East, then to the Middle East. Everyone was aware that there was action brewing in both North Africa and on the strategically located island of Malta.

For a few days things seemed to be in limbo while Turner awaited his final orders but Buck was to have an odd experience. The Squadron was landing back at Hornchurch in the dark one evening. The flarepath had been lit and Turner went onto the airfield with some signal flares to help bring the pilots in. Buck landed safely and had taxied to the hangars. Still sitting in his Spitfire, he saw a French-Canadian pilot coming in at an angle to the flarepath and yelled over the R/T for him to go round again as he was off track. However, the pilot kept on coming, heading straight for Buck and his Spitfire.

Buck throttled up his engine in a hurry, and got out of the way smartly just in time, as the other machine crashed into the hangar just where he had been sitting a few moments earlier. According to Buck, prangs were not uncommon. He noted that 11 aircraft had crashed on the airfield during 11 successive days.

That the Americans had entered the war made little or no impression of any kind on the Canadians and was largely ignored except for the desire, perhaps, to get to where the action was. A day or so before the famous Channel Dash operation, 12 February, the day on which the Geman Navy sent three of its big ships racing through the Channel from Brest (the *Scharnhorst*, *Gneisenau* and the *Prinz Eugen*), Buck had remarked to his CO that the weather was bloody cold. Turner had responded by saying: 'Well, it won't be cold where you're going.' He retorted with something about the Devil hadn't got him yet, and Turner laughed. Then Turner told him that he was being sent out to Malta to take over a squadron there, and that he wanted Buck to go with him as a flight commander. Buck was surprised, but without hesitation asked eagerly: 'When do we go?'

Squadron Leader R B Newton had arrived as CO designate of 411 in early February, coming in from 72 Squadron RAF. Buck spent his last few days mostly involved with local flying, his last operation being a Channel Sweep on the 11th. Then came the order to proceed overseas.

**The Journey Out**

Buck McNair had several days of leave, then prepared for the trip out to
Malta. At this time Malta had been struggling against Italian and German air
attacks, its defenders greatly out-numbered. Everything the defenders needed
had to be taken to the island either by ship, by air or by submarine. Following
the initial epic stand by a handful of Gladiator biplane fighters, Hurricanes
had started to arrive in the summer of 1940, and had then become the island's
main fighter.

By the end of 1941 it had become clear that the Hurricanes could no longer
survive against the Messerschmitt 109F fighters and the need for Spitfires
became paramount. The plan was to take the first batch in by aircraft carrier,
fly them off when still some distance from the island, and at the same time
send additional Spitfire pilots to Malta in a Sunderland flying boat.

This initial batch of tropicalised Spitfire Vb, would be the first of this
historic fighter to see operational service outside the United Kingdom, with
the exception of a few photographic reconnaissance types. Sixteen machines
had been loaded on board HMS *Eagle* and she had sailed from Gibraltar; by
7 March they were near enough, using long-range tanks, to be launched.
Fifteen became airborne, one failed to start.

\* \* \*

Stan Turner and a number of other Spitfire pilots had already arrived on the
island by flying-boat, ready for the Spitfires to arrive. An earlier attempt in
February to fly in the new fighters had failed. With Turner was Flight
Lieutenant P B 'Laddie' Lucas, an American by the name of Hiram 'Tex'
Putnam, Harry Fox and 'Tim' Goldsmith from Australia, Raoul Daddo-
Langlois (Daddy, or Daddy Longlegs, who had also been on the troopship
from Canada with Buck) and Bob Sergeant.

Buck McNair travelled down to Plymouth for the start of his trip. Calling
in at Air Ministry in London on the way to sign a number of documents, he
had been given a large grey envelope which he was told to guard with his life.
The envelope had written on it a list of the contents (which would save his
curious nature from opening it as he had done with that envelope he was
given at Grangemouth). These included official letters to Lord Gort at
Gibraltar and Air Marshal Tedder in Alexandria. He was to hand the envelope
over when he reached Gib, and was glad to do so.

Together with a handful of other fighter pilots – all sergeants – they
clambered aboard a Sunderland from No.10 Squadron RAAF, piloted by
Flying Officer B F Gaston from Cottesloe, Western Australia, on Sunday 1
March 1942. It was a seven hour flight, and Buck asked if he could fly some
of the way. He was allowed to do so and in fact he noted five of those hours
as second pilot in his flying log book. After a two-night stay, the Sunderland
departed for Malta on the 3rd, but this time Buck could only log ten hours as
a passenger. The reason it took so long on this last leg was that they were
forced to turn back to Gibraltar with engine trouble but once this was sorted
out, they were off again.

Buck was impressed by his first view of Malta, and how desolate and uninhabitable it seemed. There was an eerie, forbidding quality about it, looking more like some flat rock sticking out of the beautiful Mediterranean. It certainly did not look to him, seeing it for the first time, as if anyone lived there.

The Sunderland pilot brought his huge aircraft down on the waters of Kalafrana Bay situated at the most southerly tip of the island. Everyone hopped out in a hurry urged on by the mostly Australian crew. There was the constant grave danger of air attack by roaming Me109s eager for such a juicy target. They were put into a launch in short time, since the flying-boat's captain was obsessed with the need to put his aircraft under cover as fast as possible. In no time it was towed out of the water and wheeled into a hangar. The time was still early, around 4 am in the morning.

Breakfast was not until 0700 so he and his companions sat around waiting. While they waited a few Ju88 dive-bombers came over, dropped some bombs not far away, and then flew off. As Buck recalled later: 'We thought that very exciting, but nobody else paid much attention. Certainly nothing momentous happened.'

After a meagre breakfast, during which he met an old friend, Canadian Bud Connell, who was a flight commander with 126 Squadron, Buck set out to find Stan Turner after he'd got himself settled into the commandeered Pointe de View Hotel, which was used as the officers' mess. He found him in bed with bandages over one eye and round his head, together with sundry scratches. During a landing his cockpit canopy had jammed half open and as he looked out of it, it suddenly became unstuck, catching his head and jamming his face against the metal framework. Buck quipped that he couldn't leave Stan alone for five minutes without him getting himself into trouble!

Later, after he had risen, Turner and Wing Commander A C 'Sandy' Rabagliati DFC (known as Rag-Bags), the wing leader at Takali airfield, came over to the mess to collect him. Stan Turner had on an old battledress with no rank badges of any kind. Driving to the airfield Buck was impressed at the devastation and amazed at so much rubble, as well as the number of bomb craters all over the place.

At the airfield Buck was told that the most urgent requirement was the preparation for the arrival of the Spitfires, which were expected in a few days' time. While the Hurricanes and Spitfires had the same Merlin engine, there were some subtle differences in various other ways, and on the assumption that there would be few spares and tools with the new aircraft, it was decided to have the airmen make some special tools for the Spitfires which they knew they'd need.

Buck settled into a routine, getting used to the climate, the dust, and the food – which was not great. If he had been impressed by all the rubble and bomb holes on that first day, he was even more impressed seeing all the bomb damage in Valetta, the island's main town which sprawled around the great harbour. It was from this harbour that the few ships and submarines operated against German convoys, taking much needed materials to the German Afrika Korps fighting in North Africa. This was why Malta was so important. Just as Malta had to be supplied constantly to survive, so too did Field Marshal Erwin Rommel's army fighting in the desert, as it tried desperately to achieve the major goal – the oil fields of the Middle East Arab kingdoms.

Everything had to be taken across by sea, and Malta's prime objective was to sink, cripple or stop as much of the Axis shipping as possible. Every ship that failed to reach a North African port slowed down Rommel and made it that much easier for the British troops to thwart the moves east.

As they waited for the Spitfires, roads and taxi-ways were constructed off the runways, some of these extending for more than half a mile. Army personnel many of whom manned the AA guns, helped with this work, crushing rock, moving rock – eating rock!

## The Spitfires Arrive

Finally on the 7th, that first handful of Spitfires arrived. It was quite a moment for the tired defenders as they began to drop their wheels and curve onto the runway, its bomb craters filled with rubble and earth, then packed down by a steam-roller. The Spits were led by Squadron Leader Stan Grant DFC, a Battle of Britain veteran, and among those landing was Johnny Plagis, a Rhodesian, who would do well on Malta in the coming months. Amongst the others were Philip 'Nip' Hepple DFC, who had flown in Bader's Tangmere Wing in 1941, and Peter Nash. He too would make a name for himself before being lost; in fact he would also make the first Spitfire claim from the island. Of the rest, Doug Leggo, Paul Brennan, and Norm MacQueen would stand out.

The first problem was the Spitfires' camouflage. They were in desert warpaint – sandy brown. This was highly unsatisfactory, Malta was not a desert, and they would be operating largely over water. As soon as possible various colours of paint that were to hand were mixed to produce a sort of dark grey which was then hurriedly applied to the aircraft. Buck later remembered the one-colour grey made the Spitfires look more beautiful and entrancing than any of the pilots had ever seen one before. It was also most effective as camouflage over the sea. It was the colour followed thereafter, although in future the Spitfires were re-painted at Gibraltar first.

Another snag was to find the Spitfires' guns had not been properly harmonised, so for the first two days everyone was kept busy getting the machines in shape, while roundly cursing those responsible (irresponsible?) for not having the aircraft prepared properly at Gib where tools and other facilities were more readily available, and the ground crews were not under constant threat of bombing.

Finally on the 9th, Stan Turner telephoned Buck at the Mess. He wanted Buck to fly with him to air test the first serviceable Spitfires, each taking a wingman with them. Turner, of course, was commanding 249 Squadron, to which Buck and Laddie Lucas had both been posted as flight commanders. The newly painted Spits were cleared for take-off, Buck taking one marked GN-B off for a 30-minute test hop. While they were up some Ju88s came over and bombed the two other airfields, Hal Far and Luqa. Buck recorded:

'The Huns were at 18,000 feet, we were at 500. We couldn't climb as the island was studded with guns firing at them. We were afraid we would be shot down by our own guns if we did climb towards them. We set a course for our own airfield at

Takali and landed safely, as the Huns were not bothering with it on this sortie. Stan was waiting for us and watched our approach. He later reprimanded my No.2 for flying too far behind me.

'There was an uncomfortable situation in 249 Squadron at this time. Stan Turner, an extremely good pilot and fighter leader, was CO, but Stan Grant had been told as he left for Malta that he would be CO. There remained a feeling of embarrassment until it became known that Turner was to be promoted to Wing Commander Flying on the 15th, Rag-Bags being tour-expired.

'Grant was a good type of Englishman, quite a good flyer, but his personality was of far greater value to him as CO than his flying ability.'

Buck had his first Scramble this same day, but did not make contact, although the squadron had Pilot Officer Ken Murray, a young Australian, recorded as the first Spitfire pilot to be lost over the island. Next day three more Scrambles. Buck located two Me109s but failed to catch them.

With the scarcity of aircraft, it was not always possible to fly each day, nor was it desirable. The pressure was always on and unless pilots had regular breaks, they would soon burn themselves out. It wasn't just a case of constant action, but even trying to get back onto the airfield was often a major problem. German fighter pilots would hang around just waiting for the opportunity to pick off a landing aircraft, and the Hurricanes and Spitfires could obviously not stay up indefinitely. And this always supposed that the runway was not littered with bomb craters, shards of shrapnel and unexploded bombs. Buck did not get airborne again until the 16th; again there were bags of 109s about but he didn't get amongst them. Two days later he did – and nearly shot down Stan Turner!

Part of the offensive arm of Malta was the ability to locate ships to attack. While it was still a great secret, the commanders on Malta did receive Ultra intercepts and knew something of the movement of Axis shipping, but it was still necessary to send out reconnaissance aircraft to confirm their presence and number, as well as show the Germans the RAF was looking, thereby protecting the Ultra intelligence information. PRU Spitfires were used and so were twin-engined Martin Maryland machines. Adrian Warburton DSO DFC became legendary on Malta flying one of these.

On the 18th Spitfires were Scrambled, in part to give protection to a returning Maryland, Turner and Laddie Lucas leading two sections (four aircraft). A few Me109s had been reported and so the lunch break had been interrupted. South of the island they spotted a similar number of 109s and McNair made a head-on attack on the first one, but without discerning results. Turner attacked the same 109 and saw cannon strikes, claiming a damaged. McNair, meantime, had turned tightly onto the tail of another Messerschmitt and emptied his guns at it, seeing strikes too. However, Turner had drifted to one side and nearly ran into Buck's line of fire. It was a close thing, and not an event to encourage promotion. Buck later recorded:

'We were flying a finger-four formation, almost line abreast, with Turner slightly ahead. I was on his left as his No.2, while on his right were Laddie and Daddy. I saw a couple of 109s off at about 10 o'clock, right on the water, flying towards us. We were at about 500 feet and I was very lucky to spot them because their camouflage was exceptionally good.

'They continued toward us and having warned the others, we made an almost head-on attack. I missed my target, so we wheeled around and up to 2-300 feet, finding the 109s 6-700 yards ahead of us. I aimed at one, found my fire was falling short, eased the nose up a bit, then saw strikes on the tailplane, but nothing else happened.

'As I first started to fire, Stan was about 100 feet below me and firing at the same 109. We were converging as we aimed our planes at the same target. The first he knew of me opening fire was seeing my shell cases starting to fall in front of him. He eased back to cover me.

'I had the emergency tit pulled completely out for maximum speed in an attempt to gain on the Germans, but couldn't close an inch. Suddenly they zoomed up in front of us; they had pulled their emergency tits too and great streams of black smoke poured from their exhausts as they pulled away from us with ease. Our Spitfire Vs couldn't come near them for speed.

'I was still following the one Hun but Stan ordered me to break off. Stan felt as disheartened, as I did, by the way the 109s had pulled away from us so easily, and he commented: "It looks as though we'll never get any 109s at this rate."

'Stan and I were both credited with a damaged – his in the head-on attack, mine in the tail attack. It was just on dusk as we landed and Daddy was ecstatic about the beauty of the fire pouring from our cannon and machine guns; he had never seen gunfire in the air just at dusk. The Spitfire Vb had two cannon and four machine guns. Each cannon had 60 rounds of 20mm shells which gave about 6-seconds fire, each machine gun enough ammo for about 12 seconds.'

**First Kill**

Laddie Lucas led four pilots off as top cover to some Hurricanes at 0805 hours on the 20th. Patrolling at 11,000 feet they saw some Me109s coming in from the south over Filfla Island, 2,000 feet below. Checking there were no other 109s lurking above, the Spitfires peeled off and dived towards them. Buck singled out one firing at it as its pilot turned away from him. Caught by cannon shells the enemy fighter went into a spiral dive, Buck following it snapping bursts into it all the time. Smoke began to trail back from the stricken machine followed by a splash on the water south of Delimara.

Another 109 curved round onto the tail of Pilot Officer Doug Leggo, who was lagging behind, and shot him down near Siggiewi. Daddo-Langlois went after this 109, chasing it north and firing at it but without result.

The fighters had been from 7/JG53, and 'White 4', piloted by Unteroffizier Josef Fankhauser had been Buck McNair's victim; his body was washed up on Sicily seven weeks later. Two other JG53 pilots made claims for Leggo and another Spitfire, but 249 only lost one in this action. The two claimants were Leutnants Hermann Neuhoff and Ernst Klager.

What made the loss more painful was that as the Spitfires were reforming, they had spotted Leggo below on his own, looking for someone to join up with. In that moment the 109 had swooped down, fired and the Spitfire rolled over and went earthwards. Seconds later a parachute appeared, but within a heartbeat a second 109 flew by then headed away. The luckless pilot was found to be dead by soldiers from the nearby 4th Heavy AA Regiment, RA, who were the first on the scene, but he was still grasping the parachute harness. As Buck later recorded, there was more behind the story:

'On this day Laddie, Daddy, myself, and a Rhodesian named Doug Leggo were due to be on Readiness at dawn. The evening before they were at the Union Club in Valetta where they could occasionally acquire a black-market egg or steak; while there they would drink brandy and ginger ale.

'Doug was with a girl at the Club and didn't leave with the others. In fact he did not return to the airfield until it was about time to go on Readiness. Doug had drunk a fair amount, and had had no sleep. As pilots on Readiness could expect at least one Scramble call during their four-hour shift, Johnny Plagis suggested he take Doug's turn on this first Readiness period, and Doug take Johnny's place on the second, after getting some sleep. But Doug was obstinate, partly from drinking, partly from pride in his ability to keep himself fit to fly, and he insisted he was fit.

'We four got our Scramble call and soared up to 10,000 feet. We were just turning down into the sun, when Daddy called on the R/T that there were 109s at 6 o'clock – behind and above. We had time to turn around and break into them and I screamed round to the right and found I had turned too quickly and the Huns were still some distance away. I eased up a bit on my turn, for if I had continued it I would have put my belly to a 109, so I straightened up and he would have to turn his belly to me. He did, and I let off a great squirt at him. The 109 went into a spiral dive, and looking round and finding no other Huns about, I went down after it, having no trouble in following.

'I waited my chance to fire again, and got a good burst into it. I saw hits on the starboard wing, pieces came off, but he still didn't take any evasive action, just continued with the spiral dive. Down to 3,000 feet I started clobbering the 109 all over. I emptied my cannon and continued with the machine guns. Oil and glycol from its cooling system poured out. The white glycol looked beautiful streaming out into the clear air; it was a really lovely day.

'Looking round there was still nobody behind me. The German now pulled up over the roofs of Valetta, reached the sea and crashed into it. As I was turning back I heard Doug Leggo call up Daddy and ask where he was. Daddy said he was at

12,000 feet, then Doug said he was at 8,000 and would climb
up. I called up and said I was on the deck and told Doug not to
climb up by himself. Daddy also called, telling him not to climb
but go down.

'Daddy saw Huns behind Doug down below and immediately
yelled for him to break. But Doug was slow in breaking and was
shot down. He came down near Valetta, got out of his machine
at around 300 feet but his parachute did not open.

'I was unaware of the tragedy happening above me, and was
feeling good about having destroyed a 109. I was so happy I
roared across the airfield almost touching the ground, then
zoomed up into a victory roll. Stan Turner was waiting for me
when I climbed out of my Spitfire. He looked pleased but was
trying to look very angry. He yelled at me for doing aerobatics
so low, and such sloppy aerobatics at that!

'Leggo was a grand chappie and Johnny Plagis was extremely
upset at this loss. He blamed himself for not having forced
Doug to stand down. I was angry that Johnny felt he should
shoulder the blame; they had all tried to convince Doug he
should rest before going up and when he did go he disobeyed
orders by climbing into trouble.'

## Bombed

The officers' mess – the Pointe de View Hotel, at Rabat – in which Buck
lived, was a two-storey, country-style hotel, built on different street levels.
The front had two or three sub-basements where the street receded. It had
Maltese cooks and waiters, one of whom was known as Joe. Buck thought
him a good chap, but most of the others were thieves. They'd steal anything
and everything they could get their hands on, he noted.

Part of the hall was made into a bar, and off this was a room with a pool
table. The dining room would usually seat about 20 people, and the bedrooms
were of different sizes. Buck shared a fairly small one with Joe Crichton, of
126 Squadron, while larger rooms were each shared by four or five pilots.

Pilots could also go out onto the flat roof and sunbathe. There was a
splendid view over Malta, looking out over all the airfields to the north. Parts
of Valetta could be seen too. Pilots not on duty could stand there and watch
the raids in progress right in front of them – just like the movies!

The day after Buck's first victory over the island came an event that was
to remain with him for the rest of his life, although it was also an event which
almost claimed it. It was known that a supply convoy was on its way to the
island and that things would be busy and hectic in a day or so. This 21st day
of March the Luftwaffe made a concerted effort against Takali. Generally
they dive-bombed such targets but this day the Ju88s remained at 16,000 feet
or so which caused some of the bombs to spread away somewhat from the
target area. Some bombs overshot the airfield, landing in the vicinity of
Mosta, to the north-west, but one of substantial size, undershot and scored a
direct hit on the hotel.

Five pilots were killed, two from 249 Squadron (Pilot Officers Booth and
Guerin), and two from 126 (Flying Officer C Baker and Pilot Officer W H

Hallett), as well as an RAF intelligence officer. A third 126 Squadron pilot, the American Pilot Officer E Streets, lost a leg and his sight, and died later. It might have been much worse, for three other pilots of 249 Squadron – Buck, Bud Connell and Ronnie West – had been to the local cinema in Rabat, where the air raid alarm had interrupted the show. During the bombing the three had ambled back towards the hotel, occasionally dodging into doorways. Buck had just reached the hotel entrance lobby as the bomb hit.

'When I came round, I didn't know where I was. I didn't feel I was dead, but I didn't feel whole. My eyes were open, but my jaw and chest didn't seem to be there. There was no pain, I just didn't seem to have jaws or chest. I felt for my tin hat, then I started to be able to see just as if the sun was coming up after a great darkness. I explored myself with my fingers and found that I had a face and a chest, so I felt better.

'It started to get light – the darkness had been due to the showers of dust from the stone building. I felt for my revolver, the one Stan Turner had given me at Hornchurch, back in England. I mucked around and found it, knocking the dust off it and checking it to make sure it was loaded.

'As I became more conscious, I found I was upstairs; but I knew I shouldn't be upstairs – I should be downstairs. Then I realised I had been blown upstairs, either through a door or through an opening at the turn of the staircase. I'd been thrown up 20 or 30 feet.

'I went out onto the roof and back down the main staircase which was barely hanging in place. I saw the bodies lying at the foot of it. They were in a heap. There was no blood. The raid was still on – the All Clear hadn't sounded – but everything seemed very quiet. Heavy dust covered the bodies. I looked down at them, studied them. One was headless, the head had been cut cleanly away from the top of the shoulders. I didn't see the head, but I could recognise the man by his very broad shoulders.

'I heard a moan, so I put my hand gently on the bodies to feel which of them was alive. One of them I noticed had a hole, more than a foot wide, right through the abdomen. Another's head was split wide open into two halves, from back to front, by a piece of shrapnel. The face had expanded to twice its size. How the man managed to still be alive I didn't know. I thought of shooting him with my revolver. As I felt for it, I heard Bud Connell's voice behind me: "Look at this mess!"

'I put my hand against the wall, but it slithered down it. It had seemed dry with all the dust, but when I took my hand away I found it was covered with blood and bits of flesh stuck to it – like a butcher's shop when they're chopping up meat and cleaning up a joint. I turned to Bud. "For God's sake, don't come in here." Then I noticed that my battledress and trousers were torn and ripped.

'Ronnie West appeared. It seemed natural to see him. He had been in the building with us, but he didn't say anything about me being there. He didn't seem to want to talk.

'Now an ambulance and a doctor arrived. The doc asked me to help him with the bodies. I said, "Get someone else, I've seen enough." But I did get one chap onto a stretcher. He was still alive, but I couldn't recognise him. I put a cloth over his face and then a stupid orderly took it off. It was the most horrible sight I've ever seen and I've seen chappies with heads off and gaping wounds and horrible burns.

'The realisation of what had happened began to dawn very slowly. My left arm had gone out of joint when I was blown upstairs by the bomb, but I had shoved it back in place. Ronnie and I sat on the kerbside and talked about it. As we discussed it we began to understand the awfulness of it all. Then we started cursing the bloody Huns; it was maddening that all we could do to them was curse. We were inwardly sick, sick at heart.

'We decided to get drunk. When we got over to the mess, the orderly refused us anything to drink and wouldn't open the bar. We broke our way in and each took a bottle ... it helped relieve the tension.'

Buck was a tough hombre but this had been a traumatising experience. Yet he knew he had to carry on and so by sheer will-power forced it to the back of his brain. As Laddie Lucas was later to write, it was the measure of Buck's courage that forced him on, but Laddie knew it had changed him. The brash, complaining exterior was still there, but he was now a quieter, gentler man, but ever the fighter. Fighter pilots know death, but usually at a distance. This had been too close.

When Doug Leggo had been killed the previous day, his friend Johnny Plagis had promised to avenge him. There is no record that Buck openly spoke in similar vein after the bomb raid, but no one can say what he was thinking.

What is certain is this horrendous experience scarred Buck McNair for the rest of his life. During and after WW2 there was no counselling as there is in present day conflicts, no soothing words, no effort at understanding, no laying of ghosts. Like WW1, fighting men were supposed to keep a 'stiff upper lip' – play the man; everyone was in the same boat was the theory.

Be that as it may, there were many who tried to keep their own counsel and failed and even more, like Buck, who bottled it up and in the main, kept a tight lid on it. That doesn't mean it didn't affect them. As for him, he had to continue the fight. Nobody would have even contemplated anyone going home from Malta merely because they had been bombed, however near to death they had come. This was almost a daily occurrence. Keep going lad, you'll get over it!

Buck may outwardly have got over it, but inwardly it had traumatised him. In some ways he was lucky that he could still function, and function well. Probably that is what helped him to keep going. At least he was able to hit back and in flying he could focus on something else rather than how near he had come to death. And in the same way he could expel the sight of his dead comrades. Years later, Laddie Lucas said he thought Buck should have been sent back home after the experience, but it was not the time or place. Malta needed every pilot she could get.

Fighter pilots didn't often come face to face with dead people, unless someone crashed an aeroplane on an airfield. While they could send out streams of death with their cannon and machine guns, many focused on the hostile aeroplane that had to be destroyed. Few wanted to think of the pilot or crew in that aeroplane. And anyway, they were the enemy. They needed to be stopped – destroyed.

Buck McNair set his jaw, and got on with it.

# CHAPTER SEVEN

# FIGHTER PILOT'S PARADISE

Apart from the constant danger, the constant action, the poor living and eating conditions and the thought always in the back of the mind as to whether the Germans would invade, as they had invaded Crete, Malta was a fighter pilot's heaven. There were no boring patrols, escorts, and sweeps, wondering if action was likely. Action was here, up close and personal.

While one could occasionally relax, even go for a swim or sunbathe as the spring sunshine got warmer, prior to the summer's blistering heat, the battle was always there. Every day, whether flying or resting, death was nearby. In England, if one had a day off, one could easily forget the pressures. Sleep was fairly easy, in a soft bed in a cool mess bedroom, go into a nearby town, have a quiet pint. On Malta the bombs found airfields and buildings alike. There were few hiding places, and few places to go for peace.

Buck McNair had little time to get over his shattering experience. He and the others were needed. He was back in a Spitfire three days later, twice Scrambled into action. On 26 March he was off again. There was 8/10th cloud. The convoy had arrived, ships were in the harbour and being heavily attacked by bombers; every Spitfire serviceable was engaged during the day.

In the early afternoon 249 Scrambled four machines from Luqa – the only four available – to intercept more than a dozen Ju87 Stuka dive-bombers of III/StG3 and three Ju88s from I/KG54, escorted by Me109s. Sergeant Brennan went for the 88s and claimed hits on one which broke away. Bud Connell picked on another, probably the same one, and believed his fire hacked its tail off. Buck went after a Ju88, seeing his cannon and machine gun fire splatter all over it, then watched as it dived away and disintegrated as it went into the sea half a mile off Xlendi Bay, Gozo. The four-man crew clambered into a dinghy and were later rescued by Maltese police. In all probability all three RAF pilots had attacked the same Junkers.

The four-man crew of this 88 (coded B3+KH) were Leutnant Johannes Rottmann, Obergefreiters Heinz Feuerfünger and Franz Riemsche, plus Gefreiter Willi Stornbach.

In the book Paul Brennan and Ray Hesselyn wrote after they left the island (*Spitfires over Malta*, Jarrolds, London, 1943) Brennan relates:

> 'On the afternoon of the 26th I took off again. Bud Connell,
> Buck McNair and Junior Tayleur were with me. We climbed

south of the island and went up sun, being joined by Johnny Johnston and another Spit from 261 Squadron. We were at about 18,000 feet when a big bunch of 88s, heavily escorted, arrived over the harbour. As Connell led us in, Woodhall called up: "Take it easy boys. I have a lovely party for you. There are some 87s on the way." Bud however decided to attack the 88s. They seemed to be everywhere, and there were so many I could not decide which to attack. After a few seconds' hesitation I turned on one, opening fire when well out of range. It was the first 88 I had attacked, and it seemed much closer to me than it was. The 88's rear gunner also opened fire. . . . I thought I had hit him.

'Just then I had a quick look behind. Two 109s were coming down on me. I had to leave the 88 and turn towards the fighters, but instead of engaging, they rolled on their backs and went down. I turned back to my 88, which, travelling parallel with the coast, was streaking over Filfla. Buck McNair also gave chase. He was about 200 yards ahead of me and 500 yards from the bomber. The 88's throttles were wide open, and a streak of brown smoke was pouring from each exhaust, due to the pilot's heavy demand on his motors. Buck caught the bomber south of Gozo, and gave him a short burst. I could see spent cannon shells falling out of Buck's wings and the black smoke coming from his guns. He gave the fleeing bomber a second and longer burst. Its starboard wing root and motor caught fire. The 88 commenced to disintigrate and, as Buck broke off his attack, crashed into the sea. Buck and I joined up and, without further incident, returned to base.'

Buck's recollection of this action was:

'Bud Connell was leading, Junior Tayleur his No.2, with Paul Brennan as my wingman. We came across a bunch of Huns diving and bombing. It was then a case of each man picking a target. I selected one, decided it was going too fast and that I couldn't catch it. I saw another and went full-out at it.

'Brennan was above me, and had a go too and he thought he'd hit it, but then he saw another Spit going for it – me – so pulled off to give cover. I was 800 yards behind the 88 and could scarcely gain on it. He nipped into cloud 1,000 feet thick. I followed on course and when I came out he was still ahead of me. If he'd had any sense he would have turned and foxed me, but he just tried to out-run me; the Spit didn't have that much speed advantage over a fleeing Ju88.

'I chased him full out, and had a difficult time catching him, so I fired short bursts at various sights, first up, then down with the nose of the Spit. Brennan stayed behind and above, called to me: "Spitfire chasing an 88 – it's a Spitfire behind you", in case he thought I might think him a 109. I said OK. One of my bursts

hit the 88; glycol came out of one engine which then burst into
flames. I started to gain on him now – I knew I had him. The
rear gunner kept firing at me, I could see smoke from his bursts.
I put my face right behind the sight. Even if a bullet hit my
windscreen and shattered it, the glass would be deflected by the
gunsight. I fired another short burst and he dived down towards
the water, but the rear gunner was still firing at me when the
bomber woomped into the water. The machine seemed to
disintegrate.

'I flew over the spot, circled and could see a rubber tyre and
odd bits of wreckage floating about. Two or three fellows were
hanging on to bits and pieces, then I saw a fourth. They
managed to get out a dinghy which they held on to.'

Bud Connell then joined up with McNair in attacking the Stukas; Buck
claimed one probably destroyed, which was later upgraded to a destroyed.
However, Buck does not mention or record an attack on a Ju87 in his logbook, so the probability is that Connell made the claim.

At 1725 249 Squadron again Scrambled four Spitfires, McNair, Connell,
Brennan and McHan, an American. 'Sunday' McHan's aircraft was peppered
by 'friendly' AA fire but he managed to land at Takali. The other three
engaged a formation of Ju88s and four were claimed as damaged, two by
McNair, one each by the other two. One of Buck's was last seen heading
north on fire, and was more likely a probable. Me 109s then engaged the
Spitfires and they had to break off pursuit. Later a Ju88 of 3/KGr806 crash-
landed at Comiso, Sicily, with its rear gunner dead.

Richard McHan was called 'Sunday' because he was always well turned
out, always spruce, as if wearing his 'Sunday Best'. He had previously been
an Eagle Squadron pilot in England. George Buchanan was a Rhodesian and
former policeman. He was known as Buck too but this was derived from the
Buchanan name, not Robert.

**Desperate Times**
The situation by the end of March 1942 was far from rosy. A number of the
Spitfires had already been lost or damaged, and the food and ammunition
states were again low. There were rumours that more Spitfires would soon
arrive but until they did so, it was decided that with the few Hurricanes that
remained serviceable, their pilots should, whenever possible, attack the
bombers while the more manoeuvrable Spitfires should engage the fighters,
hoping to keep the Hurricane pilots from being molested.

It became the practice for four Spitfires to be used as top cover for as many
Hurricanes as could be put up. At one stage there was hardly a Spitfire left,
with the exception of one or two that might be made serviceable after
extensive repairs. Sensing the RAF's difficulty the enemy raids appeared to
increase in number. Two or three raids daily seemed to be about average.
These would blast the airfields, the harbour, revisit the harbour, then the
airfields.

During one period of having so few aircraft, everyone set to work building
bays to accommodate those they had. All the pilots worked together on one

bay, known as the pilots' bay, partly to give more purpose to their work and partly because they didn't want to work with the Maltese. Buck recalled:

'We had trouble with some of the Maltese. In addition to their regular wages, they got danger pay for working on the airfield. But they wouldn't work unless there was transport standing by to rush them away to a shelter in case of a raid. They would rush away as soon as the sirens started, while we kept on working until the bombs started to fall, then we would hop into a ditch and hope for the best.

'We were annoyed at them. For one thing, we could hardly get petrol for our ambulance, but they used gallons of it to rush them to an air-raid shelter. We hardly had enough gas for our Spitfires sometimes.

'Our airfield at this time was in a shocking state. There were scores of bomb holes, dozens of unexploded bombs with little flags stuck up near them. Wrecked aircraft littered the place. We were bombed nearly every day, and no attempt was made to repair the damage. I thought later that this was a deliberate policy in order to deceive the Hun reconnaissance people into thinking we were abandoning not only the 'drome, *but possibly the island, and were not planning to bring in any new aircraft.*'

## Crash Landing

'Our mechanics', wrote Buck, 'were always working at the disheartening job of repairing aircraft. They might work for days taking parts off two or three wrecked machines in order to repair one. Then it might be bombed before it had a chance to take off. One foul day when the fog was up to the top of some hills, Bud Connell said the mechanics had finished making a Spitfire from the wrecks of others, but had to wait until a second was ready before we could air-test it. Nobody ever flew off on their own.

'We told Stan Turner we were air-testing these two and he said: "For God's sake don't smash either of them." We found the two aircraft, mine was farther along than Bud's, and we got them started. Bud took off OK, but I couldn't find any place I could taxi for a take-off. There were holes everywhere. Finally I decided to go over to where Bud had flown off from on the other side. I noticed as I taxied that my engine was getting quite hot and I would have to shut it off soon unless I got airborne.

'It was still alright as I reached marks in foot-high grass where Bud had taken off. I opened the throttle wide to get off as quickly as possible so I wouldn't run into any holes. I was almost airborne as I felt a great bump and thought I must have hit something. It wasn't a hole, but it sure was a bump. I got off alright, both wheels up, but the undercarriage lights weren't working and the machine didn't trim properly, but it seemed generally OK.

'Then "Gonda" – flying control – called up and said: "To the pilot of the second Spitfire to take off; don't land until you get further instructions." I asked: "Whatsamatter?", and the controller replied: "You lost a wheel on take-off!"

'This was sobering news. I joined up with Bud and asked him to fly underneath me, and sure enough, the starboard leg and wheel were missing. My heart sank to my tummy, I was so unhappy. Just two Spitfires available, repaired after so much work, and I'd done this. Bud and I talked over which landing would do the least damage, one wheel down or a belly landing without wheels. We went back over the airfield and I wondered how I'd be able to land even if I had two wheels, the strip was so full of potholes. I even began feeling sorry for Bud having to land with two wheels!

'I thought that if I tried it on one wheel, a landing that is difficult to control anyway, I might go into a big pot-hole and completely wreck the aircraft. Some holes were as much as 20 feet across and six feet deep. So I decided on a belly landing. I knew it would wreck the propeller but I planned to stop it so that the shock of the prop on the ground would not be transmitted to the engine, as it would be if the prop hit while it was still revolving.

'Coming in I tightened my safety belt more, braced my knees against the instrument panel and stopped the engine as I came in over the edge of the field at about 90 mph. I got down alright although the shock of landing bruised my left knee, but it barely broke the skin. However, an infection later set in, the leg swelled, and later, on Gibraltar, I went into hospital. A couple of years later the leg still bothered me.

'Although I had got down pretty well I felt sick at heart and didn't have the strength to climb out for several minutes. I felt so badly at having smashed the Spitfire that tears came to my eyes. When I finally got out and looked at the little thing in the weeds and grass, which were 18 inches high or so, it seemed squat, so forlorn. I thought of the aircraft as a pathetic, poor creature, sitting there all broken up.

'I then discovered that someone had happened to see the wheel bounce off while watching me become airborne, and had notified flying control. We went over to investigate the spot and found I had hit an unexploded bomb, almost completely buried in the ground and obscured by the weeds and grass. There was a little flag beside it, but that was just for pedestrians walking near it, and was not big enough to be seen at any distance. I was told I was lucky the crack of the wheel against it hadn't set it off, blowing up both me and the Spitfire, so I guess I had been lucky.

'The Station Commander rushed out, angrily demanding to know why a precious Spitfire had been landed with its wheels up. I explained why, he seemed grudgingly satisfied and stomped off.'

All this had occurred on 16 April, and with his injured knee and the lack of Spitfires, Buck did not get airborne again until the 20th. Six Hurricanes had been flown to the island from North Africa on the 19th. However, more help was on the way and in fact on the 20th not only more Spitfires arrived, but they came in the shape of two new squadrons, 601 and 603, of the Royal Auxiliary Air Force. A total of 47 Spitfires took off from the American aircraft carrier USS *Wasp*, which had been steaming from the Straits of Gibraltar since the night of the 18/19th.

To the surprise of Buck and others in 249, it was the Maltese who told them that an American carrier was part of a convoy heading towards Malta, bringing with it more Spitfires. They always seemed to know all the secret gen long before they did! However, on the 20th, the few aircraft available were made ready to support the arrival, and the pilots – those who would fly and those who would not – congregated in the dispersal huts on the airfield.

The squadron had two dispersal huts, where the pilots waited for their turn at Readiness. The airfield was bombed so often that the pilots didn't bother to leave the huts during a raid. The attitude was, if we're hit, well, that'll be too bad. One day the west dispersal hut was bombed while two pilots were in it. One was reading, the other was over by the door. After the bomb hit, the chap by the door, who had been blown out, went back inside, seeing his companion still sitting with his book on his knees, although he seemed asleep. The other pilot touched him to ask if he was OK and he fell over. He had been killed by the concussion. Buck related a similar story later:

> 'One night the AOC called us together and told us some aircraft would likely be in on the following day. We had half expected this news because of what the Maltese civilians had already told us! He had every fighter pilot on the island in that one mess – probably around forty of us. We had no electric light, just candles.
>
> 'While the AOC was talking, a raid started. Whistling of falling bombs could be heard and the AOC was immediately disregarded as pilots dived under tables, got behind chairs and so on. One bomb landed close, shaking the building. I thought afterwards that if a bomb had made a direct hit on that small building at that time, Malta might have been lost.'

Because all the petrol had to be man handled, the pilots got together, and with some army types assigned to them as helpers, arranged that enough petrol would be stored in each aircraft bay to refuel each aircraft twice, as well as enough oil and ammunition. Each bay had a team of three, including a rigger, a fitter and a pilot. In some cases army men who never had been near an aircraft became riggers and fitters in the three-man teams.

They had a couple of rehearsals to prepare for the next batch of Spitfires to arrive and they inaugurated a system of flags hoisted at a bay as soon as the Spitfire was ready to go. By the morning of the expected arrival, all the airmen and soldiers were waiting in position. Buck continued:

> 'The next day we were sunning ourselves out on the roof. We

were expecting aircraft and were looking out for them.
Suddenly we spotted them – we counted about 20 – and we
cheered. We were deliriously happy when we saw they were
four-cannon Spitfires, the new Mark Vc. This would give us
twice the strength of fire and we should be able to shoot down
more Huns, we thought.

'We dressed and rushed to the aerodrome. Everyone was
excited and happy as kids at a party. We placed the first aircraft
that landed into one of our new bays. The second Spitfire to
land went to the right, off the runway, and crashed into the
Spitfire in the bay, completely wrecking both machines. It was
heart-breaking.

'Another pilot had broken the tail wheel off his aircraft when
he left the carrier. After he landed he began taxying around. We
cursed him and soon got him stopped, put a dolly under the tail
so the machine could be pushed into position without bumping
it to pieces. We had hungered so long and so much for new
Spitfires it made us hopping mad to see them mis-used.

'A lot of the new pilots were immediately grounded because
of their limited fighter experience. It seemed to us as we talked
about it in the mess that England was sending out some men just
to get rid of them. There were others who were wonderfully fine
pilots, but we grounded those who didn't have enough on the
ball – and sent them back to Gibraltar.

'After these Spitfires had landed, we saw another group of
about 20 nearing the aerodrome. It completely threw us, we
were so happy. It seemed as though our bitching was finally
bearing fruit. Up to that time two pilots had gone back to
England to persuade the authorities to send out more Spitfires –
Squadron Leader Gracie and our own Stan Turner. Jumbo
Gracie led out the first batch, while Turner stayed in London to
do some more importing.

'Pilots helped ground crews to fix up the Spitfires for flying,
but the next day, before they were ready, the Germans bombed
the airfield and ruined some of them before they had a chance
to be flown in action.

'Pilots decided to use only two cannon in each Spitfire
harmonised for flying, deciding the other two cannon could
wait. Everyone groused that the guns should have been
harmonised before they arrived on Malta. Some effort had been
made apparently, but some guns were not even working
properly.

'The first time I flew a Vc I noted how heavy it was and
cumbersome. I was sure it would not out-turn a 109, just knew
it wasn't as fast. Generally speaking, fighter versus fighter, we
were in a much poorer position with the Spitfire Vc against the
109 than we had been with anything before. We were all greatly
disappointed.'

While four cannons were better than two in fire-power, the extra weight of the two guns and ammunition was affecting the Spitire's performance. Eventually the two extra guns were taken out.

## Reinforcements

The 20th was a big day and Buck McNair was Scrambled twice. Squadron Leader E J 'Jumbo' Gracie DFC led the first group of Spitfires from the carrier; 601 Squadron was being led by Squadron Leader John Bisdee DFC, 603 Squadron by Squadron Leader Lord Douglas-Hamilton.

On the island everything had been prepared for their arrival that could be done and it was up to the handful of Hurricanes and Spitfires to help protect them as they landed. No sooner had each Spitfire touched down than it would be refuelled and sent off with an experienced Malta veteran; (a) to get it off the ground before it was bombed or strafed, (b) to help in the protection of the airfields and other Spitfires still arrriving.

Six Spitfires of 249 were Scrambled at 1300 hours led by Buck McNair, climbing to 17,000 feet. Seven miles south of Delimara he saw some Ju87s heading for Hal Far airfield, but in the attack the Spitfires became split up by several Me109s. Buck turned on to a 109 which was attacking Daddo-Langlois and scored strikes along its fuselage. The German pilot stall-turned his fighter, then dived into the sea. Heading back over the island Buck went for three Stuka dive-bombers but without visible results. He also fired the last of his ammunition towards a Ju88, seeing some hits on its wings and fuselage. This last 'official' terse statement hides a longer story, as Buck was later to relate:

'I chased this Ju88 at full speed calling to my sprog No.2 to hang on to me, and we headed north for Sicily, throttles wide open. The 88 started a 20-degree gentle dive and I was doing everything to get more speed. I didn't want to go to Sicily – I wanted to shoot him down long before we got there. We had never left the island area before this, there was too much danger from roaming 109s.

'I went into a steep dive to get speed, then levelled out. The 88 pilot kept in his gentle dive until he was down to my level; he was only 400 yards ahead of me, but we were more than half-way to Sicily. I started firing and great chunks started coming off and it caught fire. A body came out, either he jumped or been blown out, but there was no parachute.

'The 88 slowed down a bit and there was an explosion and it spiralled down towards the sea on fire. I was making a wide orbit looking for my No.2 but I was too close to Sicily to stay around and watch the 88 go in.

'I was also too twitchy to climb up for a homing – it would be asking for trouble to climb where I was. I got down on the deck, checked all my instruments and dials to make sure everything was alright. I was using 8+ boost but finding the Spitfire okay, I throttled back to +4 for more economical flying. I was safer now, with a sea haze to protect me.

'I kept going for some minutes with no sign of any aircraft, or
of the island, so I climbed to 500 feet and asked for a vector but
there was no answer. I climbed higher, but still no sign of Malta.
I was getting really twitchy now, keeping a sharp look out for
109s. I went up to 1,500 feet, got a vector and altered my
course. I would have missed the island by 20 miles if I'd
maintained my original course.

'Jeff West was up giving me cover as I was so short of fuel and
I put down on Luqa, the bomber base, very happy.'

Daddo-Langlois had attacked the same 109 McNair was attacking, and as
McNair's fire caused it to stall, it clipped 'Daddy's' wing-tip. Daddy saw the
pilot take to his parachute. Getting back to Takali, Daddo-Langlois had to
make a wheels-up landing. He later described how he and the 109 pilot had
flown at each other head-on, neither in the mood to break – hence the
collision. Ronnie West attacked a Stuka which went down south of Hal Far
and damaged another on its wings and fuselage.

At 1800 hours came Buck McNair's second Scramble. In all 11 Spitfires
got into the air, five from Luqa and six from Takali, heading up to between
15,000-17,000 feet south-west of Gozo where there was a fight with several
Me109s. Sergeant Paul Brennan shot down one Messerschmitt, which went
into the sea seven miles west of Gozo, then he attacked a Ju88 over Takali,
setting both its engines on fire; Bud Connell saw this too go into the sea.
Sergeant Ray Hesslyn also destroyed a 109 and then damaged a Ju88.

Buck attacked a 109, his fire shredding the fighter's tail but he was unable
to see what happened to it so could only claim it as probably destroyed. Pilot
Officer Bob Sergeant attacked a Ju88 north of Grand Harbour from dead
astern, using all his ammunition from 100 yards. The bomber's port engine
caught fire and it dived pouring smoke and in flames; a splash noted its
assumed crash point. Laddie Lucas damaged a 109, Flight Lieutenant
Norman MacQueen destroyed a Ju88, which brought 249 Squadron's score
this day to eight destroyed, one probable and six damaged. Buck recalled this
action:

'Junior Tayleur, an English sergeant-pilot, was my No.2, and we
climbed to 10,000 feet south of the island. We flew back over to
the north side and were turning back into the island as some
109s attacked us. We'd seen Huns around, but hadn't the
opportunity to get into position to attack them.

'Junior got a bullet in the perspex of his hood and small pieces
went into his forehead and eyes. Blood gushed from his small
wounds and he was temporarily blinded, but he managed to get
back home and to land safely with wheels-up. I went after one
of the Huns and it went into a vertical dive. The German pilot
pulled away from me and then he thought he had lost me. He
throttled back to come out of the dive and I shot at him from
400 yards before he realised he hadn't lost me.

'He went into a steep dive again. I fired a long burst at him
and hit him around the wing roots and pieces started to come

off. He kept on going. We were going so fast I couldn't steer the Spitfire straight. Suddenly he pulled up, much tighter than I would try because I didn't want to black out. I couldn't chance blacking out because there were probably other Huns about.

'I pulled out to one side to come out of my dive with less strain – on me and the aircraft. If I had stayed right behind him there would have been a danger of collision. In the very middle of his pull-out, where the worst strain or most was, pieces started to come off his aircraft, then more and more pieces came off. Then his aircraft flicked over and dived straight into the sea. I went down in a great spiral dive to watch him go in – nothing came up.

'If he was conscious when he tried to pull out, he was certainly unconscious when his machine started falling to pieces and still unconscious when he hit the water. I made my pull-out much shallower and was almost blacking out all the time. He may have been unconscious before he started to pull out or he may have been wounded while in the dive and relaxed on the stick which he had pushed forward to dive.'

Buck's first victory had been a 109 from I Gruppe JG53. Its pilot did indeed bale out and was fortunate enough to be picked up and rescued by a German air-sea-rescue craft and returned to Sicily. Daddo-Langlois lost 18 inches from his wing-tip and in trying to get down was hit again, forcing him to whip up his wheels and crash-land. He was then strafed on the ground but not hit, while other pilots had also to dive for cover as they ran to help him. The second 109 – credited as a probable, probably because he had nobody to witness the crash – has not been identified. Buck certainly claimed most of its tail had broken away.

Buck had a break on the 21st but was in action the day following. The first Scramble came at 0915: four Spitfires led by Buck McNair, in charge of three newly arrived pilots, Pilot Officers G M Briggs and W J E Hagger (Rhodesian) of 601 Squadron, and Sergeant L F Webster from 603. They chased a recce Ju88 from 6/KG77 and all had a crack at it, seeing many strikes, most of which were probably scored by the experienced leader. Buck, in a dead astern attack, saw it begin to burn and spin down. The pilots were credited with a probable but in fact this aircraft failed to return. This must have been discerned at the time as Buck McNair's log book notes one Ju88 destroyed, ten miles south of Sicily. Sergeant Webster then engaged a 109 which he claimed as damaged.

The Junkers, coded 3Z+FM, was crewed by Unteroffizier Wilhelm Schrieber, with Obergefreiters Heinrich Neumann, Walter Horn and Rudolf Spitter.

The second Scramble call came at 1010 am: seven Spitfires, three of 249 and four from 603, got airborne to engage 20 Ju88s coming in over St Paul's Bay. Led by McNair, they attacked these as well as a lone recce Ju88 they came upon later. Pilot Officer J G West damaged two Ju88s, one of which was the assumed recce machine, Paul Brennan another. Flight Sergeant Johnny Hurst shot down a 109 but one of the 603 Squadron pilots failed to return.

On the 25th – Saturday – Buck was up again. He was leading 249 with Squadron Leader Lord David Hamilton, (the brother of the Duke of Hamilton) CO of 603 Squadron, as his No.2. Hamilton had arrived with the recent batch of new pilots and Spitfires and was flying wingman to gain experience of Malta's air war. In some very mixed and confused fighting, Buck later put in claims for damage to two Me109s, a Ju88 and a Ju87 – noting in his log book that there were: *'Hundreds of the B . . . .'* and just *'Four Spits up!!'*

Paul Brennan was caught in the slipstream of a Ju88 which flicked him over. Buck saw this and called over the R/T to see if he was alright; Paul confirmed he was. Buck then told him he was going to have a crack at some Ju87s which Paul could see bombing the harbour area, with 109s above. Paul warned him of the 109s, but was unable to help as he was out of ammunition. He circled above Takali despite the presence of more 109s, but flak was forcing the German pilots to stay high.

Buck then joined him, having also run out of ammo, and the 109s began making passes at them through the ground fire. Things were getting hot so the two Spitfire pilots headed for the other end of the island. After flying through exploding bombs from Ju88s attacking Luqa, the two pilots climbed to make dummy attacks on the 109s in an effort to scare them off. It was then that Woodhall called up to say some Hurricane pilots were short of fuel and needed to land, and asked if they could help.

Over Hal Far airfield, they spotted the returning Hurricanes and several Me109s hanging around. Upon Buck's and Paul's arrival two Hurricane pilots attempted to get down but one of them thought the other was a 109 and pulled away, while the other pilot mistook the two Spitfires as Messerschmitts and also hesitated.

An irate Buck McNair knew that he and Paul Brennan were now in danger from the lurking 109s, and were themselves now running short of fuel, while these two 'clots' were messing about. Rarely being short of a few succinct words, he yelled over the R/T: 'For Christ's sake pull your f . . . hook out and land next time. If those 109s don't get you, I will!'

Paul Brennan also wrote of this in his book:

> 'Buck's language over the R/T was lurid, and he kept telling the Hurriboys that if they didn't get down he'd shoot them down. We were running short of gravy [petrol] and were thoroughly annoyed. The Hurriboys hurled back some affable abuse, but eventually all got in and we beetled off back to Takali.
>
> 'I still had no airspeed indicator, and Buck had to formate me in. I got into position in echelon starboard on Buck and we started a circuit. The upwind end of the landing-path was a maze of bomb-holes, and I realised I would have to land very short. As we approached Buck called, "You're doing 120 now," and a few seconds later, "Now you're down to 100, but I think you're too high. Go round again." I was too brassed off to worry whether I pranged or not, so I decided to go on in.
>
> 'We were rather anxious about the new boys but they landed shortly afterwards. Neither had got anything but Buck and I had

each shot down two confirmed. We celebrated in front of dispersal with a war dance – a cross between a Maori haka and an Australian corroboree. Buck, a Canadian, knew neither of these native dances and couldn't do them very well, but that didn't worry us.'

In his book *Malta; The Thorn in Rommel's Side* (Stanley Paul, 1992), and quoted here by kind permission of his widow Jill, Laddie Lucas wrote of Buck:

'Robert Wendell McNair, was . . . a Canadian of easily recognizable calibre. He was, by nature, a critic of anything or anyone he thought to be sub-standard. He spoke his mind and never hedged his bets. He did not suffer fools gladly.

[When being told reinforcements were coming . . .] 'Over his customary pink gin [G/C Woodhall] confided the news: "Jumbo says it won't be long now before reinforcements are here." Buck McNair gave the Group Captain the collective reaction. "And about f . . . . . . time, too . . . Sir!" Buck had a ready knack of picking up the mood and giving it graphic expression.

'He was, of course, a first-rate fighter leader, aggressive to the extent of being ruthless, yet inside him was a private worry which he confided in me – that his eyesight was deteriorating and might not last the war. He lived in fear that at some point the medics would discover his defect and take him off ops. For Robert McNair, in the middle of World War II, that would have been worse than the end.'

After Buck landed, Group Captain Woodhall spoke to him. asking him to watch his language over the radio in future; it wasn't nice for the young clerks and girls in the Control Room to have to listen to it!

## Life on Malta
On one occasion during April Buck McNair, Laddie Lucas, Raoul Daddo-Langlois and Paul Brennan were making their way to the airfield from the mess at Medina when their journey was rudely interrupted by several Ju87 dive-bombers and Me109s. They began an attack upon Takali so the four pilots waited by a gunpost until the Stukas had departed. As the four finally arrived at the airfield several 109s began to appear above the base, obviously lurking around until returning RAF fighters appeared. As the quartet began walking across the airfield some of the German pilots decided to beat it up. Buck and his pals felt very conspicuous in their bright yellow Mae West life vests and felt sure the 109 boys could not fail to notice them. For the first time they felt grateful for all the bomb holes on the airfield, the four soon leaping into one. The next ten minutes seemed like hours.

As Buck confided to his would-be biographer more than 50 years ago, communications on the airfields on Malta were very primitive during his time there. Different coloured Very lights would be fired off as warnings to pilots to Scramble. Distances were too great for an ordinary sound system of warning.

Often the German fighters would come over and machine-gun men on the airfield. One day Buck and Ronnie West were on Readiness, wearing their bright yellow Mae Wests as they picked up shrapnel pieces off the runway areas to lessen the risk of punctures. Several Me109s came over and started to strafe the 'drome. Both men quickly hugged the dirt, feeling very conspicuous in their life vests. Bullets splattered all about them but they were not hit.

Another day Ronnie had a Hurricane up with a hot engine. He managed to take off but the windscreen became covered in oil and it was doubtful if he could land it again. Ronnie did not want to ditch the machine as it was far too precious, so he tried to land it. His canopy was open and the oil was spraying into the cockpit, getting into his eyes, over his head and clothes. He couldn't use his goggles as it would be difficult to constantly try to wipe them clean.

Ronnie made a splendid effort, landing but overshooting, then crashing into a Beaufighter which was covered with camouflage netting and set in a bay near the end of the runway. Unhurt, he got out of the two wrecked aircraft and proceeded to take off every stitch of oil-stained clothing after clearing his eyes and face. He then walked to dispersal for fresh clothes, as if this was an everyday occurrence.

On their off days the pilots enjoyed swimming. One day Bud Connell, Jeff West, Ronnie West, Nip Heppel and Buck got some bicycles and rode over to St Paul's Bay where they rented a boat from a fisherman in order to go over to nearby St John's Island. They found masses of ants there and they watched in fascination their various manoeuvres. Buck:

> 'There were millions of them and they acted in someway like cattle going to pasture. In columns they would pour out from their home and go down what they probably termed a road, picked up stuff at their pasture, then started dragging it back home along the other one-way road. It was fascinating to see the column moving quickly along from their home, another column returning laden with goodies.
>
> 'There were hundreds of lizards too. If anyone stepped on a lizard's tail it would shake the tail off and hurry away. It probably grew a new tail, for I never saw one without a tail except those that had just shaken a damaged one off.
>
> 'Returning from the island, we five pilots were in the middle of the bay and almost completely undressed, as a raid developed. Flak started exploding above and shrapnel hissed into the sea nearby. We were getting a bit twitchy about the shrapnel as it splashed into the water around us.
>
> 'Having had a few beers on the island, and now getting twitchy, we started rowing around in circles. However, we finally began moving in a straight line and reaching the main island, sheltered under some rocks until the raid was over.'

The pilots also had a rest home available. It was a lovely villa on the island rented by the RAF for flyers needing a break. Maximum accommodation at any time was twelve. This usually included a few Fleet Air Arm pilots, who flew the Swordfish torpedo planes. Buck visited it a few times, staying a few hours, but only once did he stay overnight.

One day Bud Connell, Ronnie West and Buck were working on bays, and decided to go for a swim. Two bikes were found but Buck couldn't find one. Then he came across a superb bike at the mess with lots of gadgets – a de luxe model. Upon their return, the CO was waiting for them and asked Buck: 'What the hell's the idea of taking the colonel's bicycle?' he demanded, 'Take it back to him right now. And just for that you will work for a full week with the army on their bay construction.'

Buck was upset as the army mess was quite a distance away and it meant he would have to walk back. But he returned the cycle to the colonel, finding him a most jovial Scotsman who insisted on treating him at the bar. He laughed when Buck told him of his punishment but made no comment. Buck found the army officers – Durham Light Infantry – a fine bunch of lads, but he had to drink so much at the colonel's insistence that he felt like singing most of the way back to his own mess.

Next morning he reported for work with the army. However, he found the soldiers took the attitude than any pilot in uniform on Malta at that time was much too splendid a type to have to do construction work. Buck felt lazily disinclined to dispute their feelings, so spent the week's 'punishment' in pleasant conversation with the soldiers interrupted at intervals with even more pleasant visits to the army mess.

# CHAPTER EIGHT

# GIBRALTAR INTERLUDE AND THE END

On the last day of April 1942, Squadron Leader Stan Grant, Laddie Lucas, Ronnie West, Raoul Daddo-Langlois and Buck McNair were detached to Gibraltar. To get there they were passengers in a Lockheed Hudson for the nine-hour flight from Luqa, piloted by Flying Officer Matthews. They were being sent to help prepare the next batch of Spitfires for the island fortress. Meantime, Buck sent off another telegram to his folks on the 4th: 'Thanks for letter, am feeling fine and having good time. Robbie McNair.' And he was. He recorded that once at Gib, they had nearly made themselves sick eating so much fruit and other foods they had not been used too, or even seen for weeks. Buck and the others tested aircraft that arrived in crates by sea and were assembled at the Coastal Command sea base. Each aircraft was placed on a small raft and towed to the aerodrome at Gib, to be loaded onto an aircraft carrier.

It was at this time he was notified of the award of the Distinguished Flying Cross. The citation referred to five German aircraft destroyed and seven others damaged. The signal actually arrived on Buck's birthday!

There is no doubt that he felt tremendously pleased and honoured by the award. It seemed a long way from Battleford, Saskatchewan. With no little pride he sent a telegram to his parents, which they received on 12 May: 'Got my DFC at last, stop. Love and stuff. R McNair.'

This rather sounds as if he felt it was a foregone conclusion that he would get one, or perhaps someone had let it slip that he had been recommended for it. In any event he had achieved recognition in a tangible form and he soon bought a piece of DFC ribbon to have sewn beneath his RCAF wings. It was not long before his picture and reports began appearing in Canadian newspapers, one of which (in Halifax) read:

> PO Robert Wendell McNair of Springfield has been awarded the Distinguished Flying Cross by the Air Ministry in recognition of his exploits in the air war against Germany. PO Robert McNair has two uncles living in Halifax: S P Grimm, 32 Inglis Street, special agent for the Canadian National Railways and R O Grimm, 17 Victoria Road, CNR trainman. He also has a cousin, William Roop, living at 33 Cornwall Street. McNair, 23, has destroyed at least five enemy aircraft during dogfights

and damaged seven, four of them during a single combat. The citation added: "skilful and courageous" pilot and that he invariably pressed home his attacks with the greatest determination regardless of the odds.

The family lost no time in notifying the local newspapers of their son's achievements and soon his name was in print here too.

Wednesday, June 10, 1942. *NORTH BATTLEFORD FLIER PROMOTED AND DECORATED*. Robert Wendell (Bob) McNair is awarded DFC and advance to rank of flight lieutenant for daring exploits defending Malta.

North Battleford: A promotion from pilot officer to flight lieutenant over night, and the DFC award to boot, was the experience of 'Bob' McNair of North Battleford. Robert Wendell McNair, second son of Mr and Mrs K F McNair of 1562 Victoria Street, North Battleford, topped his amazing exploits in the 1941 Battle of Britain [*sic*], with equally daring exploits in Malta this spring that earned him two jumps in rank and the coveted air officer's award. News of his recent promotion was received by his parents last weekend.

The article then described his background and service thus far. Other news headlines heralded: '*NOVA SCOTIAN BAGS 5 HUNS; IS DECORATED. INTREPID AIRMAN GETS DECORATION.*'

\* \* \*

Meantime, he and the others were enjoying their break at Gib. They had met Wing Commander J S McLean DFC, who was in charge of the preparations now underway, for reinforcing the island. He had already helped with previous Spitfire fly-offs and was now well-versed in the procedure. This time the plan was to fly 64 Spitfires from the carriers *Wasp* and *Eagle* in two batches. The first would be sent off from the carriers in about a week, then *Eagle*, having returned, would take out another load. Stan Grant and Ronnie West would lead the first, Laddie, Daddy and Buck the second, after sweating out several more days on the Rock. John McLean was quite a press-on type; in 1941 he had won his DFC while operating from North Weald on fighter operations.

It seemed, therefore, that the latter three men would be enjoying the relaxing atmosphere of Gibraltar for a couple of weeks. It would be a nice rest, although Laddie Lucas was sure Buck was eager to get back into the action. Laddie recorded that Buck was quick to complain about what, operationally, they might be missing 800 or 900 miles away. As Laddie put it:

'He was soon at his restless worst, putting excessive pressure on McLean and Stan Grant to let him take part in the first fly-off instead of having to kick his heels with us and wait for the second. Inactivity was anathema to McNair.

'One morning, down on the airfield by the Rock, he exploded in front of McLean. "Let's get on, Sir," he gibed, "and get ourselves a slice of this f . . . . . . piece of goddam cake that we hear so much about." Mac played it deadpan. "All in good time, Buck," he said, "all in good time." The additional chuckle diffused the tension. McNair didn't know it, but the words of the preacher would turn out to be wise.'

While at Gib, Buck met Noel 'Buzz' Ogilvie, with whom he had trained and who had come overseas as a sergeant-pilot. Buzz, and Jimmy Lambert – both RCAF – had both volunteered in England for Malta, and while waiting, an order came through on 1 April, for the entire squadron to go. Their CO wouldn't believe the order, thinking it must be an April fool's joke, and telephoned Group HQ for confirmation.

Whilst at the Coastal Command base, the Station Commander there took exception to visiting pilots calling their CO 'Bill' in the Mess. As a result, Squadron Leader New asked his pilots to 'Sir' him whilst there. Pilots thereafter, would 'Sir' him loudly, twice in every sentence, if the Station CO was within earshot. Of course, as soon as they left the Station, the Bill relationship resumed.

As the time to go approached, Buck briefed the pilots about Malta, its shape, the runways, the dangers and so on. He warned them too that anything might happen near to or over the island, and that they might easily be attacked in the circuit, so not to get careless preparing to land. He also advised them to take as many cigarettes and bars of chocolate as they could stuff into their aircraft. Amongst the pilots was Norman Fowlow, who would be Buck's best man two years later. In fact there were at least 25 RCAF pilots in this batch, including four Americans.

## Carrier Fly-off

Otherwise the inactivity was heightened at Gib for Buck, with the news from Malta of brother pilots being shot down, killed and wounded, which made him even more eager to get back. However, the time passed and on 7/8 May the first phase of 'Operation Bowery' got underway. In all there would be 50 Spitfires embarked on the *Wasp*, and 17 aboard the *Eagle*, as the two carriers and their escorts headed out into the Mediterranean for the first fly-off. The carriers would get them to within flying range of the island.

The *Wasp* was designed as a carrier and was fairly easy to leave because of her wide bow, but the *Eagle* had been converted into a carrier and her deck came to almost a point at the bow. It was vital for the pilot to take off from the extreme centre of the deck, both to get the longest run and to have both wheels leave the deck at the same time.

The first fly-off, on the 9th, went off successfully and 60 of the 64 fighters launched arrived, although one pilot was killed landing at Hal Far. One of the four not to get to the island was Jerrold 'Jerry' Smith. Once airborne he had a problem and knew he would never make Malta so landed back on the *Wasp*. This was very creditable and saved a valuable Spitfire, especially as there had been no plans or instructions for any of the pilots to actually land back on. Jerry Smith was the older brother of Rod Smith, who had arrived in Britain with Buck in 1941. Jerry eventually got to Malta later, only to die in action there.

Buck and the others at Gib spent some of their time air testing the final batch of 17 Spitfire Vc machines, each with not two, but four 20 mm cannon. One of the pilots to fly off the *Wasp* was John Sherlock, who a year later would be in Buck's squadron in England. He relates:

'We were 48 pilots who boarded the USS *Wasp* on 20 April 1942 at Glasgow. We did not know at that time that we were to meet up with another carrier somewhere along the route to Malta. It was carrying 12 more Spitfires and pilots so altogether there were to be a maximum of 60 Spitfires to help out on Malta, which at that time was almost destitute of fighter planes. We took off early on the morning of 9 May and after a flight of somewhat under four hours, we arrived.

'One chap, a Canadian – Sergeant Sherrington – was killed on take off, crashing into the sea off the prow of the carrier. Two other Canadians – Flight Sergeants Valiquet and Rounsefel, failed to arrive. It was not until years later we learned that these two had attacked an Italian Fiat RS14 floatplane near the island of Lampedusa and had collided with each other, both being killed. An Aussie pilot in my group, Flight Lieutenant Ray Sly, landed at Hal Far and then attempted to take off again as the field was being bombed by Ju88s and strafed by Me109s, but he collided with an aircraft pen and was killed. A fifth pilot, Jerry Smith, had trouble with his 90 gallon belly tank and landed back on the carrier, ending up less than ten feet from the end of the flight deck as he had no arrester gear. He was the first Spitfire pilot to land on a carrier without a hook.'

This was a major feat by Jerry Smith, quite apart from saving a valuable Spitfire.

*   *   *

Meantime, back on Gib, it was soon time to get more aircraft on board the carrier after it returned, and the convoy sailed again on 16/17 May under the command of Squadron Leader W G New. In the early hours of the 18th Bill New and Buck led off the first group as dawn appeared. Laddie and Daddy led off the second batch about 30 minutes later. These feats were something in themselves. None of the pilots, and certainly not any of the Malta veterans, had ever taken off from a carrier, which was not a matter to take lightly in any event. Among the pilots was Jerry Smith, who made it this time. Now all they had to do was to fly 700 miles and hope they found the island, and that the 109s would leave them alone. In order to get the required 30 knots of wind speed over the deck so that the pilots could take off, the *Eagle* had to steam at full speed. Buck McNair recorded:

'The ship was straining and the voice over the loudspeaker announced a wind speed of 29 knots and was this OK? McLean said yes, but Bill New, who weighed 220 pounds and was to be first off, yelled No.! The carrier was vibrating trying to get that extra knot. The next call was that the wind speed was 29 and one half knots; McLean again said OK, but New parried this with No, thirty or no dice!

'The loudspeaker voice then said that the Captain was refusing to take the ship any farther towards Malta, and that they either took off now or they returned to Gibraltar with him. Faced with this, Bill New released his brakes and shot forward, making his take off OK. So did all the others. Each was carrying an additional 1,000 pounds of extra gasoline for the long trip.

'We flew down to the north of Tunisia, then near Pantelleria where I took command of the formation prior to landing. At 10,000 feet I called Malta Control, only to find I could hear them but they could not hear me. I recognised Woodhall's voice and called, "This is Buck." "What are you doing?" was his reply [finally]. I told him I had some friends with me and he said OK.

'I could see some Huns making smoke trails off Sicily but I wasn't bothered as I dived down with the formation and landed. Flight Lieutenant R M Lloyd of 185 Squadron knew Lambert and Buzz, having met them in England, so he asked for them. 185 were predominantly Canadian, including Shorty Reid from Windsor Ontario; MacNamara, John Sherlock, Cy King, Claude Weaver of Oklahoma, and B W Andrews. In fact when I arrived back on Malta, the pilots in all squadrons on the island were mostly Canadian. It continued that way until I left.'

It had been a three and a half-hour flight for Laddie, and three hours, 40 minutes for Buck, but both formations landed intact despite a number of Me109s buzzing around. The island had been mightily reinforced over the last ten days or so, but by the time Buck and Laddie arrived, a number of these reinforcements, both pilots and Spitfires, had already become casualties.

Pilot Officer F J Sherlock did not fly with Buck McNair on Malta, being assigned to 185 Squadron, while Buck was with 249, but John recalls:

'Malta was very hectic and the bombing never ceased, day or night. Our flights were usually short ones and we were not only outnumbered on every occasion, but usually the enemy were above us and a distinct disadvantage. Our food was inadequate and consisted of bully beef three times a day, seven days a week and we would also have one or two slices of black bread each day. I weighed just over 140 pounds when I arrived on Malta, and upon my return to the UK, I was down to 109 pounds.

'One of the main reasons for weight loss was due to what was called "Malta Dog" which was a very severe form of dysentery. This was due to the water which was simply rain water stored in wells drilled out of limestone and contained a large amount of salts. It remained so and all boiling did was to concentrate the salts. Any tea or food cooked in water was simply another dose of salts. To put it crudely, the definition of the "Dog" was being able to shit through the eye of a needle 50 feet away at least 15 times a day. There was no relief from it.'

## Back in the Swing

Buck McNair was raring to go and it certainly showed. His first Scramble came the next day, mixing it with some Italian Macchi 202 fighters but without success. He was equally unlucky the next day, this time in a scrap with Italian Reggiane 2001 fighters: 'Spun off at 32,500 feet trying to squirt a 2001!!' he noted in his log book.

On day three his only flight was to 'escort a sprog' – presumably taking one of the new pilots up to show him what was what. On day four – the 22nd – he scored. Scrambled at 1100 hours leading four Spitfires, they intercepted two Me109s off Kalafrana and Buck shot one of them down. A Scramble on the 23rd brought no contact, then he had his first day off. He was back in the air on the 25th.

At 1420 eight Spitfires were Scrambled to intercept enemy aircraft. Three Savoia S.84s escorted by 109s and Re2001s found themselves under the full attention of the RAF fighters. Squadron Leader New damaged a bomber as did Norman Lee. Ronnie West bagged a Re2001, Paul Brennan damaged another while Buck and Sergeant deNancrede each scored hits on 109s, McNair being credited with a destroyed. It seems however, that the RAF pilots were rather over-optimistic in their claims; 5/JG53 did have one of its 109s severely damaged but it got back to Comiso.

This ended Buck's May flying, and on the last day this 'veteran', who was regularly leading other pilots into action, was notified of his promotion to Flying Officer, although he appears to have become an acting flight lieutenant, at least as far as the squadron was concerned.

## Trials and Tribulations

Buck remembered that sometimes the armourers got careless and would leave belts of ammo unfastened to the small belt in the gun itself. The procedure was to place the belt, of probably 150 rounds, in an ammo box, then reload the gun with the small belt of ten rounds, finally linking the two belts together with a shell. Buck checked his guns, found none of them linked up properly, and would have been left with two rounds for each gun. Thereafter, Buck never flew until he had first checked his guns. Whilst waiting he would also check petrol, oil too – and his parachute. He continued:

'We wanted to take out two of the four cannons. The two additional guns were cutting down the performance of the aircraft and we were simply having twice as much gun trouble. Partly this was due to faulty ammunition, partly to weak recoil springs and partly to sloppy maintenance.

'Sloppy maintenance was because the work was so heart-breaking. It was becoming progressively more difficult to keep the aircraftmen under control. Some of them were most exemplary, showing in many instances more of the qualities of officers than some of the officers themselves. But it was heart-breaking work for them. They would work for weeks and weeks, without proper tools and equipment, making tools in many cases to do a job, and then a bomb would drop on the Spitfire before it had a chance to fly. It was most discouraging for them, and quite a number simply walked away, going absent without leave for several days.

'There was little relaxation for either officers or men. The pilots weren't getting results. Time after time we would get into position to fire at the enemy only to find our guns jammed. This would lead to words between the pilots and armourers, although generally speaking the pilots and ground crew got along amicably. The "erks" did an amazing job on the whole.

'The food was bad, and the airmen did not have decent quarters. They marched three miles to and from their billets, coming to the airfield at dawn, returning at night. Their noon meal, such as it was, was brought to them in a truck – the same issue to them and we pilots alike. And the food was foul; there were always flies and bugs in the damn stuff. We would swat flies all day long. If we tried to play cards while on Readiness, it really became a fly-swatting exercise.

'There was little room in our dispersal. We had no radio, victrola, tables or comfortable chairs as they had in dispersal huts in England. The inside of our dispersal was just a heap of rubble. For chairs we used a piece of rock, and for a table to play cards we used part of an old aeroplane wing on top of the rubble.

'All the fellows were amazingly good. Everyone pitched in to help the others. Pilots, officer or NCO, were glad to help the airmen. We had no great bowsers to carry the fuel. All petrol had to be lugged by hand to refuel every Spitfire dispersed all around the airfield – we could not spare the gasoline to truck it around. And it takes a lot of petrol to fill even a fighter when you have to manhandle every drop.

'But there was a great spirit among those who stayed on Malta. It really was amazing. Everyone was proud to be in the service with men who were carrying on under such miserable privations without any recognition. Officers and men felt like brothers to each other – we all shared work, foul food, poor lodgings, filth – and we all shared each other's worries.

'When I first arrived the officers had extra messing, paid sixpence a day for it, but that soon stopped. We all lived then on straight rations. For weeks on end the rations were a chunk of dry bread and a hunk of corned beef, and that would be our complete rations for the day. We thought we weren't getting our proper rations and complained to the messing officer. He called a meeting and with a great flourish, like a master of ceremonies, he had the chef come in with a tin of corned beef and a huge butcher's knife.

'With equal ceremony, the chef opened up the tin, placed the corned beef on a large plate, then with his knife cut off a sliver of meat. The messing officer, pointed to the exhibit on the knife, and said: "Are you each getting that much meat a day?" "Oh, yes," the pilots chorused. "Very well, gentlemen, then you are getting your ration."

'Our losses still mounted. One reason was due to new pilots not heeding our advice. For instance, one officer out from England, and who had a good deal of Spitfire experience over both France and Britain, might be paired off with a sergeant-pilot who had never flown any operations over Europe, but had been on Malta for some weeks and knew the score. In several instances the officer took exception to being told by an NCO what he should do. Consequently, a number of new pilots were shot down and killed – more than should have been.

'The more experienced pilots were extremely annoyed by this. They didn't care so much about the "know-it-all" getting himself killed by resenting advice, but they did resent the loss of a Spitfire! One day I was leading a section of four, with Paul Brennan, and two other new officers. Paul had been my No.2 but as he became more experienced, became a No.3 with his own wingman (No.4).

'We went up to 4,000 feet and saw 15 or 20 Ju88s just below. I looked round and saw nothing else and said, "OK, let's have a go at them." We started diving but just then I spotted some 109s above coming down too – the bombers had been bait. I ordered everyone to pull up, that there were these 109s coming from behind.

'Paul's wingman saw all the bombers, wanted to get one on this, his first trip, and yelled, "I'm going to get these bastards!" "Come back you . . . fool," screamed Paul, but the new officer kept diving. A 109 kept on his tail, out-dived him and shot him down in flames before he even reached the bombers.'

Buck told Ivers Kelly that although the island had been reinforced and they had passed a turning point, fuel was still in short supply. They couldn't send up all the fighters at once, and only sent those needed when really necessary. Life became a little dull, with food still bad. The Squadron was split into a group of eight. Stan Grant, Laddie Lucas and Buck generally led a two-man section, and each acted independently once engaged. Sometimes only four aircraft could be made ready for action. When the enemy did come over it usually resulted in a bit of a fight among the Spit boys to get to the Huns first.

The enemy tactics were now to send over four bombers with a tremendous fighter escort; the fighters diving like stink and getting away again, is how Buck put it. Some time earlier the Italians had tried high-level bombing, but it was not very effective.

On the ground pilots were rationed to one bottle of beer per man, per week. 'If you were lucky enough to get it, it was foul, but it washed away the dust.' Cigarettes too became so precious that often a butt, with a matchstick stuck in it, would be passed to two or three persons each taking a couple of puffs. Buck also recalled meeting one of the German Me109 pilots, shot down back on 10 April:

> 'When we pilots visited the hospital to see some of our own chappies, we would call on some of the German wounded too. Some of them were not too bad, others were surly or worse. One of them was a damn fine man. He was never bad tempered or foul-mouthed. His name was Neuhoff and he'd been shot down by Buck Buchanan.
>
> 'He was a damn fine soldier. When we asked him how many pilots were in his squadron, he'd say with a smile: "You know I can't tell you that." He had been wounded by a cannon shell, his plane had caught fire and his face and arms were burned. He suffered, but never complained.
>
> 'Only one thing annoyed him. He had destroyed 40 allied planes – Buck Buchanan just one. Neuhoff was disgusted with himself and with his No.2, that he had been shot down by an amateur. He said his No.2 had left him or it wouldn't have happened; he would like to lay his hands on his wingman.
>
> 'Curiously enough, his wingman was shot down sometime afterwards by Norm MacQueen, and was taken to the same hospital, but the two never met to my knowledge while I was in Malta.'

Leutnant Hermann Neuhoff had only been promoted to lead JG53's sixth Staffel the evening prior to being shot down. Buchanan was presented to him when the German asked to meet the man who had got him. However, there is some doubt, and in fact another pilot may have been his victor. The Germans also thought he'd been brought down by the fire from another Me109 pilot, who admitted firing on another Messerschmitt. After the war Neuhoff seemed to subscribe to this latter view. He had been shot down the day before his 24th birthday, and his Knight's Cross was awarded after his capture. Twenty-one of his kills had been made on the Russian front.

*   *   *

Although Buck McNair was still very much in the midst of heavy fighting over the island, and despite the influx of many new Spitfires, the month of June only saw him airborne on ten occasions between the 3rd and 16th. All were Scrambles.

First real contact with the enemy came on the 10th, an evening Scramble by eight Spitfires at 1810 to cover the arrival of some Beaufort torpedo bombers of 217 Squadron. They were heading in from Gibraltar and nearing the island reported they were under attack by a hostile fighter. Once airborne they were vectored towards four Italian bombers instead, escorted by fighters, with some German 109s nearby. In the fight with the escorts which ensued, Stan Grant shot down a Re2001, Flight Sergeant Williams damaged another, while Buck destroyed a 109. This was probably Unteroffizier Heinrich Sedlmaier of the 5th Staffel, JG53, who went down north of Valetta, baled out wounded and was later rescued. This is the event which Buck recorded thus:

'We were sent out to pick up Beauforts but once airborne we could hear reports on the R/T of a raid coming in which had been picked up by radar. I asked if we could go for them but this was refused, we must rendezvous with the Beauforts. I could hear all the plots of the raid and knew the Huns were coming in from the north so started positioning myself while looking for our bombers.

'I could see no sign of the Beauforts at the rendezvous, and reported this and asked if it was alright to climb. This was agreed. I got up-sun and saw a gaggle of 20 Me109s escorting bombers. The 109s weren't acting like the German flyers we were accustomed to seeing. They had no formation of any kind, but bunched together in a way that made me think of a bunch of cattle all trying to get through a gate at the same time.

'By now they were right under us. One of them turned and I turned with it, giving it a squirt as I dived. He dived too, with me after him. I pranged him again and he baled out. My section had followed but they didn't get any but Stan Grant did.

'As I saw the fighter going down, I saw a Spitfire going down too, both in the same area. I called up control and said two were going into the drink, one of them ours, one theirs. Then I went to escort the launch because sometimes enemy fighters machine-gunned them and sometimes the launch crews refused to go out without an escort. I directed the boat to the green colour which marked where the Spitfire pilot had hit the water. We couldn't find the German pilot.'

The downed pilot was Pilot Officer Innes of 601 Squadron, rescued by HSL107; the German pilot too was later rescued. McNair's next sorties came on the 12th and 15th. This latter day he took off three times.

This was his part in Operations 'Vigorous' and 'Harpoon'. The first, which took place between 12-16 June 1942, consisted of 11 merchant ships making a supply run to the island from Alexandria, closely escorted only by destroyers as no larger ships were available. More distant cover was provided by eight cruisers to ward off any hostile surface vessels. The other operation consisted of a convoy attempt from Gibraltar.

Action over the former convoy, as all Malta convoys were, proved intense. By Monday the 15th much air action had been seen over the ships, by German and Italian aircraft from Crete, and covering RAF and SAAF aircraft from North Africa. Elements of the Italian Fleet had also sortied and had been under attack by RAF aircraft, but the strength of the Italians forced the already damaged convoy to abort and return to Alexandria. However, the chance to attack the Italian ships was too good to miss, and the RAF struck at them late on the 14th and again on the 15th.

On the Monday morning a Beaufort put a torpedo into the battle-cruiser *Trento*, and another attack claimed hits on a battleship. Later still a RN submarine finished off the crippled *Trento* with two torpedoes. RAF Wellingtons, Beauforts and Liberators, plus USAAF Liberators, had all made attacks, escorted on occasion by Beaufighters. No. 249 Squadron provided escort to Fleet Air Arm and RAF aircraft, often at extreme range, and Buck's log book entries for his three sorties record:

> 'Escort Albacores to Italian Fleet – three hits.'
> 'Escort Beauforts – they blew up Iti Cruiser, some show!!'
> 'Patrol 140 miles west of Malta and 45 miles south of Pantelleria!!'

Unfortunately the 'hits' he observed on the Italian cruiser, were near-misses from bombs dropped by Liberators; all the torpedoes missed. The final patrol, as indicated, was flown to the west of the island – Operation 'Harpoon'.

## More Reinforcements

By this time more Spitfires and pilots had arrived. On 3 June 31 Spitfires had flown off HMS *Eagle*, although four had been shot down by marauding Me109s as they arrived over the island. On 9 June, 32 more had left *Eagle*'s deck. Among the first batch was Sergeant R G Middlemiss RCAF, and on the latter, Sergeant G F Beurling.

George Beurling was to gain undying fame over Malta during the next four months, and he would meet up again with Buck back in England in 1943. Bob Middlemiss would also fly under Buck back in the UK. Bob recalls:

> 'I first met Buck when I joined 249 Squadron in Malta in 1942. By the time I arrived on the island he had already made a name for himself in the Squadron with some six victories and already been awarded his first DFC. It was in Malta I discovered what a fine fighter pilot he was.
>
> 'I would describe Buck as being a very skilful, tenacious, determined and confident person. A great leader with fighting spirit and a great devotion to duty towards King and Country. He led his pilots with outstanding ability and by personal example. A true Air Force officer, a gentleman and later a good husband and father to his children.'

However, Bob's time with Buck on Malta was to be brief, about two weeks. Two Scrambles on 16 June, the first against a raid of 20+ in which they were ordered off too late, and the second covering the return of a PRU Spitfire, ended Buck McNair's Malta air war. As he noted in his logbook, during the period 10 March to 16 June 1942, 249 Squadron had claimed 96$\frac{1}{2}$ Axis aircraft destroyed, 17$\frac{1}{2}$ probables, for the loss of nine pilots.

There was an immediate lull after the recent activity, so much so that Buck felt it was perhaps a good time to be a little more offensive, as he later recorded:

> 'One day at dispersal I thought it would be a good idea to organise a sweep to Sicily with two sections of eight Spitfires. It would be a break from boring inactivity. The idea was well received so I 'phoned Group Captain Woodhall and gave him an outline of the plan. He said: "I'll let you know in half an hour." I asked him: "Will we get our 'chutes ready?", but he just said, "I don't know – I'll let you know."
>
> 'We thought the thing was a cinch and were very happy. But we got impatient after about 20-25 minutes, but at 30 minutes the phone rang. Woodhall said: "You're going, but the rest are not." I said I thought it would be a bit lonely, but the Group Captain replied, "Not where you're going. You're off to England. You are to be returned to England immediately at the request of the Canadian authorities. We'll emplane you tonight."
>
> 'I said I wanted to go on the Sweep before I went, but the Group Captain merely said: "No, you can't!"'

It must have been quite an anti-climax. One minute he thought he would be leading a raid on Sicily, the next he was told he was going home. McNair turned in his equipment, leaving most of his non-essential stuff behind for general use by the others, preparing to travel just in his blues, and taking just his personal stuff with him. There were around 20-30 guys at headquarters and he drank some beer with them. Most were flyers to whom he'd felt very close for the last few months. He had no desire to leave and felt strongly that he should stay, but he was quickly told there was no chance.

For him it was much more moving than any other farewell he ever made in the air force. They had been through so much together, and in desperation they all agreed they would get together in six to eight months' time for a slap up dinner in England, but fate was against it and it never happened.

He and another couple of chaps who were also leaving the island, talked of what they would do once they were back in the UK. Talk was of food and sleep, staying in bed for days, ringing bells for waiters to bring up food and whisky. Their one thought of luxury was a clean comfortable bed, quiet – and food.

On 1 July, Buck climbed aboard a Hudson aircraft for the 15 hour flight to England, landing at RAF Hendon, north of London. Since his arrival on the island he had personally claimed seven German aircraft destroyed, probably destroyed four others and damaged another six. This brought his official overall score to 8-8-7.

**Recollections**
Buck noted a few fleeting recollections of his intense time on Malta. He recalled how often if aircraft could fly but were not fit for combat, pilots would fly them away from the island and wait for the 'all-clear' before flying them back. This was far better than leaving them on the ground to be bombed.

On one occasion six German aircraft crossed right in front of him. He took a squirt at each in turn, and one took a squirt at him. Buck saw strikes on all four but made no claim as he could not get close enough. On another sortie, the pilot flying on his wing yelled over the R/T: 'Our own guns are firing at us!' Buck looked behind and beyond him, and saw it was a 109 firing at them. The new pilot hadn't bothered to turn his head to look behind.

Air Marshal Tedder, the AOC-in-C, RAF Middle East, had made a quick visit to the island, and had watched an airfight, in which Buck had shot down a 109 over Valetta. As Buck landed, Tedder was there to greet him, and the Air Marshal said: 'Well, McNair, I saw you shoot down that 109; what happened?' Buck never talked much of his score or his combats, certainly not to senior officers, so merely replied: 'Oh, I don't know; he was acting like a clot so I shot him down!'

A New Zealand pilot was badly shot up at 12,000 feet, dived down and was shot up again at 2-3,000 feet, stayed in his dive and made a good crash landing. However, his Spitfire caught fire. Buck and some others were walking on the road nearby, saw what had happened and rushed to the scene. Some army types were there, and although they attempted to get the pilot out, they couldn't undo the straps. The pilots rushed into the flames and got him out. He was burned and charred to the waist; blood was pouring from his ears. He was still alive and tried to talk but they could not make out what he was saying. A few moments later he died and they rolled his body in the silken shrouds of his parachute. Not the best of experiences, and yet another to prey on Buck's already jangled nerves.

One day the pilots saw a lot of smoke on the horizon. Someone said it was ships – an invasion! Buck and the others readily believed it, indeed, they had been expecting such a move. Everyone got out their pistols, then someone said the smoke was from a German bomber burning on the far side of the island. Panic over!

CHAPTER NINE

# BACK WITH FIGHTER COMMAND

If Buck McNair imagined he was going to have a long, luxurious stay in some hotel bedroom, with room-service and so on, he was quickly disillusioned. On 2 July he found himself at RAF Hornchurch where he flew a Miles Magister to North Weald and then down to RAF Tangmere. The next day he went to his old haunt at RAF Digby, returning once again to No.411 Squadron.

The squadron was still commanded by Squadron Leader R B Newton DFC, and still flying Spitfire V aircraft. It was using West Malling as a forward base for sweeps and escort sorties over France and the Low Countries. He returned as a flight commander, taking command of the Squadron's B Flight, replacing Flight Lieutenant D J Smith, but luckily missions were few which gave him time to re-adjust to operations so far removed from the helter-skelter of Malta. At least here the Germans didn't keep dropping bombs on you, and the food was 100% better. And one could take a bath much more readily – and regularly – even if there were regulations on how many inches of bath water one was allowed.

Also with 411 Squadron was Buck's old school chum Douglas Matheson, with whom he had also trained back in Ontario. Doug Matheson recalls:

> 'In the summer of 1942 Buck was posted back to 411. He was pale and skinny – looked really unwell – but he rapidly seemed to get well again after a rough go in Malta. He was now my flight commander, and our CO was Bob Newton, a RAFVR type, a really good man, and the last RAF chap to command a Canadian fighter squadron.'

His first flight with 411 was in fact a 'ride' being flown by Flight Lieutenant Tripe in the Squadron Magister to collect some mail at West Malling, but at least on this occasion he decided to stay in the aeroplane and not to have fun baling out!

Those first couple of weeks at Digby were interspersed with a relaxed routine. First came flights in his personal Spitfire – BL750 DB-L – some air-to-air gunnery, a few convoy patrols, the odd Scramble, and generally getting back into the swing of things. On 19 July came the first bit of excitement.

Buck McNair with Sergeant Dawson as No.2, went off at 1530 hours to fly a late afternoon convoy patrol off the Lincolnshire coast. They located the 25 ships of convoys 'Casing' and 'Banter' but were unable to make radio contact with any of them. So they sat back and patrolled at 800 feet, below a cloud base just 100 feet higher, no doubt hoping any gunners on the ships were able to identify them as friendly Spitfires and not hostile Me109s.

At 1615, flying north on the seaward side of the convoys, which at this time were some 15 miles east of Skegness, Control warned them of bandits, and then three aircraft became faintly visible through the clouds at 1,000 feet, heading towards the ships about a quarter of a mile from the two Spitfire pilots. Buck and Dawson pressed the auxiliary boost control and through a break in the cloud, they identified them as Dornier 217 bombers flying in a vic formation.

Buck called a 'tally-ho' to Control and immediately opened fire on the nearest Dornier, making a stern attack 20 degrees to its starboard side with cannon, firing from 600 yards but with no visible effect. Return fire was experienced, with tracer fire zipping back past the two Spitfires, then the Dorniers were swallowed up into cloud once more.

Buck followed, firing three short bursts of cannon, and as the bombers again came into view, he saw one shell burst on the starboard engine of one Dornier, and smoke began to pour out. Dawson was unable to bring his guns to bear but confirmed seeing the smoke from the damaged engine. Buck opened up again with machine gun fire on the second Dornier from 400-500 yards but again could not see any effects; however the bombers did drop their bombs over the convoy while still in cloud, and therefore unable to make a proper bomb run because of the two fighters. They were last seen turning east, one still trailing smoke. On landing Buck could only claim a damaged, and he also discovered that his starboard cannon had packed up owing to a blown cartridge cap, which of course had reduced his hitting power to just one cannon.

A Dornier 217 from II/KG40 returned to Soesterberg with 10% damage.

**Back in the Press**

Back home in Canada, Buck was again in the news, and so was his aircraft fitter, Corporal Manley 'Red' Francis RCAF, who also came from North Battleford:

'*NORTH BATTLEFORD FLIER KEEPS IN NEWS.* Corporal Manley "Red" Francis RCAF likes his job. He is fitter to the plane "Old Faithful" that Flt Lt R W "Buck" McNair flies when he is dishing out the "licks" the Nazis don't like. Both of them are from North Battleford, which makes it all the better.

'A newspaper clipping received on Thursday by Mrs L Francis, Norton Farm, Battleford, mother of Corporal Francis, tells of McNair's first brush with the enemy after his return to Britain from Malta where he won the DFC. "He was on patrol off the coast over the North Sea," it set forth, "when he saw three shadows in the clouds above him. Going up to investigate he saw three Dornier 217s flying in line astern between two layers of clouds. He opened fire with his cannons at about 600 yards. Then he began a game of hide and seek in the clouds, emptying his entire load of cannon shells at the fleeing Germans. In one attack he saw hits on the starboard engine of the rear aircraft in the line. The enemy returned fire, but the young Canadian's plane was undamaged.'

The following day McNair flew four times, in a variety of sorties. First was a Scramble, which resulted in 100 minutes of flying in and out of clouds to no avail. Then came a 20- minute flight to RAF Wittering, 'To pick up ammo' – which seems a strange log book entry. Then in the afternoon a 20-minute flight to RAF Digby from where a sea sweep was flown for 1¹/₂ hours. On this sortie there was some brief excitement as the Spitfires located four Avro Anson trainers, the fighter pilots thinking they had something to shoot at, but the moment soon passed.

For the rest of July little of any real interest developed. Scrambles, sea sweeps and convoy patrols were the main feature, with just a few brief encounters with Dorniers over the North Sea. Squadron Leader Newton found one on a night patrol on the 30th but lost it in clouds. Next day McNair chased a 'bogey' for 40 miles but was unable to close with it.

Obviously Buck had an inkling that he might be able to get home for a rest, as on the 11 July he cabled his parents: 'Address RAF Digby. Hope to get away from here soon. Will let you know. Love and kisses. McNair.' He was obviously short of some kit from Malta, as he then cabled home: 'Have you received any kit of mine? Please cable answer. Love and kisses. McNair.'

By the end of July, Buck McNair could boast a total of 556 flying hours, 370 on Spitfires, but amazingly, still only 150.45 total operational hours.

**August and Dieppe**
The month of August 1942 continued much as July had done. A Rhubarb sortie from Martlesham was cancelled on the 2nd, scrambles and sea sweeps produced no joy and he was lucky during an air test on the 7th, finding after take-off that his control lines on the undercarriage had been crossed. No doubt he had something to say to the mechanics on landing!

Then on the 16th the Squadron headed down to West Malling in Kent, from where they flew a Wing show the next day, but as Buck put it – 'No soap!!' Another Sweep came on the 18th, without contact or results, but that evening everyone was suddenly called to briefing. Having already been joined by 610 Squadron and 485 New Zealand Squadron, they formed the West Malling Wing, under the command of Wing Commander Pat Jameson DFC. They heard that the next day, that mainly Canadian troops, plus British commandos, would be assaulting the harbour town of Dieppe on the French coast, in an attempt to hold it for the whole day, during which certain objectives would be taken and destroyed, prior to a late afternoon withdrawal.

The whole show would be covered extensively by RAF light bombers, fighters, fighter bombers and recce aircraft, the objective being to fill the sky with aircraft both to swamp any opposition the Germans might put up, and to protect the ships taking troops to and from the town and beach area. Marked down as a trial of strength, and a feeler to gauge enemy reactions against any future invasion along the French coast, nobody was left in any doubt that it was going to be a busy day, and by the looks of it, a dangerous one too. The pilots of 411 Squadron were told to be ready to take off at first light. Their specific job would be to take over the job the Hornchurch Wing was marked down for in the event of that Wing being unable for any reason to take off.

In the event, the Hornchurch Wing was able to take off, so Jameson led his pilots off at 0740 for a fighter sweep, providing additional fighter cover for the assault vessels heading in to the beach. The last 411 Squadron Spitfire landed back at 0915 after a hectic half hour over Dieppe. They had been greatly outnumbered by enemy fighters which had reacted quickly to the 'invasion', and were operating between 4,000 and 7,000 feet. The squadron's Red Section had suffered most. The pilots on this first show were:

| Pilot | Spitfire | Pilot | Spitfire |
|---|---|---|---|
| S/L R B Newton | BL385 | F/L R W McNair | BL735 |
| P/O D Linton | BL542 | F/L P K V Tripe | BM358 |
| P/O P R Eakins | BM406 | P/O E G Lapp | W3318 |
| P/O Reid | BM652 | P/O J A Stock | BL750 |
| F/L Ramsay | AD352 | P/O Connolly | BL464 |
| P/O G C Semple | P8971 | F/Sgt S A Mills | AD263 |

Squadron Leader Newton, after about 15 minutes above Dieppe and having made several head-on attacks on FW190s without result, saw a 190 coming down from the sun at great speed. Once in range, Newton made a steep turn to the left, closed in to 250 yards behind the 109 and fired. Strikes were seen around the cockpit area and the fighter stall-turned to the left. Another Spitfire got behind it and scored more strikes, whereupon it dived into the sea.

Red Four, Pilot Officer Reid, was hit by cannon and machine gun fire but he managed to get home. Red Three, Pilot Officer P R 'Tubby' Eakins, was also hit; a cannon shell blew off his radiator, and he failed to return. Red Two, Pilot Officer D Linton, also failed to get back. He called to say he'd been hit but was OK, but after forming up he broke away after another enemy fighter and was not seen again. Later Flight Lieutenant P K V Tripe and Pilot Officer Stock heard him call 'Moleskin' (base call-sign) for a homing but no record of this was heard by West Malling Control.

Blue Four, Flight Sergeant S A Mills, got back although he had been slightly wounded in one heel. He too had got behind a 190 and was just about to fire as his aircraft came under cannon and machine gun fire. His radio was knocked out so he set off for home, weaving to avoid two 190s which began to follow him part of the way.

As they landed and reported, the pilots complained at being outnumbered three to one, and that the cover squadrons above had been too high to help, and that in any event their Spitfires were too slow to compete with the FW190s. The only other pilot to put in a claim had been Buck McNair, in his Spitfire – still DB-L – but BL750 had now been replaced by BL735 (someone having damaged Buck's BL750 on the 14th).

Buck had seen a FW190 on the tail of Tubby Eakins and warned him over the radio but whether he heard the call or not will never be known. It appeared unheeded and Buck watched, seeing hits on Eakins' Spitfire's undersides, and the radiator fly off in pieces. Eakins called briefly, saying: 'I've had it!' Another 190 came across in front of McNair and he opened fire on it, seeing bits fly off before it half rolled and dived. After this attack, Pilot Officer Lapp saw a 190 hit the sea, but was not sure if this was the 190 fired on by Newton and another Spitfire, or McNair.

Meantime, Flight Lieutenant Tripe, Buck's wingman, broke to port to avoid a couple of 190s, then saw a Me109 coming in from the sun head on. The Messerschmitt turned, exposing the whole underside. Tripe fired and the fighter half-rolled away. Whether this was the same fighter Newton fired at is not clear, although at the time, since each pilot claimed to have fired on different aircraft – a 190 and a 109 – this may have not been acknowledged.

A second sweep was timed at between 1055 and 1225; this time the Wing intended to make rendezvous with three Blenheims over Selsey Bill. After circling for ten minutes with no Blenheims in sight, the Wing picked up two Bostons and escorted them over instead. These two medium bombers went in at sea level, laying a smokescreen for the withdrawal. They both came under fire from the ships, and the Spitfire pilots watched in numbed silence as one Boston was hit, dived into the sea and disintegrated. Other reports say it was shot down by German fire from the coast.

By this time, although it was not clear to the squadrons above, the Canadians had been severely mauled as they landed on the beach, and had been pinned down, taking heavy casualties. Very few soldiers had got into the town, and a withdrawal was brought forward. The afternoon would see still more air battles over the ships as they brought the survivors home.

The Wing's third sweep came at 1400 hours; 411 Squadron flying in the middle of the other two at 10,000-12,000 feet above the ships. While there was plenty of action going on, the Wing was not engaged and it landed at 1530. Buck must have swung round near to the enemy coast, for he noted in his log book: 'Bags of dead on the beach!!' The final sweep took off at 1745, again flying middle squadron over the convoy. One Dornier 217 nosed in and was engaged by Squadron Leader Newton and Flight Sergeant D R Matheson. It quickly dropped its bombs one mile from the convoy and headed away damaged. The squadron landed at 1915. In all this historic day the squadron had amassed over 73 operational flying hours.

The squadron did not achieve much, and had lost two pilots, but many other units had seen considerable action. It just depended where one was and what was going on. Several squadrons saw less than 411, while others were hotly engaged several times. At the time it was thought that despite the massive losses, killed, wounded and prisoners of war, sustained by the attacking force, lessons had been learnt, and the RAF had scored a great victory. It had been the greatest air battle since 1940 and the RAF and Navy gunners claimed well over 100 German aircraft, with another 180 odd probably destroyed and damaged. Actual losses had been fewer than 50 with 24 others damaged. On the other hand the RAF had lost 100 aircraft during the day, with another 60 damaged.

The day following this exciting and hectic event, the Wing escorted USAAF B.17s on an afternoon attack on Amiens. McNair led Blue Section and at just after 6 pm he left the Wing just inside the French coast and positioned himself up-sun. Three FW190s had been seen at 3,000 feet above, and other 190s came in at 27,000 feet flying a wide line abreast. McNair swung round on the nearest ones, firing at the No.2 head on but without seeing any results. The 190 pilots seemed unwilling to fight but McNair got a second burst from 600 yards and one cannon strike was seen on the starboard side of the Focke Wulf's fuselage near the tail. The fighters quickly turned east and McNair could only claim one damaged despite firing off all his cannon ammo (120 rounds – 60 ball and 60 incendiary) and 830 rounds of .303 (18 tracer and 282 incendiary, 530 ball).

Meanwhile, Jack Stock, flying BL735 'L' as Blue 4, was in trouble with engine problems, but managed to glide back over the Channel to make a forced landing at Friston. As he recalls:

> 'After my glide across the Channel, Buck quietly took me aside and tore a gentle strip off me, saying I should have jumped as I had now missed a chance for a caterpillar! Buck was my flight commander on 411 Squadron during the summer of 1942, a straight forward, no nonsense type and a good friend. He would always show the way himself first – a real leader.
>
> 'I can offer two anecdotes to illustrate his approach and wry sense of humour. One was the caterpillar business. On another occasion we were doing practice interceptions with Buck and myself, with No.2s in sections. Just as Buck was making his first attack, my No.2 began screaming on the R/T about smoke and fire in the cockpit. After the panic and confusion died down and we returned to Digby, it was found that my No.2's IFF unit had exploded.
>
> 'The man was still shaking and had indignantly accused Buck initially of shooting at him. Buck just smiled and then remarked: "If I had been, you wouldn't be here now!"'

Doug Matheson also remembers Dieppe:

> 'You will know that we got the can kicked out of us at Dieppe, in the air as well as on the beaches. Buck, unusually, got only a damaged that day, as I did. We were faced with FW190s in force for the first time and they out-performed a Spitfire Vb by a mile. I well remember after that bad day that Sholto Douglas, C-in-C Fighter Command, came calling on all the squadrons to see just what the hell had happened. Flight Lieutenant Buck McNair bearded the old boy, and said: "Sir, we just can't cope with 190s with our Vbs!"'

Gordon Lapp also recalls Buck in 411 Squadron:

> 'I had first met Buck when I joined 411 Squadron in December 1941 at Hornchurch. Buck was one of the colourful pilots. He had been with 411 since it was formed a few months before, and was involved in a few adventurous escapades that seem to have

left the other pilots in awe.

'Buck was a debonair, natural leader and a non-conformist. After going to Malta, he appeared back with 411, and I flew as his No.2 many times, including four trips over Dieppe from England. The first trip was in the early morning and we met a wall of German fighter planes. Although thoroughly involved we had no success.

'I am convinced that his fearlessness in action, yet light hearted and friendliness to all, greatly influenced other pilots, inspiring them to put supreme effort into defeating the enemy airforce.'

On the 21st the squadron flew back to Digby and slipped back into the dull routine of sea sweeps and convoy patrols. However, they were allowed moments of excitement, such as escorting B.17s to Rouen on 5 September, operating from West Malling and again to St Omer on the 6th. Squadron Leader Newton received the DFC on the 5th and the Station Commander, Group Captain Campbell, left, his successor being the legendary leader of 1 RCAF Squadron in the Battle of Britain (later renumbered as 401 Squadron RCAF), Group Captain E A McNab DFC. Newton too was about to be rested, and so was Buck.

On the 21st Buck was sent for a medical board. He was found unfit for flying duties by the RAF Hospital at Rauceby, as well as by the squadron MO. Flight Lieutenant George B Murray DFC came in from 401 Squadron to replace him. It was obviously time for a well-earned rest. He should really have had one following his return from Malta, but that hadn't happened. Now it had been forced upon him.

On 16 October he boarded a Boeing Stratocruiser at RAF Hendon and headed for Washington, via Prestwick and Ganda (20 hours). Four days later he was in a Lodestar from Ottawa, Toronto, Halifax, Regina and North Battleford (18 hours). He was going home. On the 18th he had cabled home from Washington DC: *'Arrived last night, be seeing you in a week. McNair.'*

The family were not slow in letting everyone know. In the local North Battleford newspaper there appeared: *'HERO OF MALTA IS ON WAY HOME.* October 19 – Mr and Mrs K F McNair have received word that their son Flt Lt R W 'Buck' McNair DFC, hero of Malta, arrived in Washington and may be expected home in a few days.'

**Civic Banquet**

If Buck McNair imagined he was in for a quiet time he was wrong. No sooner was he back home than he was the local hero returned. Then, on Wednesday 18 November 1942, the North Battleford Council put on a Civic Banquet in his honour, held that evening at the Library Auditorium, North Battleford.

The Mayor, J D Deans, introduced Buck to the assembly and a toast was proposed by Paul Prince MLA, followed by an address by Flight Lieutenant J M MacDonald, from No.4 Recruiting Centre, RCAF. Three lots of community singing no doubt had Buck feeling he'd rather be back on Malta, but he took it all in good part. The meal and the evening ended with the song 'O Canada'.

The event was covered by the *North Battleford News* the next day,

including the speeches made by the Mayor and Mr Prince. No doubt they had
been well prepared in advance so the newsman had no difficulty in getting
copies for his paper. Unfortunately, the really interesting speech would have
been that made by Buck himself, which was mostly about his time on Malta.
As this was no doubt an 'off the cuff' dissertation, it was not printed up in the
newspaper.

\* \* \*

**Bond Tour**
One of Buck McNair's first jobs was to go on a bond tour, which was far
from his liking although he soon began to appreciate that in order to win this
war, the more people who became involved the better. And if that meant him
touring round encouraging people to buy war bonds, so be it. He was later
joined by Buzz Beurling, back from his successes on Malta; they would meet
again in England the following summer.

Buck soon tired of the bond business and was eager to get back to the war,
particularly the Middle East. He upset quite a few senior officers and the
AOC of Western Command, who happened to be the father of someone Buck
had become rather friendly with, Chester Hull, a retired lieutenant-general.
The AOC was a delightful man but Robert rubbed him up the wrong way.

Buck went into his office one day and said, 'Sir, I don't like this work; I
want to get back to the war!' His approach irritated the AOC so much that the
man told him so. The exchange ended with the AOC picking up an ink-well
from his desk and hurling it across the office at Buck, who beat a hasty
retreat.

**RCAF Squadron**
After just over a month of home leave, Buck McNair was posted to No.133
Squadron of the RCAF. It was based at Boundary Bay, near Vancouver, BC,
and flew Hurricanes. One of the pilots there was Don Laubman, later to
become a great friend of Buck's and an exceptional fighter pilot once he got
to England. Don Laubman recalls his first encounter with Buck:

'My first encounter with Buck occurred after I had been
instructing for about 1 1/2 years and had finally got posted to a
Hurricane squadron. The camp was brand new and we were
quartered in a building which also housed the officers' mess.
This particular evening several of us decided to go to the gym
after dinner to play some basketball. Appropriately attired we
were heading out of the quarters when I noticed the most
decrepit old officer's hat I had ever seen or imagined, sitting on
the rack. Thinking that it was a discard, I placed it on my head
and went over to the gym. We played basket ball with me
wearing my 'new hat' and after that we had a short game of
soccer using the hat as the ball. When we returned to the
quarters, I replaced the hat. The next day we learned that we had
a new member on the squadron, a fellow named Buck McNair,
who was home on a between-tours rest. It was Buck's Sunday-

*Top left*: The oil painting of Buck McNair DSO DFC** by Robert Hyndman, sat for at Bény-sur-Mer, Normandy, July 1944.

*Top right*: The McNair brothers, Franklin, Kenneth and Robert, working on a floatplane on the Saskatoon River, aged 18, 13 and 16.

*Middle right*: Norseman with floats for use on Canada's rivers, seen here at Yellowknife, 1939. Robert was allowed to fly these aircraft and fell in love with flying.

*Bottom*: U/T pilot McNair, R W, the day he flew solo in this Fleet Finch II No.4515.

*Top left*: A Fleet Finch II with Bob Middlemiss in 1940 at No. 13 EFTS, St Eugene. Bob would later know Buck on Malta, and in 126 Wing.

*Top right*: In England, Robert was posted to 411 Squadron RCAF where his first CO was S/Ldr Paul Pitcher who had seen action in the Battle of Britain the previous summer.

*Middle left*: Buck (giving the hand manoeuvres) and W F Ash with 411 Squadron in 1941. Bill Ash flew the Magister from which Buck decided to jump, so he would know how to do it!

*Middle right*: The Miles Magister (L8270) from which Buck McNair baled out.

(D Matheson)

*Bottom*: Tex Ash shaking hands with the Canadian Prime Minister, Mackenzie King, 27 September 1941, during a visit to 411 Squadron – the day Buck damaged a 109.

*Top*: Spitfire of 411 Squadron at RAF Digby 1941.

*Bottom*: Pilots of 411 Squadron at Hornchurch 16 November 1941;  (l to r): Buck, Sgt C I Nutbrown, Don Blakeslee, Tex Ash, Sgt G A Chamberlain, Sgt E E Green, Paul Pitcher, Ralph Weston, Sgts W J Curtis, T D Holden and R M Booth.

*Top left*: Buck with his new CO, Stan Turner, and Ralph Weston, one of 411's flight commanders. Early in 1942 Turner took Buck with him to Malta.

*Top right*: F/Lt Laddie Lucas seated in the Sunderland on the flight to Malta, 16 February 1942. Among those on board was F/Lt Buck McNair. *(Lucas Album)*

*Middle left*: Malta 1942. Three of Buck's companions during the defence of the island: Paul Brennan, Wingco E J 'Jumbo' Gracie and Ray Hesselyn. *(Lucas Album)*

*Bottom left*: Three of those killed by the bomb on the Hotel were F/O C H Baker (126 Sqn) ...

*Bottom right*: P/O W H Hallett (126 Sqn) ...

*Top left*: and P/O J C M Booth (249 Sqn).
(all Lucas Album)

*Top right*: The bombed-out mess (Point de Vue Hotel, Rabat) 22 March 1942, where Buck was nearly killed the previous evening. (Lucas Album)

*Bottom*: Watching the action from the mess quarters at Xara Palace, Mdina. (L to r): Pete Rathie, Raoul Daddo-Langlois, Ozzie Linton and Buck. (Lucas Album)

*Top left*: Buck and Ronnie West, Xara Palace. *(Lucas Album)*

*Top right*: Stan Grant DFC watches 109s above the airfield. *(Lucas Album)*

*Middle left*: Nip Heppel and Buck, St Paul's Bay. *(Lucas Album)*

*Bottom*: Spitfires at Gibraltar awaiting transport to Malta. *(Lucas Album)*

*Top left*: Buck ready to go;  on HMS *Eagle*, May 1942. *(Lucas Album)*

*Top right*: Spitfire ready to go, HMS *Eagle*. *(Lucas Album)*

*Bottom left*: Bud Connell and Norman McQueen, 249 Squadron. *(Lucas Album)*

*Bottom right*: John Sherlock and Cy King, 185 Sqn, Malta.  John later flew with Buck in 126 Wing. *(J Sherlock)*

*Top left*: Relaxing on Malta, top to bottom: John Sherlock, Ken Charney, Johnnie Plagis, Ron West, Dave Kent and Buzz Ogilvie. Buzz later nominated Buck for Canada's Aviation Hall of Fame.

*(J Sherlock via Malta War Museum)*

*Top right*: Back in England (Digby) summer 1942, Buck McNair DFC (right) with John (Jack) Stock, 411 Squadron.

*(D Matheson)*

*Middle right*: Buck and Doug Matheson, Digby 1942, 411 Squadron RCAF.

*(D Matheson)*

*Bottom*: Back home in Canada, 1942, Buck with his mother and father.

*Top left*: Back on the job with 403 Squadron early summer 1943. Centre front is S/Ldr Charles Magwood with George Aitken (left) and Norm Fowlow (right). Behind are Sgts G R Brown and W C Uttley.

*Top right*: Buck's good friend Rod Smith DFC, Biggin Hill, January 1944.

*Middle left*: Deane MacDonald DFC and Art Coles, 403 Squadron.

*Above*: Flight Lieutenant Hugh Godefroy and Flying Officer Tommy Brannagan, 403 Squadron RCAF.

*Left*: George Aitken, 403 Squadron, Kenley, May 1943. *(Aitken Album)*

*Top left*: Willie Lane, 403 Sqn, in J-Johnny, pointing to a bullet hole in his canopy. He was lost on 15 May 1943.   *(Aitken Album)*

*Top right*: Flight Lieutenant Art Sager, 421 Squadron RCAF.

*(A H Sager)*

*Above left*: F/Os W E Harten and A E Fleming, 421 Squadron.

*Middle right*: 403 Sqn, Sunday service at Dispersal, just before Les Ford's departure. Front (l to r): G D Aitken, Dean Dover, Charles Magwood, G/C Fenton, L S Ford, Norm Fowlow, Johnson (adj) and Berger (I/O); rear four faces belong to F/O R Wozniak, Chevers, Deschamps and W C Uttley.

*Right*: The Red Indian Squadron crest.

*Top left*: Two Bucks! Robert McNair and Robert Buckham DFC.

*Top right*: Bob Middlemiss and George 'Buzz' Beurling.

*Above left*: Wing Commander Hugh Godefroy DSO DFC CdG.

*Above right*: Flying Officer Tommy Parks (right) helped save Buck McNair's life on 28 July 1943 by staying over his dinghy despite emptying fuel tanks. S/L J F Lambert is the other pilot, a later CO of 421, killed in action December 1943.

*(F J Sherlock)*

*Left*: Squadron Leader A D Grace of 277 Squadron ASR, who landed his Walrus on the sea to rescue McNair on 28 July 1943.

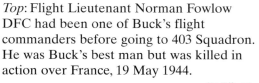

*Top*: Flight Lieutenant Norman Fowlow DFC had been one of Buck's flight commanders before going to 403 Squadron. He was Buck's best man but was killed in action over France, 19 May 1944.

*(R Elliott)*

*Middle left*: Wing Commander Buck McNair with his golden retriever pup, Peter. The original photograph clearly shows his facial burns over the areas not protected by goggles and oxygen mask.

*Bottom left*: Wingco McNair and Norm Fowlow 1944.

*(R W Orr)*

*Bottom right*: Don Laubman DFC, knew Buck in Canada and in England.

*Top left*: Barbara and Buck on their wedding day, April 1944.

*Top right*: Relaxing from operations, Wingco McNair, summer 1944.

*Middle left*: Bob Hyndman, the Spitfire pilot turned official artist. He painted Buck's portrait in France in 1944.

*Middle right*: Buck and George Keefer outside Buckingham Palace with Barbara, 7 November 1944. Both men had just received the DSO from the King.

*Bottom left*: Senior RCAF officers (l to r): Buck McNair, George Keefer, Keith Hodson, and G/C Bill McBrien.

*Bottom right*: Group Captain R W McNair DSO DFC & two Bars.

*Top left*: Seated, Johnnie Johnson and Buck; behind to the right is John Sherlock.

*Top right*: Buck McNair with his former Wing Leader, Johnnie Johnson DSO DFC, Officer's Mess, St Huberts, Quebec, 1947.

*Bottom*: The North Star (17503) which crashed at Vancouver Airport on 30 December 1953.                    *(L Milberry)*

*Top left*: Robert McNair greeting HRH The Duke of Windsor at Baden, August 1957.

*Top right*: Robert and Barbara at Baden-Baden.

*Middle*: Robert, with Air Commodore Gilchrist (Air Division Chief of Staff), and his three squadron commanders in 4 Wing, Wg Cdr O Brown (419), Sqn Ldr G Murray AFC (422) and Sqn Ldr E Garry (444), in November 1959. The event is the winning of the Lloyd Chadburn Trophy, for the Wing attaining the highest air firing average at the APC, Sardinia.

*Left*: OC No.4 Canadian Fighter Wing, Germany, 1957.

*Top*: Re-visiting the island of Malta, September 1970. Welcomed by Colonel Heid.

*Middle left*: Keith and Bruce McNair; sons to be proud of.

*Above*: Wartime photo of Baron Michael Donnet CVO DFC CdG, fighter pilot with the RAF who knew Robert in war and peace, lastly when both were with their respective embassies in London. At Robert's funeral he gave the eulogy.

*Left*: Last visit home, Robert (right) says goodbye to his brothers Ken and Frank.

go-to-meetings hat! I don't think he ever learned about my folly.'

## The Buckerfield Family

While in Canada Buck made several friends. Being in the public eye helped. One was Ernest Buckerfield, head of Buckerfield Seeds in British Columbia, and a multi-millionaire. Ernest Buckerfield had a lovely family, with a daughter Mary, and it was the great man's wont to invite young RCAF pilots back to his home, and in due course, Buck became one of them. Buckerfield and his wife Amy took a shine to Buck and they became firm friends. This friendship between Ernest and Buck lasted to the end of their lives. In fact it has been said that Buck was as close to Ernest as if he'd been the latter's son.

In later years Ernest used Buck as a confidant, and Ernest's brother, Robert Bruce Buckerfield, head of the Canadian Imperial Bank of Commerce, was also a good friend. Immediately after the war the Buckerfield family were to be a great help to Buck's family.

CHAPTER TEN

# BACK TO THE WAR

Robert 'Buck' McNair finally made it back to England, and the war. His logbook while in Canada had shown his flying hours had increased to 612 but the beginning of his next book starts with the total at 714 in April 1943. In this book – No.3 – he states that the previous book was lost in the Mediterranean, but the reasons are not clear, nor does the Med feature in his movements at this time. However, the intelligence officer of 403 Squadron RCAF, confirmed Robert's summary of claims as eight destroyed, five probables and eight damaged, between September 1941 and September 1942.

So at this stage, while he was beginning to be well known as a useful fighter pilot in the RCAF, he was little more than an experienced Spitfire pilot, with a DFC, looking for a job following a rest period in Canada.

In April 1943 he received a posting to No.403 Squadron at RAF Kenley, part of the Kenley Wing led by Wing Commander J E Johnson DFC and Bar. His squadron commander was Squadron Leader L S Ford DFC and Bar, from Hamilton, Nova Scotia, but almost as soon as Buck arrived, Les Ford was given command of the Digby Wing, and Squadron Leader C M Magwood took over.

Wing Commander Johnnie Johnson, who would end the war as the highest scoring RAF fighter pilot in the European theatre, had commanded 610 Squadron during the Dieppe Operation the previous August, and was now Wing Leader at Kenley with 403 and 416 Canadian Squadrons. As a matter of interest, Johnnie himself only had nine confirmed victories at this time, but was fast establishing himself as a good and aggressive leader, with the happy knack of being able to keep tabs on two dozen Spitfires well into a battle situation. In this way he was generally able to retain tactical control for several minutes before the vagaries of combat began to split up the various sections. However, those initial moments were vital in gaining the most out of any given situation, both offensively and defensively.[1]

No.416 Squadron (known as the Wild Cats) was commanded by Squadron Leader Foss Boulton, from Alberta, and together with 403 (the Wolf Squadron), were known as the Canadian Wing. Squadron Leader Charles Magwood came from Toronto. Older than most, 29, he had already notched up a few kills with 403 as a flight commander.

---

[1] Johnnie Johnson died 30 January 2001, aged 85.

The Wing was operating with the Spitfire Mark IX, which no doubt Buck found a lot handier than the old Spitfire V which he'd flown the previous year, both in England and over Malta. The Wing had previously been led by Keith Hodson DFC and Bar, who was to become a friend of Buck's. Keith Hodson was born in the Channel Islands but had grown up in London, Ontario. A pre-war pilot he had been an instructor early in the war, but in 1942 had become operational with 602 Squadron, part of the then Kenley Wing. In May he took command of 401 Squadron RCAF, and flew during the Dieppe show and later from Biggin Hill.

**The Air War**
The Spitfire IX was a vast improvement over the Mark V and was able to combat the FW190 on something like equal terms. The early IX with the Merlin 61 engine was superior to the FW190 in speed at most altitudes, although the 190 had a better rate of climb at 15,000-25,000 feet. It had first seen combat at Dieppe but not all Fighter Command had the IX as yet. In fact in the spring of 1943 Fighter Command only had ten squadrons equipped with the IX, and the V was still being produced!

In order to fill that vital gap between 15,000-25,000 feet, Rolls-Royce improved the engine, resulting in the Merlin 66. One initial advantage for the Allied pilots flying the IX was that it looked exactly like the Mark V, but with the Merlin 66 engine, its second stage cut in at 13,000 feet, so really its best combat height was at medium altitude. So until the Luftwaffe pilots began to be more cautious, the IX gave them some nasty surprises.

As the German fighter pilots had by this time conceded the sky above 20,000 feet to the RAF, there were few 190s or 109s found above that height, mainly because the previous HF Spitfires had been operating up to 30-35,000 feet. This of course meant that the IXs would find more action at medium altitude, which was what their pilots wanted. For too long the fighter pilots had seen loads of Me109s or FW190s at lower altitudes and by the time they'd got down to them, they had flown off.

Buck was soon to learn how the air war over Europe had changed since the summer of 1942, and bore almost no relation to that of the summer of 1941. In those far off days squadrons and wings were quick to engage enemy aircraft, but by the spring of 1943, the wing leaders were less likely to dive headlong into a fight. Johnnie Johnson and the like preferred to size up the situation and send down sections or squadrons to make an engagement while still retaining a top cover. Air combat had matured.

By this time too Fighter Command had discovered the limitations of range with their Spitfires. The Americans were beginning deeper and deeper penetrations into Germany with their four-engined B17 and B24 bombers, and even their twin-engined bombers – B25 Mitchells and B26 Marauders – were heading deeper into France. Fighter Command could not provide total escort, but could only help by using relays of squadrons or wings, some to take them in, others to bring them out, with others to cover the target area. With the 'heavies' Spitfires could only take them as far as the German border, and others would meet them as they crossed back over the border some time later. The Germans knew this and rarely engaged them until the bombers had shed their fighters.

Long range tanks helped, but not with long range sorties, especially if they had to jettison them before they were empty as German fighters came into view. American P47 Thunderbolts were starting to cut down the range problems but it wouldn't be until the P51 Mustangs began to arrive in numbers that the US 8th Air Force could escort its own bombers to such targets as Berlin – and back.

### Back in the Saddle

Buck McNair's first operation following his return to operations came on 24 April, with what he described as a 'stooge patrol' between St Pol and Amiens. His first flight in a Spitfire had been that same morning, the first time he'd been in a Spit since the previous August. On the late afternoon of 3 May, came Rodeo 212. Despite his experience he was still deemed both rusty and lacking in up-to-date combat knowledge, so on this trip Charles Magwood put him down as his No.2. Norm Fowlow, whom he had known on Malta, was a section leader, and Hugh Godefroy, a brother flight commander. The three sections comprised the following pilots:

| Blue Section | | Red Section | |
|---|---|---|---|
| F/O N R Fowlow | BS534 | S/L C M Magwood | BS383 |
| F/O T A Brannagan | BS533 | F/L R W McNair | BS474 |
| F/O J I McKay | BR632 | F/O R Wozniak | EN129 |
| Sgt W C Uttley | BS104 | Sgt D C Hamilton | BS396 |

| Yellow Section | |
|---|---|
| F/L H C Godefroy | EN130 |
| P/O W T Lane | BR986 |
| F/O G D Aitken | BS148 |
| P/O H J Dowding | BS540 |

Take-off was at 1720 hours and Johnson led both squadrons to Nieuport, climbing to 18,000 feet. They made one orbit between Cassel and Poperinghe at 20,000 feet and then climbed through cloud over Samer to 22,000. Warned of enemy aircraft, Johnson searched the sky, finding the hostiles. He ordered 416 to make an attack on four FW190s approaching Samer from the south-east as the Wing approached from the north-east. No. 416 shot down two, one by Foss Boulton and the other by Flight Lieutenant R Buchan, also of 416 Squadron. The Wing came out south of Hardelot and re-crossed the English coast over Pevensey Bay. It had been a text-book operation with no losses and two claims – a good baptism for Buck McNair even if it had not been his squadron that had been engaged. It certainly did not impress him enough to even make a comment in his log book!

The opposition had been aircraft of JG26, Feldwebel Karl Ehret had been wounded, and a crash landing caused further injury. Unteroffizier Heinz Gomann force-landed his damaged 190 on Etaples airfield.

Buck was equally unimpressed on the 7th, on Rodeo 213, but at least on this occasion he led a section:

**Blue Section**

F/O N R Fowlow — BS246
W/O A V Hargreaves — BS533
F/O J I McKay — BR632
F/O R D Bowen — BS534

**Red Section**

S/L C M Magwood — BR623
Sgt W C Uttley — BS104
F/O K P Marshall — BS396
Sgt D C Hamilton — BS396

**Yellow Section**

F/L R W McNair — EN130
P/O P K Gray — EN129
P/O H J Dowding — BS540
P/O W T Lane — BS474

Johnnie Johnson led the Wing out east of Hastings on the south Sussex coast at 12,000 feet and crossed the French coast south of Berck at between 22,000 and 24,000 feet. The Wing orbited Bruges, and were then vectored by Appledore control south towards Abbeville, then north at 27,000 feet, where 6-8 German fighters were spotted diving away. Appledore control reported more hostiles over Abbeville itself but they were engaged by pilots of the Biggin Hill Wing so the Canadians flew home. They crossed back in over Rye.

Circus 295 was put on the board on the 11th, with Buck flying Yellow 3 in Hugh Godefroy's section; Johnson led the Wing. Hugh Godefroy had actually been born in Java, the son of a Dutch father and Canadian mother. Educated in Ontario he volunteered upon the outbreak of war and his first operational tour had been on Hurricanes with 401 Squadron in 1941. Going then to 403 Squadron he became a flight commander in March 1943 and received a DFC in May.

Johnnie Johnson led the Wing out at noon, making a wide orbit of Dunkirk from where Appledore vectored them to Mardyck, then to St Omer and finally they withdrew at Gravelines. Some FW190s were then seen and the Wing turned at the coast as some red marker flak came up. Red Section of 403 attacked a dozen Focke Wulfs, and 416 engaged several more 190s, claiming one shot down. Disengaging, the Spitfires came back over Deal and were back on the ground by 1335.

On this operation, No.3 to Charles Magwood had been Squadron Leader L V Chadburn DFC. Lloyd Chadburn, from Montreal, had been flying with the RCAF and RAF before joining 416 Squadron, becoming its CO in 1942. He had just returned from leave in Canada and was flying as a supernumerary with 403 before taking command of the Digby Wing.

Two days later, on the 13th, an event occurred which was to affect Buck in no small way before the week was out. Circus 296, led by Johnson, got into a running fight between St Omer and the French coast with 20 German fighters. Charles Magwood shot down one and damaged a second. Later, Johnson led Ramrod 71, escorting B17s during which they met an estimated 50 enemy fighters. Sergeant Uttley was shot down east of Doullens and Sergeant C W McKim of 416 went into the sea 15 miles west of Le Touquet. Not only this but Foss Boulton failed to get home too.

Pilot Officer Dowding shot down a 190 while another went down to Johnnie Johnson, Bowen and Dowding over the sea on the way back.

Dowding and Lane were also credited with one damaged apiece, while Hugh Godefroy and Flight Lieutenant H D MacDonald also claimed damage to 190s.

Once again they had been up against JG26 whose pilots claimed three victories. The Geschwader commander, Major Josef 'Pips' Priller, got one for his 87th kill, Hauptmann Hans Naumann, the leader of the 6th Staffel, another for his 15th, while Leutnant Rudi Leuschel, leader of the 10th Staffel, claimed his 2nd victory. JG26 lost one pilot killed – Unteroffizier Werner Lonsdorfer – but JG2, JG54 and JG27 had been in action too. JG2 reported four pilots lost during the day, and JG54 had a pilot bale out. JG26 also shot down two B17s.

At 2020 403 Squadron mounted an Air Sea Rescue sortie looking for the missing pilots, Buck flew Blue 1 with eight other pilots, including Magwood and Chadburn. Also in the sortie was Flying Officer R G Middlemiss. Bob Middlemiss had been on Malta at the same time as Buck. They flew over the Channel for an hour but failed to find any signs of the downed airmen.

It had been a bad day for the Wing. In the event, Foss Boulton had been wounded and had baled out to become a prisoner. Uttley crashed near Grevillers, south of Arras and was buried there. McKim was seen to ditch but was not found. Two other Spitfires had been damaged. Bob Middlemiss recalls being re-united with Buck:

'On my return to England I completed my tour at an Operational Training Unit as an instructor, and was then posted to 403 Squadron at Kenley. The squadron at that time was composed of a great number of experienced pilots starting out on their second tour, including Buck McNair. Some went on to become great squadron commanders and wing leaders. When he left 403 he became CO of 416 Squadron, and then a month later CO of 421, sister squadron to 403 at Kenley.'

**Buck is re-united with Rod Smith**
Rod Smith had returned from Malta towards the end of 1942 and had become an instructor. In the spring of 1943 he ran into his old friend again, the first time they had met since their Digby days. Rod recalls:

'Buck and I ran into each other again in the late spring of 1943. I was down for an investiture for my DFC and Buck was at Kenley, so I went there to visit him. He introduced me to Johnnie Johnson, their wing leader. I'd seen Johnnie on a show back on 8 November 1941, a dreadful do we went on; the first time we saw the FW190. Johnnie devotes two pages of his famous book 'Wing Leader' to that show.

'Buck was moping at Kenley; he was still a flight lieutenant a year after he'd left Malta. A bunch of flying instructors were starting to come over from Canada, a lot of them flight lieutenants and Buck's contemporaries but who had also risen to his rank. Buck, of course, wanted a squadron and was highly qualified to have one, because of his leadership ability and having been a flight commander on 249 Squadron. He had far more experience than any of these new guys.

'The Sweeps being flown were pretty damned hard and dangerous; you were evading all the time, and didn't often get a chance to go after the enemy. Gus Edwards had become AOC-in-C of the RCAF Overseas, and he was something of a politician. He wanted everything to be RCAF[1].

'One of the wing leaders was Keith Hodson, a training command chap – in fact I'd checked him out in a Spitfire at Wellingore – nice guy but not spectacular. Buck told me that he'd been complaining a bit, so he was summoned to Gus Edwards' office at Lincoln Inn Fields, in London, and Keith Hodson was there along with some other officers. Buck asked to be transferred to an RAF squadron.

'Edwards said he understood that Buck was not satisfied with the Canadian Wing, and wanted a transfer, etc, and Buck told Edwards that the pilots were not experienced enough and pointed to Keith, saying that here was a very nice guy but he doesn't really know anything! Relatively speaking, to Buck, this was so, but rather off for a flight lieutenant to say to an AOC-in-C in his office.

'Gus Edwards said they were grooming Buck to be a flight commander in one of the Canadian squadrons. Well, this was a terrible insult to Buck, having been a flight commander for over a year; it was ridiculous. Buck responded by saying that if they gave him the Wing he might stay! The upshot was he was given 416 Squadron in the Kenley Wing.'

The next operation, on 14 May, was another Ramrod (No.73). On this show, Buck's IFF (Identification Friend or Foe) blew up during a skirmish with some Me109s over France and the Spitfire's cockpit door panel was torn off, which must have caused an interesting few moments. They had been escorting American Fortresses over Dunkirk-Ypres-Nieuport, led by Johnson. Hugh Godefroy shot down a 190, while Deane MacDonald put a 109 into the sea.

On the 15th came Circus 297, escort to 12 Bostons attacking Poix, the home of I Gruppe JG27. Flight Lieutenant L B Madden and Pilot Officer Lane failed to get back although the squadron claimed one victory and a damaged. Willie Lane's brother Gordon, who was in the Royal Canadian Engineers, had arrived at Kenley on a visit. It was hard to tell him that his brother had not come home. They had been in combat with JG2 who claimed both Spitfires plus another Canadian of 421 Squadron.

For the third day in a row the Squadron were on ops. This time it was Circus 298, that began at 1640. Buck's sortie is not listed in the squadron records as it seems he was acting as Wing Leader – certainly he was flying the Wingco's Spitfire, marked with Johnnie Johnson's initials, JE-J, a wing

---

[1] Air Vice-Marshal Harold Edwards CB RCAF.

commander perogative. He had also test flown it earlier in the day. There is
a good reason why he was not in the Squadron records for Circus 299 on the
17th, and that was because he was no longer with 403.

By this time it was obvious that Foss Boulton, missing on the 13th, was
not going to be found in a dinghy in the Channel, so that he was either dead,
or down in France, a prisoner or on the run. A new CO had to be found for
416 Squadron, and Buck got the job. As Johnnie Johnson, who would have
had a hand in the appointment, recorded in his book *Wing Leader* (Chatto &
Windus, 1956):

> 'During one hot fight over the target area Foss Boulton was
> wounded and shot down. His place at the head of 416 Squadron
> was taken by the burly, assertive, Buck McNair, who had already
> been through the thick of the air fighting over Malta . . . .'

Perhaps, too, Buck's forceful attitude with Gus Edwards had something to do
with it!

**Squadron Commander**
At least Buck did not have to travel far to take up his new post and new
command, the 'Wild Cats' were in the other hangar and they all shared the
same messes. One of his flight commanders was another 'Buck' just to
confuse matters. This was Flight Lieutenant R A Buckham DFC, and like
McNair, a Robert.

He was also known as Bob at times, and he came from the town of Golden,
British Columbia. He was nearly three years older than his CO but had
enlisted in the RCAF in 1940, joining 416 Squadron in time for the Dieppe
operation. On 14 May 1943 he had claimed his fifth victory, and added a
damaged to his score on the 16th.

Acting Squadron Leader McNair did not have any time to get used to his
new job as orders for Circus 299 were already clattering out from the HQ
printer. The Wing would be led by Charles Magwood, as Johnson was still
away, although McNair would still be flying the Wingco's JE-J. The Wing
acted as first fighter echelon heading out over Shoreham and crossing into
France above Port en Bassin. Reaching Caen at 1038, then sweeping over the
Cabourg area, all eyes were scanning the spring sky. Above Bayeux and Caen
red marker flak exploded near them at 30,000 feet. The top squadron was
marked by these bursts until the fighters were some 15 miles back over the
coast, but they did not herald an attack by the Luftwaffe.

If Buck thought he had finally made it to command position, it suddenly
felt short lived, for this same day 416 was declared non-operational. Not long
after the Spitfires had landed back, the pilots took over the Spitfire Vs from
421 Squadron, while they – smiling – took 416's Spitfire IXs. No. 421
Squadron then prepared to take over 416's dispersal hut and area, as they
moved in from Redhill.

Buck did not stay non-operational for long! The next day he flew as No.2
to Johnnie Johnson on Rodeo 218 and on the 19th again as the Wingco's
wingman on Rodeo 220. However, his new squadron was starting to break
up. On the 21st Pilot Officers H A Terris and B S Siddall, together with

Sergeants H F Packard and K R Linton moved to 421 Squadron. Five days later Buckham left to go to Digby – after a spot of leave – as Wing Gunnery Officer. Finally on the 29th, 416 took its 'new' Spitfire Vs to Wellingore and then to Digby on 6 June, becoming part of 12 Group's Digby Wing.

The squadron was now in the backwater of operations, but on 10 June Buck McNair and eight of his pilots flew over to RAF Coltishall in the late afternoon, taking off after topping up with petrol at 2015, to fly a fighter roadstead operation off the Dutch coast. The next day Buck led his pilots and those of 402 Squadron as close escort to some Ventura bombers attacking Zeebrugge. They made rendezvous over Bradwell Bay and an otherwise uneventful trip at least produced some good bombing of the target.

On the 12th they headed south again, this time to Ford, Sussex, in the afternoon. After refuelling, Buck led 416 on an escort to Bostons on Rodeo 91, along with 402 Squadron, the Digby Wing led by Lloyd Chadburn. They met some heavy flak fire over Fécamp on the way out, but everyone got down at Ford prior to heading for Bradwell Bay for the night. This was because the next day the Wing was to escort a dozen Mitchells to Flushing in a morning show. One bomber fell to flak over the target while two others were severely damaged. 416 escorted these two back while two dozen FW190s made darting attacks on the Spitfires and the crippled Mitchells but all returned.

That was not the end of the day, for in the evening, Buck led a Roadstead, with 402, acting as close escort to torpedo-carrying Beaufighters. They attacked a convoy of ships a few miles off Callantsoog, by Den Helder; one Beau was hit, followed by a splash on the sea. Torpedo hits were claimed on two 4,000 ton ships and two smaller vessels, three of which were left smoking, and one listing over. The Beaus were from 236 and 254 Squadrons, and two of the German ships sank, the 5,180-ton MV *Stadt Emden* and the 487-ton auxiliary (VP.1109) *Mahren*.

Buck lost his other senior flight commander on the 17th, Flight Lieutenant I C Ormston DFC who moved to 401 Squadron, but word now reached Buck that he too was leaving. On the 18th he was to fly down to Kenley once again, and take over the unit that had taken his Spitfire IXs and dispersal – 421. Squadron Leader P L I Archer DFC, had just been given command of 421 but was shot down on 17 June flying one last sortie with 402 Squadron. Phil Archer had been an experienced fighter pilot with six victories, having flown with 92 Squadron during 1941.

## War in the Third Dimension

Buck McNair was about to commence an intense period of operational flying. Malta had been tense, immediate, up close and personal. Operating over northern France and the Low Countries day after day took another kind of skill and a different kind of attitude.

I asked George Aitken, who flew with Buck McNair in 1943, what it was like to fly and fight on these missions:

> 'Usually the routine was to prepare oneself, shaving, washing and getting dressed and then heading for the mess to partake of what breakfast had been made ready for us. Following breakfast most of us might check to see if we had any mail and then find

those trusty bicycles that each of us had.

'I would imagine the NCO pilots would have had a like routine as we might all meet along the perimeter track and head for our Dispersal area together. The maintenance personnel always seemed to beat us and some Spitfires had already been serviced. Our intelligence officer, doctor and adjutant, and on some occasions our padre, would be with us at Dispersal. Our Mae-Wests, parachutes, etc, were all kept at the Dispersal Hut along with our flying helmet and face mask. We would tie on our Mae-West, fitting it to an oxygen container that was provided for just such a test. Some of us might also check the parachutes, making sure that the release pin in particular was not bent in any way that might cause a failure should one have to use it.

'When I was at Kenley, 403 carried out a number of different operational functions, patrols, scramble patrols, flight scrambles, escorts, rodeos, sweeps, ramrods, high cover sorties, circuses. On any operation that might take the squadron over the Channel, we would be briefed by the squadron leader in our dispersal and it was then that we might find out who would be on that type of action, and in what position we would fly in the Flights. On patrols we would know before take-off where we were to patrol, such as Beachy Head, etc. On all scamble activities upon getting airborne, the Controller would advise you where, when, and what duty he wished the leader to proceed with.

'How were pilots assigned to the various function? A good question and I think it was the squadron leader who chose who was to be in his section and each of the flight commanders chose who would be in theirs, and what positions they would fill [Nos. 2, 3 or 4]. Since we usually had a full complement of pilots, it appeared to me that they did try to share the various functions fairly. Whilst I was keen to keep the same letter and serial number of the Spitfires I flew, I did not always keep the position that I flew in the Flight. Also, behind the dispersal hut was a place to take a nervous pee!!

'At dispersal before take-off, or if left behind (ie, not flying on the sortie) we might play cards or chess, write letters, or catch up on sleep, or, if the weather was good, take in the sunshine. It might be the time also for some of us to get to know our ground crew, who were just as keen as us to see the Spitfires return.

'On one occasion I had been left behind, I watched a perfect landing of an unmarked Spitfire. It did not head for dispersal, but further along the perimeter track a staff car seemed to be waiting for the pilot to shut down his engine. Before getting into the car, the pilot took off the helmet to reveal locks of blonde hair. She had flown in one of our replacement Spitfires – a lady member of the Air Transport Auxiliary.

'One role in these early months of 1943 was to act as a short-range "wall" for US Fortresses and Liberators engaged in attacking German targets in daylight. This meant we would perhaps give them protection part way over and then return to base, refuel, and go and cover them as they came back. On one occasion after a day of protection duties we were treated to several cases of Coca-Cola by the Americans in appreciation.'

The scene at the various dispersal areas became a daily ritual. Pilots gathered in and around the hut much like a cricket team at their pavilion. On warm days the flight hut gave off distinctive smells. Outside, warm creosoted wood from the huts, perhaps some recent mown grass; inside human odours, socks, flying boots, rubber, cigarettes.

There was a normality about everything, but an impossible normality, never seen before and not likely to ever be seen again. Only a few years, or even months, before, these young men had been at school, college or university. Now, fully trained pilots, they were Fighter Command's cutting edge, flying the world's most advanced fighter aeroplanes. Each day they put their lives on the line.

Birds twittered and chirruped in nearby trees and hedgerows behind the nearby shelters and aircraft pens. Scattered off to one side was an assortment of bicycles, leaning up against the side of the hut or lying on the ground. An old battered car or two – sporty jobs usually – open topped – each exuding the personality of their owners, generally the CO's or a flight commander's vehicle.

These boys dressed according to personal choice and comfort. Outwardly they all looked similar, but upon closer inspection each had subtle differences. Some wore RAF battledress, one or two a worn No.1 uniform, no longer used on any formal occasion because of wear or the odd oil stain. Nobody wore ties. It was all silk scarves of multi-various colours and designs, or perhaps a roll-neck sweater. Anything that would stop the neck chaffing in the air with the constant twisting of the head as their eyes kept the constant vigil. Those less vigilant were soon picked off.

Some wore flying boots, others sturdy shoes but with those gaiter-type leggings that could, if their owner came down in occupied territory, be cut away to leave a more civilian looking shoe in which to attempt to evade. A map might be stuffed in the boot or legging; perhaps a knife too, not necessarily for defence but rather to cut away a parachute harness of the control lines if one became snagged on landing or in the sea. Most pilots wore gloves of some description, not only against the cold but to help protect flesh from fire if the unthinkable happened.

They were all professionals, the regular airmen as well as the wartime-only volunteers. They were in a serious profession with death their constant companion. And the strain was made more difficult by other touches of normality.

Soldiers in the front line or sailors at sea became used to being in constant danger and each coped with it until leave – or a friendly harbour – came up. Airmen in Britain from whatever command, Fighter, Bomber, Coastal – all had one major difference. At one moment they could be in deadly combat with the enemy over occupied territory. An hour later, if they survived, they could be having a beer in a pub, taking a girlfriend to a cinema, or even be on the telephone to a wife or mother. The change was dramatic, for within twelve hours, they could easily be, once again, in mortal danger from enemy action. And this went on day, after day, after day.

War in the air was sudden, deadly; it took only a moment of indecision, a second's loss of concentration, or pure bad luck to end one's life. Buck McNair and all the others lived with this every waking moment, and sometimes during sleeping moments too. Only those who did these things, lived these things, can fully comprehend them.

CHAPTER ELEVEN

# THE CHIEF

Number 421 Squadron, RCAF, had been formed in April 1942 at Digby. Over the following months, flying the Spitfire Vb, it had seen brief action from bases such as Exeter, Fairwood Common, Ibsley, Kenley and Redhill. Now it was based at Kenley once again, had recently been re-equipped with the Spitfire IX, and as previously mentioned, was part of Johnnie Johnson's Canadian Wing. The other squadron in the Wing was 403, commanded by Squadron Leader H C Godefroy DFC, who had taken over from Squadron Leader Charles Magwood on 13 June.

Buck reported in on 19 June. His flight commanders were Flight Lieutenant A H Sager and P G Blades. Art Sager came from Hazelton, BC, and following graduation from the University of British Columbia, had worked for the *Daily Mirror* newspaper in England, and even had a spell as an actor. When war came he was in Canada as a schoolmaster but joined the RCAF and after training returned to England to join 421 Squadron upon its formation. Art recorded in his diary:

> 'Two days later (after S/L Archer was shot down) S/L "Buck" McNair DFC, flight commander in 416, took over the Squadron and inaugurated his command by shooting down an Me109 on his first show, a Circus with Bostons to Abbeville, from which three pilots of 403 failed to return. Buck is an excellent pilot and marksman, blunt, rough character and an intrepid leader.'

Commanders of 421 had their own unofficial title due to the squadron being known as the Red Indians, as Art Sager relates:

> 'The use of the term "the Chief" or "da Chief", dates from S/L Freddie Green's period of command – November 1942 to April 1943 – and originated with our first adjutant, the irrepressible Chas Chasanoff, who considered Freddie type-cast for the role. It was Chas who in November 1942, wrote to the McColl Frontenac Oil Company, requesting permission to use their company's Red Indian crest. Long before the crest and name was officially approved we became "The Red Indians" with charismatic Freddie Green our popular chieftain, widely known as "da Chief".'

Mr Pritchard of the McColl-Frontenac oil company agreed that the squadron could use its Indian head logo, and these appeared on all 421's Spitfires, just ahead of the cockpit or on the engine cowlings. Initially an unofficial badge was produced with just an Indian head upon it and it was this insignia which appeared on the Spitfires. Once the squadron had its official crest approved it became an Indian head with full war bonnet together with crossed tomahawks. Its motto was: 'They have sounded the war trumpet'.

Several of the Spitfires added a name by the insignia, sometimes an Indian word, or like Art Sager, the name 'Ladykiller'. He had meant it to describe the deadly character of the Spitfire but he came to regret it as some gave it another connotation!

Buck had met a Belgian fighter pilot earlier while with the Hornchurch Wing – Michael Donnet – who had escaped from Belgium in July 1941. They had become firm friends and oddly enough, Donnet, while flying with the RAF had an Indian head painted on his Spitfire. Asking him about a photograph of a certain (later goon) Michael Bentine painting the head on the aeroplane, Mike Donnet related to this author:

> 'About the Red Indian painted by Michael Bentine on my Spitfire, the story is that my Belgian Air Force squadron in 1939 (No.9, flying Renard 31s), with which I fought the May 1940 campaign in Belgium, had the Red Indian as its squadron badge. When I was in the RAF, I painted a Red Indian head on all my Spitfires. Bentine, our intelligence officer, did suggest he paint the one in the photograph you mention, on my Spitfire XIV, and the picture was taken at that time. The coincidence with the Red Indian head on Buck's 421 Squadron's machines is very interesting.'

Hugh Godefroy, in his book *Lucky Thirteen* (Croom Helm, 1983) records (and is quoted with his permission):

> '[Buck] was a handsome blond westerner renowned for his outspoken criticism of Headquarters personnel. His fearless aggressiveness as a fighter pilot and his natural ability to lead forced the higher-ups to tolerate him. His squadron was the most important thing in his life. He insisted on implicit obedience to his flying orders which included following his example of bulldog aggressiveness in battle. Anyone he found hesitating he turfed. Those who stood behind him he would defend even though he was threatened with Court Martial. He believed in the merit system, and he had no use for promotion based on seniority.
>
> 'On one occasion when he was away on a forty-eight hour pass, a signal arrived promoting one of his pilots to flight commander. Buck had not authorised this change in leadership. With his face white with rage, he picked up the telephone and called Air Chief Marshal Leigh-Mallory at Fighter Command Headquarters. He was put straight through.

'"Leigh-Mallory here."

'"McNair here. If you want to run this squadron, you come down here and lead it. As long as I'm in command, I'm gonna decide who gets promotion. Do you understand?"

'Without listening for an answer, he slammed down the receiver. The Air Marshal spent the next half an hour trying to find out who had called him. Fortunately he was unsuccessful. Buck made his own choice for the flight commander vacancy and the appointment was changed quietly at local level.

'When day gave way to night, he became a different person. He absolutely refused to talk shop. He mixed with everyone on an equal basis. If anything, alcohol seemed to increase his tolerance, and he drank just enough to enjoy such carefree moments to the full.

'Unbeknown to anyone, the continuous bombing in Malta had opened a chink in his armour. A raw nerve had been bared. One evening in the bar a pilot touched that nerve. This lad was a new replacement in Buck's outfit and was fascinated by his Commanding Officer. He hung on Buck's every word. While standing beside him, during a lull in the conversation, he began to whistle, initiating the sound of a falling bomb. Buck's smile evaporated. With a lightning right to the jaw, he knocked the lad to the floor, then slowly and emphatically he said:

'"I don't find that a bit funny – never do that again."

'In the early part of July, Johnnie took seven days leave and told me to lead. In leadership matters Buck gave me full support, and I drew great benefit from his counsel. We became as close friends as circumstances permitted.'

No. 421 Squadron was not without a few Malta veterans, John Sherlock and Tommy Parks being two of them. John Sherlock recalls Tommy's arrival:

'When Tommy first joined 421 Squadron, he met Buck McNair in the bar and Buck was introducing him to the other pilots. Tommy recognised me and said in a very loud voice; "Oh, I know Sherlock. I would like to fly beside him. Anybody as stupid as that SOB has to be the luckiest pilot in the world to be still alive and I would rather fly beside a lucky pilot than a good one." After that we began sharing quarters.

'The Kenley Wing flew Spitfire IXA models and which had the two-speed, two-stage super-chargers, so practically all our flights were high level, acting as escorts for Fortresses, Liberators, Mitchells, Marauders and occasionally Venturas. The summer of 1943 was a very pleasant period compared to the previous summer in Malta. We had a beautiful mess at Kenley, central heating, excellent food and the latest model Spitfires, and the best wing leader and squadron commanders available. Most of the pilots were second tour chaps or else had

been instructors back in Canada, who had been flying out of
quiet sectors before coming to Kenley.'

**First Sortie as The Chief**
Squadron Leader McNair wasted no time in flying with his new command
and slated himself for the mission on 20 June as soon as the tele-type
machines began rattling out the operational orders. Circus 313 would see the
Wing providing Target Support to the show, Bostons to Poix and Abbeville.
Take-off was scheduled for 1230, the pilots being:

*Circus 313, 1230-1405 hrs*

| A Flight | | B Flight | |
|---|---|---|---|
| F/L P G Blades | BR623 | S/L R W McNair | AD113 |
| P/O A E Fleming | BS129 | F/L A H Sager | BS290 |
| F/O J D McFarlane | MA416 | P/O P G Johnson | RS126 |
| F/O F J Sherlock | BR978 | P/O K R Linton | RS152 |
| P/O P A McLachlan | BR138 | F/O R T Heeney | BS509 |
| | | F/O W B Quint | MA591 |
| | | P/O W F Cook | MA477 |

The Wing encountered strong opposition in the Doullens area and 403
Squadron was hit hard by fighters from JG26 (who had shot down Archer and
another 421 pilot on the 17th). Flying No.2 to his CO, Flying Officer F J
Sherlock made the following combat report upon their return:

> 'Time: 1318. Six to eight 190s shot up through the Squadron
> over Doullens. The CO fired at one and I pulled off to the
> starboard side and took a short burst at him when the CO
> finished. The CO then got behind another and started firing. I
> saw cannon strikes all along the starboard side, the starboard
> oleo leg fell down, and some smoke appeared. Just then another
> 190 shot up and I broke over to the other side and took two
> 1-second bursts at him. By then the CO had started climbing so
> I rejoined him.'

FW190s of JG26 had scrambled at 1300 hours and headed south-west. The
Geschwadergruppe encountered Spitfires of the Hornchurch Wing without
result, but the II Gruppe, led by Hauptmann Wilhelm-Ferdinand Galland,
split his fighters and took two *Staffeln* into the sun. Some of the Kenley Wing
pilots spotted the lower 190s but as 421 dived to engage, Galland came down
from above and bounced both 403 and 421. No. 403 lost three pilots, one to
Galland (his 43rd victory) another to Oberfeldwebel Adolf Glunz, (his 35th)
and one to Unteroffizier Peter Crump – his 5th.

Buck's fire had shot down Unteroffizier Erwin Hanke of the 4th Staffel.
He managed to get his fighter down, crash-landing at Orches, near Douai,
with injuries. The 190 was written-off. It will be recalled that John Sherlock
had been on Malta, with 185 Squadron, at the same time as Buck.

As a matter of interest, while the squadron diary records Buck as flying
Spitfire AD113, in his logbook he notes flying one marked 'JE-J'. This

would be Johnnie Johnson's personally marked wing leader's Spitfire, which at this period was EN398. As Buck had already flown and would later fly Johnson's machine again on occasions, especially leading the Wing, it may be that at the last minute he changed from AD113 to Johnson's machine for this sortie so he could be quickly recognised as leader.

The next sortie came two days later, the 22nd. Ramrod 99 that morning was an escort mission to 240 American B17s bombing the Ruhr. There was little opposition and in the afternoon they were off on Circus 314, the Wing flying withdrawal support to Ventura bombers which had attacked Abbeville. Some German fighters were seen but none came near enough to be engaged.

On the 23rd Ramrod 100, escort to more Fortresses, but then on the 24th came three more shows. The first was uneventful, a Wing Sweep to help cover Bostons going for Flushing soon after breakfast. Over the noon period, Ramrod 103, another supporting Wing Sweep for Bostons bombing the marshalling yards at St Omer. Several enemy fighters were seen and 403 Squadron had a brief skirmish, claiming one destroyed but losing one Spitfire to JG26. In fact the Canadian claimant did so after seeing a parachute near to a 190 he had fired at. However, beneath the parachute had been his own No.2, whom the 190 pilot had just shot down!

Buck's pilots began to run short of fuel after this action. Karl Linton had to make a forced landing near Dungeness, while three other pilots landed at Redhill not risking to fly just a few more miles to Kenley with fuel warning lights burning.

The third operation of the day was mounted at 1645 – Ramrod 106. The Wing acted as target support for Venturas on Yainville, situated west of Rouen, on the Seine, by the Forêt de Brotonne. No. 421 was down to nine serviceable Spitfires, plus the Wing Leader's:

*Ramrod 106, 1645-1825 hrs*

| A Flight | | B Flight | |
|---|---|---|---|
| F/L P G Blades | MA416 | S/L R W McNair | BS152 |
| P/O T J DeCourcy | BR623 | P/O J S Hicks | BS509 |
| F/O H F Packard | BR138 | F/L A H Sager | BS290 |
| F/O A E Fleming | BS129 | F/O C S G DeNancrede | BS126 |
| | | F/O W E Harten | ? |

The Wing had crossed into France at Fécamp and flew to Yainville. South of Rouen they encountered fighters and spent several minutes milling around but were unable to bring the Germans to battle, so they headed north for home.

Buck's squadron ran into 15-20 German fighters but Phil Blades was the only one who got in a short burst although without result. On the way out, Johnnie Johnson and Buck, with their No.2s, stalked two FW190s to the coast near Fécamp, and finally shot down both. Flying Officer Hicks also got in a short burst at a fighter.

Then two 190s had appeared at their 9 o'clock and Johnson, Buck and their wingmen went after them at full bore, catching up with them near the coast. Buck was closing with one but then saw Johnson was making for it too, so he swung over and went for the starboard one. Buck began firing at 450

yards as the WingCo also fired at his target. Buck saw strikes and a flash on
the cockpit canopy and then the fighter seemed to explode. He last saw it
going down at a very steep angle.

This fight was with I/JG2 which had two FW190s damaged, one severely
(80% damage) and one with 35% damage. As a matter of interest, the
Intelligence Report (Form 'F') for Ramrod 106 recorded the operation as
follows:

> *Ramrod 106. 17.50 hours, South of Fécamp.*
> W/C J E Johnson DSO DFC & Bar, led the Wing consisting of
> 10 a/c 421 (RCAF) Squadron commanded by S/L McNair DFC
> and 9 a/c 403 (RCAF) "Wolf" Squadron under the command of
> S/L Godefroy DFC.
>
> The role of the Wing was Target Forward Support Wing to 12
> Venturas of No.2 Group bombing the Power Station at Yainville.
> The Wing was airborne at 16.45 that afternoon, and had landed
> from this operation by 18.25.
>
> Newhaven was crossed at 16.57 hrs at zero feet then [the
> Wing] commenced climbing at 17.09 hrs and when off shore St
> Valéry en Caux an orbit was made, crossing in 17.20, 14,000 ft,
> thence to Yainville 17.25 hrs.
>
> Operations warned the Wing Leader that E/A were climbing
> up inland, the Kenley Wing again orbited seeing about 40 E/A
> climbing up from Rouen towards Le Havre, a greater proportion
> of which were Me109s. Although not possessing tactical
> advantage, the Wing nevertheless engaged these E/A in order to
> keep them from molesting the bombers, but saw no conclusive
> results.
>
> The Wing reformed and tried to engage a further 3 FW190s
> but without success. They then headed for Fécamp being
> shadowed by 2 FW190s who were obviously waiting to bounce
> the odd straggler. They were about 2 miles behind the Wing so
> W/C Johnson climbed with both Squadrons steeply into the sun
> and carried out one orbit to port, the FW190s being thus placed
> down sun of the Kenley Wing and at a disadvantage. The E/A
> seemed to lose sight of the Wing for they flew beneath, thus
> presenting an excellent target.
>
> When they were 1,000 ft below and 1 mile ahead of the Wing,
> the Wing Leader, Black 1 and S/L McNair, Black 3, went down
> on these two E/As with the following results, the remainder of
> the Squadron were told to keep high in order not to scare the
> Huns. W/C Johnson (Black 1) closed on the No.2 E/A from line
> astern opening fire at 300 yds closing to 150 yds. Cannon
> strikes were seen on the fuselage and tail plane of the E/A and
> a large piece fell away from the starboard half of its tail unit.
> The E/A spun down and was seen to crash at Valmont. It is
> claimed as destroyed.
>
> S/L McNair (Black 3) 421 Squadron, attacking the starboard
> of the two E/As opened fire at 450 yds with a two second burst

but saw no results, then fired another burst and saw strikes and a flash on the cockpit, later there was an explosion in the E/A which went down on its back at a very steep angle.

P/O DeCourcy (Black 2) watched both of these two FW190s go down, later seeing two aircraft crash about 2 miles apart inland of Fécamp. Black 3 is therefore credited with a FW190 destroyed. F/L Blades (White 1) and P/O Hicks (Black 4) were also engaged but make no claims pending CCG assessment.

Throughout the operation 403 Squadron as top squadron maintained cover to 421 Squadron but were not engaged.

Wing reformed leaving France over Eletot 17.52 hrs 20,000 feet recrossing Beachy Head 18.10 hrs at 6,000 feet. Two aircraft landed at Friston to refuel.

Buck had fired 71 cannon rounds and 240 .303 rounds. By this stage in the air war, the cannon armament had been improved, and the gun was being belt fed through the old drum system which in earlier time carried 60 rounds of 20 mm per gun. The belt now fed 120 rounds per cannon, sometimes more. The .303 rounds remained the same at 350 per gun.

\* \* \*

There was no let-up. On the 25th the Wing flew to Martlesham Heath and took part in a 12 Group Ramrod (19), escorting Venturas to Amsterdam but weather forced an abort. The pilots flew back to Kenley where they learned that Joe McFarlane was off to 412 Squadron as a flight commander.

Next day came Ramrod 108, the Wing flew fighter cover to Fortresses bombing Tricquiville airfield. Several aircraft developed engine trouble, including the WingCo, so Buck led the Wing. A number of fighters were seen but they did not engage. One pilot in 403 Squadron was forced to bale out and broke an arm.

Rodeo 235 was mounted on the 26th, a fighter sweep to Boulogne-St Omer-Gravelines areas. Fifty+ enemy fighters were encountered but there was only one combat, in which Wing Commander Johnson downed a 190.

After this hectic few days it was a relief to get away, and Buck McNair went off on the 29th to London to meet his King. He went to Buckingham Palace to receive his DFC – quite an occasion for the country boy hero.

## The Daily Round

I asked Art Sager what a typical day at Kenley might be like. Firstly he recalled that Kenley had several good points, not least being female batmen – or is that batwomen? When he first went there he awoke the first morning with what he thought must be an angel bending over him with a cup of tea, trying to waken him. As he reached up she made a hasty retreat, having only entered the room as her knocking had failed to gain his attention.

Another attractive feature was that London was only 30 minutes away by train from the station at Whyteleaf, at the bottom of the hill. The officers' mess had a double lounge, and in one there was a bar, the other a piano. Other features were a billiard room, a theatre for briefings, film shows and even concerts, plus a huge dining room, gymnasium and a squash court. Bedrooms in the main building were singles.

For aircrew meals were not restricted – porridge, sausages, kippers, and frequently there were eggs for breakfast, not to mention dinners of pre-war variety. Perhaps the main problem, like most airfields, was the distance from mess to dispersals, forcing everyone to get hold of a bicycle, or even a motorbike.

One of the first things a new pilot had to do was to be photographed in civilian clothes. Taking the picture with him on Ops ensured a good likeness for a forged ID card if he got down safely 'over the other side' and was successful in making contact with French Resistance workers. Otherwise, the essentials were to carry escape kits which contained a silk map, chocolate, first aid items, phrase book in four languages – and some carried a P38 revolver in order to protect themselves in emergencies, although the pilots noted that these 'emergencies' were not actually described!

Briefings for the various missions (Circus, Ramrod, Roadstead, Sweeps and so on) usually took place an hour before 'tit pressing' time and take-off. The Wing Leader gave everyone information on the type of show, what the target was, and if an escort job, the role and tactics to be employed by each of the squadrons, with courses and timings. Watches were then synchronised.

This was followed by an intelligence officer telling everyone about assumed enemy reaction, where flak guns were sited, and action to be taken if shot down or in trouble. Then the Met man gave a weather forecast. Finally a rallying remark by the WingCo, something akin to a coach urging his team on before the start of a game. Sometimes the Station Commander would say a word or two.

After breakfast everyone reported to the dispersal area, the time varying according to the time of year and the state of Readiness. When on the ground pilots passed most of the day at the dispersal. It was their assembly and waiting point where they could lounge about, read books or magazines, play cards, listen to records, and so on. It was also the operational headquarters, as on the board were posted the readiness of each Flight or component thereof, and if a show was scheduled, the time of the briefing, approximate time of take-off and the make-up of the squadron by section and pilots' positions in them.

The waiting period between briefing and take-off was generally the most edgy and in order to take one's mind off things, one might fuss over one's aeroplane, and talk to the rigger and fitter. Once airborne the pilot became too busy to be nervous – or at least, over nervous.

Squadrons took off in formation, formed up as a Wing once beyond the airfield circuit and headed for the Channel at tree-top height. Once out over the sea the gun button and reflector sight were switched on, and, climbing, the Wing either made for the area of operations, or made rendezvous with the bombers. Each squadron would now take up its assigned position at high, close or rear cover, each unit's three sections of four spreading out in loose 'finger four' formations.

Radio silence was kept until, finally, if hostile aircraft had been picked up on radar by the Fighter Controller back in England, he would call:

'Hello, Greycap Leader (or whatever call-sign one had), Grass-seed here. Do you read me?'

'Loud and clear Grass-seed,' the Wing Leader would reply.

'There are ten plus bandits on your heading a few degrees to the right of you, now at 8,000 feet and climbing north.'

'OK Grass-seed, we'll investigate.' Then the WingCo would call everyone – 'Okay chaps, keep a look out. Turning starboard now.' The sun would be kept on our left and behind, a good spot if the Germans were ahead and below.

Everyone spread out, all eyes searching the sky. Then the Controller would come back:

'Hello Graycap Leader, Grass-seed here. Sorry, but it looks like the rascals have disappeared.'

'Thanks Grass-seed, we'll get them another time.' On other occasions, if the enemy was met, the WingCo would give instant orders and call a 'Tally-ho!' to the Controller, announcing that a fight was imminent.

\* \* \*

## July 1943

Buck McNair was now flying Spitfire IX serial number MA586, coded AU-N. He had taken it over towards the end of June and would fly it throughout July – or at least – until the 28th. July began with Ramrod 117 on the 1st, to Rouen as Bomb-phoons (Hawker Typhoons carrying bombs) raided Abbeville and Courtrai. The Wing acted as first fighter sweep together with the Hornchurch Wing, but the Typhoons didn't proceed so the Wing merely made a sweep of Berck-Merville-St Omer. German fighters came up and 421 covered 403 as they attacked and claimed three shot down.

Next day the Wing flew down to Tangmere, but the first show was cancelled, the pilots hanging around till late afternoon, at which time the Wing made a sweep over Fécamp-Bernay-Le Tréport. The Hornchurch boys engaged fighters while Kenley Wing kept high cover.

On 3 and 4 July came Rodeo 238 and then Ramrod 122, with Ramrod 124 later on the 4th. The first trip on the 4th was as escort to returning B17s from Le Mans. The Wing picked them up over Argentan, so it was one of the longest trips so far.

They had a rest on the 5th, although Buck flew down to Redhill and back, but on the 6th it was back to the action. Two shows were planned for this day. The first was Rodeo 240, a sweep at 0945 over Dieppe-Poix-Amiens-Boulogne which resulted in combats for 403 and 421. No. 403's Flight Lieutenant H D MacDonald, from Toronto, shot down a 109, his seventh victory, while Buck McNair claimed another. Art Sager claimed damaging hits on a third in the Amiens area.

*Rodeo 240, 0945-1125 hrs*

| A Flight | | B Flight | |
|---|---|---|---|
| F/L P G Blades | MA266 | S/L R W McNair | MA586 |
| F/O H P Zary | BS129 | P/O W F Cook | MA579 |

| F/O J A Omand | MA756 | Sgt F C Joyce | MA591 |
| P/O P A McLachlan | MA572 | F/L A H Sager | BS290 |
| Sgt N B Dixon | MA416 | F/O C S G DeNancrede | BS152 |
| | | P/O W E Harten | MA713 |
| | | P/O R W Isbister | MA477 |

Buck was flying as Black 1. As they reached Amiens eight to ten Me109s were seen coming in from the north-east and about four immediately dived away. Buck led his men in a climb to around 28,000 feet, closing in behind the remaining 109s. As he brought his pilots round in a slow turn to starboard, losing height slightly, Buck singled out one, closed in behind it and fired three bursts of about two seconds each. He saw strikes on the 109's fuselage and cockpit, but noted the German pilot made no evasive action. As the fighter began to go down, glycol streamed from its engine, splashing over Buck's windscreen. He called a re-form and as he looked down again saw two 109s going down, one pouring black and white smoke, and what looked like the pilot's body going down near the other aircraft.

Sergeant Dixon was Buck's wingman and he confirmed seeing hits on the 109 after firing at it from 250 down to 150 yards. He described a ball of fire round the cockpit just before it went down.

The Messerschmitts were from 3/JG27. This unit lost two fighters, one flown by Feldwebel Ernst Schneider, who was killed 12 km west of Amiens, and Unteroffizier Herbert Körser, who crashed near Petit-Camon, wounded. A third Me109 G-6 landed at Poix with 20% damage. MacDonald's claim was for a 109 south of Abbeville at 1031 hrs, after seeing it dive into the ground with a big flash. MacDonald thought his victim was the leader of a group of a dozen 109s he went for, because all the rest dived and scattered. This lone 109 pilot began to edge towards 403's Red Section, but quickly changed his mind after spotting the Spitfire approaching, and dived. MacDonald chased and was losing the race but suddenly the 109 levelled out for a second or two giving Mac time to loose off a burst which produced hits and then white smoke.

Buck put down at Hawkinge to refuel and then flew back to Kenley. Already another mission had been scheduled, Rodeo 241 for that evening, to Le Tréport-Amiens-Abbeville-Le Tréport. No. 403 Squadron again made a claim, this time for a 190 destroyed by Flight Lieutenant W A G Conrad. No. 421 was not engaged but gave cover to the Wolf Squadron, whose call-sign was 'Sunrise'.

Wally Conrad was another of the successful fighter pilots to fly in the Canadian Wing. He came from Melrose, Ontario, but later lived in Quebec. He saw considerable action in North Africa with RAF squadrons during 1941-42, returning with a DFC. He would later command 421 Squadron.

Karl Linton recalls Buck at this time:

'During the war I served under Buck McNair, and Green, Hall, Archer, Magwood, Lambert and Conrad in 421. And then on my second tour in Italy, under Goldberg. I would humbly say Buck was the greatest squadron leader I ever met.

'When he took over 421 Squadron, we were not flying as a

squadron. The A and B Flights too often flew too far away from Buck's Section but very soon Buck had us in fighting form. Once, when he first took command and I had flown 60 plus sorties, Buck called me over the R/T and said, 'Linton (or some code), get your flight in closer. We are one squadron all going the same way!'

'I was embarrassed to receive a black with the other pilots listening but things got better and I'm sure Buck liked me as a flight commander, and also as a friend. Buck, I feel certain, saved many pilots' lives as our CO. I had nothing but respect and great admiration for him. In my mind he was the best CO of any fighter squadron I flew in, with Wally Conrad a close second!'

According to Karl Linton, with Buck's arrival on 421 something clicked. In his view a depressed squadron immediately took to their new leader and caught fire! Two days after he had arrived Buck had destroyed a FW190 and four days later another. A week later came a third; he turned 421 into a fighting machine. Up until this time, 421 had only managed to score three destroyed, two probables and seven damaged.

Karl Linton also recalls another incident with Buck:

'On a later occasion, Buck saw a Spitfire blazing away at me during a dogfight and took off after him. He chased that Spit back over the Channel and almost to London but lost him in the haze. These sort of things made our relationship grow over the months.'

* * *

Rodeo 242 on 7 July to Duclair and Harfleur brought no action. On the 9th, with Rodeo 243, Buck led 421 over Gravelines and Thielt, penetrating as far as Ghent, in Belgium. Several enemy fighters were seen and one was engaged by The Chief at 35,000 feet at 1225.

*Rodeo 243, 1130-1315 hrs*

| A Flight | | B Flight | |
|---|---|---|---|
| F/L P G Blades | MA226 | S/L R W McNair | MA586 |
| P/O T Parks | BR138 | P/O P G Johnson | MA591 |
| P/O J A Omand | MA756 | F/L A H Sager | MA477 |
| F/O H P Zary | MA416 | P/O J S Hicks | BS126 |
| P/O T J DeCourcy | BS129 | P/O W F Cook | BS290 |
| Sgt N B Dixon | MA592 | Sgt J C Joyce | MA579 |

Buck had noticed smoke trails south-west of his formation and had started to climb as 403 began to descend on some more fighters below. He then saw two Me109s trying to work their way round behind 421. Buck pulled round and lined up on the leading 109 but as he got to within 500 yards, the German's wingman swung in behind his leader and came across in front of

the Spitfire in a tight turn. Buck pulled round on him and fired two bursts at
150 yards, but then his cockpit canopy iced up so he was unable to see any
results. He felt certain he had hit the 109 which went down and although
Buck rolled after him to about 25,000 feet, he could still not see clearly so
had to break off. Art Sager saw the 109 hit and begin to trail smoke near the
cockpit, and also saw it go down like a falling leaf towards cloud at 15,000
feet, seemingly out of control.

The Luftwaffe paid a visit to southern England during the afternoon. Two
or three bombers flew over Kenley at teatime and Art Sager Scrambled but
he was unable to locate the raiders in 10/10ths cloud. However, a Dornier 217
crashed five miles south of the airfield, presumably hit by AA fire.

There was an early show on the 10th, take-off being 0710 for Rodeo 128.
The mission was to cover B17s – 240 of them – bombing targets near Paris.

*Rodeo 128, 0710-0840 hrs*

| A Flight | | B Flight | |
|---|---|---|---|
| F/O J A Omand | MA226 | S/L R W McNair | MA586 |
| F/O H P Zary | BR138 | P/O R W Ibister | MA591 |
| P/O H F Packard | MA592 | F/L A H Sager | BS290 |
| F/O F J Sherlock | MA416 | P/O C S G DeNancrede | BS126 |
| P/O T J DeCourcy | MA756 | P/O T S Todd | MA599 |
| P/O T Parks | BR978 | P/O K R Linton | MA477 |

Several enemy fighters were seen in the Rouen-Bernay areas and 421 became
engaged three times. Buck claimed one destroyed, while Art Sager and Hank
Zary each put in for a damaged. Flying Officers John Sherlock and Omand,
and Pilot Officer Ibister all made attacks but could not assess results.

They had been heading back to the French coast by 0810 as 12+ fighters
were seen flying east at the same height as the Spitfires – 26,000 feet. Then
another dozen could be seen off to the west over the Canadian's left
shoulders, but 2,000 feet lower. The WingCo sent 403 round and down upon
these, while the original 12 came down between 421 and 403, just as eight
Me109s came up out of some cloud, going for the Wolf Squadron.

Buck immediately ordered his Green Section down on these 109s, but then
even more 109s appeared behind and below, so Buck took his Section down
upon them. Some of the Germans immediately descended into cloud, leaving
just two above. Buck closed in on these two, called for his wingman to take
the starboard one and closed in on the port fighter. Buck fired a 4-5 second
burst from dead astern and from slightly below, in the German's blind spot,
scoring hits throughout. The 109 disintegrated in front of him, as he kept
closing and firing.

This was another Me109 G-6, this time from the 12th Staffel of JG2,
which went down over Hectomare, taking Feldwebel Klaus Reichelt with it.
Buck had fired 100 rounds of 20 mm cannon, and 400 rounds of .303
ammunition.

**New Flight Commander**
Flight Lieutenant Phil Blades, A Flight Commander, became tour-expired,
his place being taken by N R Fowlow, transferred in from the Wolf Squadron.

Norm Fowlow came from Trinity Bay, Newfoundland and was nearing his 22nd birthday. After training with the RCAF he came to England and flew with two RAF squadrons during 1941-42. He was one of the reinforcement pilots flown off the carrier *Wasp* on 9 May 1942, for Malta. Within a few days he was shot down and baled out, but continued fighting over the island until August. Back in the UK he was posted to 403 Squadron. By the time he moved to 421 he had three or four confirmed victories, and he and Buck McNair had become good friends.

Over the next few days the Wing flew several more operations over France. Rodeo 244 with the Hornchurch Wing on the 13th proved uneventful, and Ramrod 133 early the next day, again covering Fortresses to Paris, saw no action. On Rodeo 245 in the late afternoon of 15 July, 421 covered 403 as they shot down two enemy fighters, Johnnie Johnson also getting one. No sooner had the Wing landed than it was refuelled and rearmed and sent off on Rodeo 246 at 1945 hours. It made a Sweep of Abbeville-Poix-Berck and nearing the latter place some fighters were encountered. Buck fired at one but saw no results. He didn't even bother to make any comment in his logbook.

This daily grind continued on the 16th with Ramrod 144 – a Sweep covering a formation of B26 Marauders bombing the marshalling yards at Abbeville during the early evening. They made rendezvous with the Hornchurch Wing and flew over Dieppe-Grandvillers-Abbeville and although several fighters were seen there were no engagements. This time Buck was moved to make a written comment: 'Bags of 190s, but no go!?'

The next two shows were called off owing to weather – English summers rarely change – and on the 20th Pilot Officer R J Audet arrived on the squadron from OTU. Richard 'Dick' Audet, a 21-year old from Lethbridge, Alberta, does not appear to have lasted long with the Red Indians, and soon left to fly with an anti-aircraft co-operation squadron in the south-west of England. However, his potential was realised later in 1944, when he was posted to 411 Squadron RCAF and in his first real combat on 29 December, he shot down five German fighters, followed by two more on 1 January 1945. By the end of that same month his victory score had risen to 10 and one shared destroyed, including a Me262 jet, and he had been awarded the DFC and Bar. He was killed by ground fire whilst strafing a train on 3 March, ten days before his 23rd birthday.

* * *

### A Rose by Any Other Name
The same day as Dick Audet arrived (he was to fly only four missions before being posted away) came the news that the Wing was going to have to prepare to disband and become No. 127 Airfield, within 83 Group.

This was in advance of the planned invasion of Europe, still many months in the future, whereby Fighter Command would be split into two formations, Air Defence Great Britain (with the old Fighter Command role) and 2nd Tactical Air Force, which would take its squadrons into France as soon as sufficient ground had been captured to bulldoze airstrips within the beach-head and beyond.

However, nothing was going to change in the short term, and the Wing continued on for a few more weeks as if nothing had happened. On 25 July the Wing flew up to Coltishall to fly two missions with 12 Group: Ramrod 154, flying target support to 12 B25 Mitchells to Amsterdam, and then Ramrod 158, target support for Bostons bombing Schipol airfield that evening. However, on the latter sortie four Red Indians had to abort owing to jettison tank problems. Spitfires were now flying more and more with these long range fuel tanks under their bellies, and it was not an uncommon occurrence for problems to occur as pilots switched from jett. tanks to main tanks, prior to dropping the empty – or almost empty – belly tanks. Johnnie Johnson managed to bag a 109 on this latter mission and the Wing was back at Kenley for a late supper.

Johnson led a target support mission on the 26th, again escorting Marauders, this time to St Omer – uneventful – then a Sweep over Mardyck-Armentières in the afternoon. Next day two missions again, Ramrods 162 and 164, the first a Sweep for Venturas attacking Zeebrugge in the late morning, the other a target support show for B26s to Tricquiville in the evening. Buck noted in his log book for these two sorties: 'No Huns!' then 'Still No Huns!'

In my book *RAF Fighter Command 1936-1968* (PSL 1992) Johnnie Johnson wrote about these continuous escort missions in 1943, which is worth repeating here:

'My Canadians, contrary to popular belief, were first class disciplinarians in the air – very good indeed. In 1943 we began to see large gaggles of FW190s and Me109s, sometimes up to 50 or 60. My Kenley Wing was only two squadrons, 24 Spitfires, so I got onto our AOC, Air Vice-Marshal Hugh Saunders, and . . . asked if I could try two wings? He agreed and let me have a go with the Hornchurch Wing, led by Bill Crawford-Compton.' [However, this failed to work due to Crawford-Compton wanting to get into the action just as much and if Johnson went down on some enemy fighters, Compton went too.]

'The greatest drawback to me in those days was when the American Fortresses started going out and were taking some terrible losses. We just hadn't the range to escort them all the way and it was terrible to see them struggling back, engines knocked out, huge holes in wings and fuselages, trailing smoke, and knowing that there wasn't a thing we could do to help them.

'The Spitfire was only a defensive fighter, designed for defensive work. We pressed for longer range and we got the 90-gallon tank, which meant that we then actually held more fuel externally than internally. This took us to the German border but that was all.'

### Down in the Drink

The July weather did not improve much and on the morning of the 28th fog delayed the Wing from flying south-east to Manston to refuel for a morning operation. Ramrod 165 – cover to B17s – was scheduled but the Spitfires did not get airborne until 1020. After topping up tanks at Manston, the Wing left at 1145 and headed for Amsterdam, but in the air was diverted towards Rotterdam.

*Ramrod 165, 1145-1315 hrs*

| **A Flight** | | **B Flight** | |
|---|---|---|---|
| F/L N R Fowlow | MA226 | S/L R W McNair | MA586 |
| F/O T Parks | MA416 | F/O W E Harten | MA477 |
| Sgt D V Campbell | MA794 | F/O L R Thorne | BR978 |
| F/O J A Omand | MA756 | F/L W E Quint | MA591 |
| P/O P A McLachlan | MA592 | P/O K R Linton | MA582 |
| | | P/O W F Cook | MA579 |

Not much activity, and the Fighter Controllers were not reporting any signs of hostile aircraft, so Johnson flew south-west along the Dutch coast. About 1226 pm Buck started to be aware that the normal purr of his Merlin engine was turning into an intermittent growl. He was a few miles off the coast at Knokke and handing over to Norm Fowlow, he quickly broke away and headed for England with his wingman, Pilot Officer Thurne (Tommy) Parks.

McNair lost height from 20,000 to 10,000 feet and was still only 12 miles or so off the enemy coast as the labouring engine caught fire. Control of the fighter was lost and Buck put it into a dive towards the sea, slid back the hood, disconnected radio and oxygen, released his seat harness, turned the fighter over and baled out at 5,000 feet. His final message over the radio was: 'So long you guys. I'm really gonna get my feet wet this time.'

Tommy Parks orbited nearby and gave a 'Mayday' call, then continued to orbit the spot for the next 90 minutes until relieved by 411 Squadron. The rest of Buck's squadron landed and refuelled at Manston, then took off again to help. As they arrived back at the scene, the pilots were relieved to see a Walrus amphibian rescue aeroplane landing to pick up their CO, which they proceeded to escort to Hawkinge once it became airborne. Buck had been burned about the face and had had a real close call, but was safe and quickly in hospital where his injuries were attended to.

Tommy Parks had done a man's job in staying with his CO. One of the 411 pilots to fly out was Doug Matheson:

'Buck's squadron had been on a "do". 411 was Scrambled, and we were told that Buck was down in the sea and was without a dinghy. The rest of the Squadron headed out on the vector given. Norm Keene and I were sent to Manston to pick up the Walrus, and here was some sort of misunderstanding. Norm was the flight commander, and he got the idea that Buck was down near Cap Gris Nez, 90 degrees from where we had to go. I nearly shot him down in frustration, getting him straightened out, after what seemed "too damn long". We got the dear old Walrus going in the right direction and it went straight to Buck.

'I could see him by the yellow marker. The Walrus landed and had him scooped up in no time. Buck later told me that if he hadn't got pulled out very soon something very important was going to happen!

'Buck was in hospital. In and Out really, as we would go out
to a pub or to eat somewhere, and put him back in bed when we
went home. The burns to his eyes caused permanent damage.'

According to Doug's logbook he was out for two hours on this rescue trip,
noted Buck McNair's rescue and that he had only been in his Mae West. It
later transpired that in baling out Buck had caught the full force of the
flames, which not only seared his face but also burnt the release wire of his
parachute and damaged the harness. Struggling to get the parachute to
function, and hoping the harness would hold the jerk if it did open, he fell
more than 3,000 feet, so was down to around 2,000 feet when he finally got
it deployed.

Nearing the water, he then discovered the release box to the 'chute had
been fused by the heat and could not be turned. Not wanting to contend with
the parachute canopy once in the water, he tore himself loose from the
charred harness and fell the last 75 feet into the sea. He landed on his back,
which gave him one hell of a jolt. Once he burst back to the surface, he found
that his dinghy pack had gone.

Although it was high summer, don't be fooled, the English Channel is
never warm. In winter survival in the sea is sometimes a matter of minutes.
In the summer the odds are a little better, but it doesn't take too long before
hypothermia sets in, and then that's it. Karl Linton also remembers:

'When Buck baled out returning from France, Thurne Parks –
or Tommy as we called him – and I hovered over Buck till a
Walrus or a boat could pick him up. However, I had not
conserved my petrol as well as Tommy, and after a few minutes
I had to leave, and landed dead-stick at Manston.'

Buck was to note in his logbook: 'On fire – picked up by ASR. Two hours in
Drink. Rather cool in there!' John Sherlock and Bob Middlemiss also recall
the event. John Sherlock:

'On 28 July Buck's engine quit over the Channel and he baled
out, sustaining burns to his face. Tommy Parks circled Buck
until a Walrus picked him up. Tommy had been with Buck in
249 Squadron on Malta and had himself baled out two or three
times, so he knew how lonely it could be floating around all
alone in the water. As a matter of interest Tommy became a
geologist after the war and was employed by a large British
mining conglomerate, Selco Ltd. Buck's eldest son Bruce
worked for Tommy in northern Canada one summer, as did our
son.'[1]

Bob Middlemiss, still flying with 403 Squadron, relates:

'On one of our fighter cover operations, on 28 July, Ramrod

---

[1] Tommy Parks died in early 1971 – the same year as Buck.

Mission 165 to Holland, his Spitfire developed engine trouble, and he left the Wing, losing height from about 20,000 feet. While descending through 10,000 feet, approximately 12 miles off the French coast, his engine caught fire causing the loss of control and a dive towards the Channel. He was able to climb out of his fighter and his 'chute was seen to open about 2,000 feet. He landed in the sea, a "Mayday" having been transmitted, and the ASR boys picked him up. Buck was burned about the face and lost part of his vision to his left eye. This never stopped him from continuing to fly during the rest of the war and the time he remained in the Royal Canadian Air Force.'

## Kipper McNair[1]

Johnnie Johnson, in his famous book *Wing Leader* (Chatto & Windus 1957) tells the story of Buck's bale out. He wrote that Buck and Parks had not long broken away before Parks called up to say his CO's aircraft had caught fire and he had baled out. Johnnie called back:

'Can you see him Red 2?

'Yes, Sir. He's in the sea, but not in his dinghy. About ten miles from the French coast. What shall I do?'

[Johnson knew Parks would have a difficult job keeping an eye on his CO's bobbing head in a rough sea and that it was going to be a tricky rescue.]

'Red Two from Greycap. Stay over him as low as you can. Low revs and just enough power to stay in the air. Transmit for a Mayday on "C" for Charlie and we'll get back as soon as we can. OK?'

The Wing then put their noses down and headed for Manston to refuel. Calling Kenley Johnson was informed that Spitfires were already on their way and that a Walrus had been alerted at Hawkinge. If the Spitfires could find Parks soon all might be well, but if he lost sight of Buck, or had to break off due to shortage of petrol, the chance of finding him again would be minimal.

The good news, although Buck would not know it until later, was that the Walrus pilot was an experienced pilot and air-sea-rescue man, Squadron Leader A D Grace, with his two-man crew, Warrant Officer J Butler and Sergeant J Humphreys. Alan Grace was a flight commander with 277 Squadron, and although Buck was only his second successful rescue, he would go on to rescue many more downed airmen and win the DFC.

Grace put down 40 miles east of North Foreland and his crew soon had Buck stripped, rubbed down and swathed in blankets. As they massaged his frozen limbs they also applied gentian violet to his burns. Soon after getting him back to Hawkinge he was quickly moved to Canterbury Hospital. Over the returning Walrus, Johnnie Johnson and some of the Wing provided escort, Johnson calling the Walrus pilot to ask how their pilot was doing.

---

[1] 'Kipper' was the term used by the ASR boys for a customer – a man in the drink.

'Not too bad,' answered Grace. 'He's burnt a bit and swearing a lot!' No sooner had they landed, than Johnnie landed too. As he was being transferred to an ambulance, Buck recognised Johnnie as he approached.

'Don't let me lose the squadron, chief,' he said. 'This is nothing. I'll be back in a day or two. Promise I won't lose the squadron!' Johnson promised to keep the job open for him, and hoped that he would indeed be able to do so.

It was important to Buck that he didn't lose his squadron. He felt he was on top of his form and he needed the adrenaline rush, the excitement. He was still the country-boy hero and needed so badly to keep that image. This too was important to him. He knew too there was still a job to be done. He had done much already but nobody likes a quitter. And he was determined that this slight setback would not stop him. If he had been shot down it might have been different, but engine trouble – that rankled too.

He knew, however, that he had been hurt. Not just the burns. Something was wrong with his left eye; he had known that for some time, and this had not helped. Perhaps it would clear up in time; it had to. A fighter pilot is no good without his eyes. All his skill meant little if he could not see the enemy first. That has always been true. The first to see the opposition is the first to get position for attack. Lose that and you – and others – die.

As it happens, just the previous day another Canadian squadron commander had been rescued by 277 Squadron – Squadron Leader G C Keefer DFC, CO of 412 Squadron. His Spitfire had developed a glycol leak and he too had had to bale out off the French coast – or to be correct – in the Somme estuary. The Germans hadn't bothered to rescue him as they probably thought the next tide would bring him to them. The Walrus landed and was immediately fired upon, but they got their man and flew him out.

Georgie Keefer had seen action alongside Wally Conrad in North Africa. He had been born in New York of Canadian parents and later lived in Charlottetown, Prince Edward Island, attending Yale University before the war. Back in England he flew with 416 and then took command of 412 in June 1943. He and Buck also became close friends.

CHAPTER TWELVE

# THE SUMMER OF 1943

Incredibly, Buck McNair was back with his squadron inside two weeks. After about a week in Canterbury Hospital, he went across to East Grinstead for several more days, to be looked at by the specialist burns people in Sir Archibald McIndoe's famous team. He apparently made no mention of his eye problem. Either he was hoping it would still clear up on its own in time, or he would see how it affected his flying if it did not.

Although his face still showed the scars from the flames he had been exceptionally lucky and his good looks were not permanently affected. He also had to get himself a new Spitfire IX, choosing MA831, coded AU-M (M for McNair!). He also had another reason to celebrate. On 30 July had come the announcement of the award of a Bar to his DFC.

The first notation in his logbook for August is: 'Doc dressing face a-la-Hollywood!' One must assume, therefore, that the MO was still working on his face even though he had put himself back on Ops, and the man was covering the scars with make-up. Doctors were usually quite fussy about injured flyers, but no doubt Buck talked his way back into a Spitfire earlier than most might have done.

The Wing had still been active. Squadron Leader Hugh Godefroy had led the Wing on 2 August but he had had engine trouble so Norm Fowlow had taken over, but there were no encounters. On the 9th Pilot Officer Flying Officer R T Heeney had baled out of BS290 on an afternoon Ramrod as his engine cut out 20 miles inland over France. He baled out at 2,000 feet but was later reported killed. He had just completed a fighter leader's course.

The Wing had finally become 127 Airfield and moved to Lashenden, Kent, leaving 11 Group's control and coming under 2nd TAF. Lashenden was only 45 miles from Kenley but the difference was marked. Gone were the permanent buildings and a nice solid and well provisioned mess. Now, in preparation for 'roughing it' on the Continent once an invasion began, everyone was to live, eat and work under canvas.

Johnnie Johnson got permission to have a glorious thrash at Kenley and also to have the Wing stand down in consequence. Hugh Godefroy gave me permission to quote from his book *Lucky Thirteen* concerning Buck McNair, and as so often in such books, there is a wealth of information – and humour recalled. On perhaps the last Kenley Wing show, Johnnie Johnson was leading and had come under some accurate anti-aircraft fire. One of the pilots called his attention to this, saying that it was getting 'Goddamn close!'

Johnson's retort was: 'To hell with the fuckin' flak, we're after fighters!' No sooner had he uttered these words than an AA shell exploded behind and to his left, blowing him almost over onto his back. There was a pregnant silence as everyone watched him straighten up and then dodge round for a bit, like a bird that had experienced a near miss from a shotgun. Finally Johnnie came on the R/T: 'Makes you bloody think, dun' it?!'

Buck returned to 421 – at Lashenden – on 11 August. First time back in the air for him was for Ramrod 194 the very next day. Take-off was at 0940, after waiting for fog to clear (yes it was August!!); as it was slow to do so, the Wing finally got airborne on instruments! By this time Art Sager had left at the end of July on a posting to 416 Squadron, in Lloyd Chadburn's Wing at Digby, and the new flight commander was Flight Lieutenant R D Phillip. Over Ghent, Phillip broke off to engage a Me109 which was seen attacking the B17s they were protecting, chasing it down and claiming it as damaged. As the armada came out over the Dutch coast another 109 came up on the squadron from behind. Phillip went over to identify it and it headed away and down also damaged by Phillip's fire. Meantime Johnnie Johnson shot down a 109 and shared another, both with Wally Conrad. Buck landed at Bradwell Bay, refuelled and was back in time to lead the boys on Ramrod 198 which left the ground at 1800 hours, covering Mitchells to Amiens.

Buck now had a week off, not flying again until the 19th. During his absence the Wing and 421 had flown five Ramrods and on one had lost Wally Conrad. Ramrod 206 to Ghent on the 17th had ended near the French coast with a mid-air collision between Conrad and his wingman. The No.2 had gone into the sea with a jammed canopy and was lost; Conrad took to his parachute and came down in France. However, the Desert Air Force veteran managed to evade capture and was back in England in October, via Spain.

The sortie on the 19th was Ramrod 209 and it came exactly one year since the Dieppe Raid. Take-off came at five minutes past mid-day – a Sweep but Buck was not on it. His pilots returned minus Pilot Officer Frank Joyce, who had been told of his commission just prior to take-off. At least he ended up in an officers' PoW camp, not one for NCOs – or was he still wearing his NCO stripes?

Buck flew the second mission of the day, Ramrod 210, that evening, Ghent to Flushing but nothing of interest occurred as they shepherded Fortresses back from Brussels.

Next day the Spitfires moved to Headcorn, Kent; 16 machines of 421 took off at 0755. Later the ground party arrived and then it was everyone helping to hoist tents and raise a large marquee. It was almost a relief to fly a show that evening, Ramrod 211, a forward support mission south of the Somme, but again all remained quiet. John Sherlock remembers the move to Lashenden and Headcorn:

> 'The Wing moved under canvas to a place called Lashenden in Kent, on 7 August, and then moved again on the 20th to Headcorn. The temporary runway was of heavy hemp matting covered with a heavy metal mesh laid over it. The RAF expected to use this type of runway when we invaded France.

We remained at Headcorn until returning to winter quarters at Kenley in October.

'Life under canvas was a little different from the posh quarters at Kenley as we dined cafeteria style, out in the open if the weather was good, or if it was raining, we moved into a large mess tent. There was no electricity or running water, no convenient toilets, etc. We had been used to camp cots and had to make our own beds and to have a bath, we had a small canvas contraption on a wooden folding frame. To obtain water, we were issued a canvas pail and we had to walk over to a water tank, fill up the pails and carry them back to our tents. It was fine in good weather if it was not at 4.30 and 5.00 am, but certainly not as nice as a hot shower at Kenley.'

It was rumoured that Johnnie Johnson would not be long in becoming tour-expired and in order to retain leadership and good discipline in the air, Godefroy and Buck were taking turns in leading the Wing. Buck led it on 22 August, on Ramrod 213. Sixteen FW190s were seen east of Le Havre but they did not want to play. Two more shows on the 23rd and another on the 24th also failed to find the Red Indians combat action, although Wingco Johnson and 403 saw some, as Bob Middlemiss noted:

'Extract from my log book – 23 August – Ramrod 214. "Had a go at 12+ 190s, Wingco got a flamer, I got a 190 damaged. 16+ 109s above – Buck kept them off."'

However, on the 25th, 421 did mix it with the Germans.

*Ramrod 15A, 1835-2030 hrs*

| A Flight | | B Flight | |
|---|---|---|---|
| F/L N R Fowlow | MA226 | S/L R W McNair | MA831 |
| Sgt I R Forster | BS200 | P/O R W Ibister | EN525 |
| F/O A E Fleming | MA756 | F/L R D Phillip | MA477 |
| P/O P A McLachlan | BS198 | F/O P C Musgrave | MA582 |
| P/O W M Barnett | MA794 | F/O L R Thorne | MA713 |
| | | P/O W F Cook | BS126 |
| | | F/O T S Todd | MA579 |

The Wing provided high cover to 18 Bostons attacking the airfield at Beaumont-le-Roger. Pilot Officer McLachlan engaged a 190 at close range – down to 50 yards – opened fire and destroyed it. Buck was also engaged.

Johnnie Johnson was leading, Buck flying as deputy leader. They were on their way back but near Le Havre-Caen, encountered ten FW190s, chased by 403 Squadron, but they were reluctant to be engaged. Then Buck and his wingman, McLachlan, went after a pair of 190s from a gaggle of eight flying below, heading south. McLachlan later reported:

'S/L McNair told me to take the port EA but when about 1,000 yards away, EA crossed over, so Black 1 took this one turning

to starboard. My 190 seemed to apply hard left rudder and skid
violently so I gave a 1-second burst from 300 yards – no result.
EA then half-rolled and I chased and closed in from dead astern.
Fired again but broke to avoid a collision. Whitish flash on its
starboard wing near aileron.'

McNair recorded:

'Took Black Section down on two 190s and told No.2 to take
port EA. At 700 yards port EA crossed over starboard aircraft,
so I took that one, delivering a 5-second burst while overtaking
him, from 500 yards to 50 yards. Broke off to avoid collision.
Black smoke came out just before I broke away. Some seconds
later Wing Commander Johnson observed an aircraft burning on
the ground just below combat area, and seen by others too.'

This was credited to McLachlan and a damaged awarded to McNair. Buck
had not been helped by his starboard cannon which went u/s in this action.

* * *

**Luftwaffe versus Luftwaffe**
Quite an unusual incident occurred on Ramrod S5 on the 26th – a fighter
sweep to the Tricquiville area, then on to Rouen and Caen. Fifteen to twenty
FW190s were seen flying in and out of some clouds, and over Caen one
FW190 pilot was so frightened by the sudden arrival of Green Section that he
opened fire and shot down a 109! Not to miss any chance, Pilot Officer W F
Cook decided to put in a claim for it!

Next day Buck led the Red Indians on two Ramrods, the first as top cover
to three dozen B26 Marauders. A dozen Me109s were spotted but they did
not come near enough to engage. The late afternoon show was as escort to 60
B17s to the north of St Omer but the Gemans did not put in an appearance.

An early morning Ramrod – S16 – on the 31st was another escort, this
time top cover to 36 Marauders. A dozen Me109s did sniff around over Lille
but did not come near enough to engage. Ramrod S17 came in the late
afternoon.

This show was to escort two formations of American B17s to Brussels:

*Ramrod S17, 1655-1830 hrs*

| A Flight | | B Flight | |
|---|---|---|---|
| F/L N R Fowlow | MA226 | S/L R W McNair | MA831 |
| Sgt I R Forster | MA334 | F/L R D Phillip | MA477 |
| P/O H F Packard | MA230 | F/O L R Thorne | MA525 |
| P/O W M Barnett | MA794 | F/O R W Ibister | MA713 |
| F/L J N Paterson | MA592 | F/O T S Todd | MA577 |
| P/O J Bamford | BS129 | | |

Johnnie Johnson led the Wing. Rendezvous with the 120 Forts was made over
Blankenbergh, the Wing going with the first formation. Ten miles south of

Ghent at around 1750 the bombers turned north-east, forsaking the original target due to weather. No. 403 Squadron stayed with the bombers while Johnson positioned 421 up-sun as five Me109s were spotted slightly to the south-west.

Buck led his Red Indians down into the bounce but three of the 109 pilots saw the danger and immediately dived away, but the remaining two were hit by Buck, and Phillip (leading Green Section), and shot down. Johnson had led them down but it was Buck who was in position to line up on one as the others scattered. He opened fire at 350 yards, held the button down for about two seconds, overshot slightly but throttled back to regain position. He fired another couple of seconds-worth of cannon and machine gun fire but then had to skid off to one side.

Levelling off just 50 yards to one side of the Messerschmitt he could see white smoke, followed by black, followed by flames coming from underneath the 109's engine as it slowly nosed downwards. Buck could see the pilot slumped over in an attitude suggesting that he had been hit. Blue 4, Flight Lieutenant Paterson, confirmed seeing the 109 go down in flames.

Buck had fired 40 cannon shells and 84 machine gun bullets and the Red Indian's war diary noted that it brought their CO's score to 13 destroyed, five probably destroyed and eight damaged. At least at the moment his damaged eye was not hindering him too much. During August he had flown 13 major operations, and as he recorded in his logbook, his total Ops from England since returning from Malta had reached 110, while his total flying hours had topped the 850 mark, of which 273 had been on operations. Phillip's score now stood at $2^1/_2$ destroyed and five damaged.

## September 1943

On the evening of 1 September, Wing Commander Keith Hodson DFC, OC 126 Airfield, and his Wing Commander Flying, B D Russel DFC, visited 421 Squadron. Dal Russel, from Toronto, was a veteran of the Battle of Britain, having flown with 1 RCAF Squadron in that conflict. Until fairly recently he had commanded 411 Squadron. No. 126 Airfield, together with 127, were the two main Canadian 2nd TAF Spitfire Wings.

In overall command of the two Airfields (Wings) was Group Captain W R MacBrien, known as Iron Bill (but also Tin Willy behind his back). No. 126 Wing had three squadrons, 401, 411 and George Keefer's 412 Squadron. Overall command of 127 was Wing Commander M Brown, Johnnie Johnson was the WingCo Flying, with 403 and 421 Squadrons. Up to now these Wings had claimed 96 German aircraft destroyed.

MacBrien had only recently been promoted, and John Sherlock recalls a story about this, involving Buck:

'We were at Kenley at the time Bill MacBrien 'phoned from Redhill advising that he had just been promoted to Group Captain and he wished to celebrate. There was not a squadron at Redhill at the time, and as MacBrien was to come to Kenley in the very near future as the CO of 127 Wing, he wished to meet some of the pilots and requested Buck to come down with a bunch of the squadron for a get-together. There would be a dinner laid on, plus a free bar. The only stipulation was that we were to bring money down as the usual crap game would take place.

'We put on our best blues, collected all the loose cash we could, and then had a couple of beers before leaving Kenley as it was a long drive – at least half an hour or so. Buck had the use of a Humber shooting brake and a bunch of us piled in. I remember Tommy Parks, Wally Conrad, Red Omand, Mac McLachlan, Paul Johnson, Pat Packard – there must have been at least ten of us.

'Parks sat in the front beside Buck and remarked: "Now, for Christ's sake, McNair, take it easy. The last time I went out with you, we ended up in the . . . . ditch!" At this moment, there came a quiet voice from the back, Wally Conrad: "Yeah, McNair, why don't you start out in the . . . . ditch and maybe we'll be lucky and end up on the road."

'Anyway, we found our way to Redhill without any difficulty and the bar room was set up beautifully with a barman in attendance, and a sumptuous meal laid on. Buck, who was a tall chap, jumped up on the bar, leaned over and grabbed a couple of bottles and threw one in my direction and told the barman to just charge them up "to the Groupie". On top of this, the best part of the evening was the crap game as we cleaned out the Groupie; we must have left Redhill with about 500 quid of his money! I think I had a large portion of this and he never forgot it.'

Buck's first four September sorties brought no action, but on the 3rd – the war's fourth anniversary – Ramrod S26 was slated to start shortly after 0900. The Wing provided top cover to Marauders attacking Beaumont-le-Roger airfield.

*Ramrod S26, 0915-1045 hrs*

| A Flight | | B Flight | |
|---|---|---|---|
| F/L N R Fowlow | MA226 | S/L R W McNair | MA831 |
| F/O R W Nickerson | BS398 | P/O W F Cook | LZ924 |
| F/O J A Omand | MA726 | F/L R D Phillip | MA477 |
| F/L J N Paterson | MA794 | F/O A R MacKenzie | EN525 |
| P/O M C Love | MA334 | P/O W E Harten | MA713 |
| Sgt I R Forster | MA582 | F/O C S G DeNancrede | MA579 |
| | | P/O J S Hicks | MA591 |

Johnnie Johnson again led the Wing, making rendezvous with the bombers four miles north-east of Fécamp and together headed for the target. Shortly after 1000, north of Evreux, near the target, a pair of Me109s were seen and Johnson detached McNair and his Black Section. These 109s were shadowing some B17s returning from a bombing mission to the Paris area. However, the two German pilots saw the danger and evaded but then another pair were spotted.

Pilot Officer M C Love, Buck's wingman, was in a good position to attack but closed in very fast on one of the 109s. His first burst smashed pieces off the fighter and it went down but it appeared that chunks of Messerschmitt crushed into Love's Spitfire and punctured his radiator. Love reported to Buck that he was on fire and losing glycol, so there was no way he was going to get home. Buck ordered him to fly inland and bale out, and he was last seen heading for Argentan. His last words were: 'See you in Gib.' As most downed pilots who managed to avoid capture headed south for Spain and then Gibraltar, Love's words were an attempt to lift his own spirits as he headed down.

Meantime Buck had lined up on the other 109 as it turned to port and he fired a 3-second burst from 300 yards. The 109 turned to starboard and dived slightly as Buck closed to 100 yards dead astern and let go a 5-second burst. This time his fire struck home decisively and the fighter blew up and he saw the wreckage go down and crash north of Evreux.

The opposition had been JG2. They lost two fighters, with one pilot killed and another wounded. Buck probably shot down the 109 G-6 flown by Unteroffizier Günther Borrusch, who was killed, while Love got the G-6 flown by Oberfeldwebel Paul Marx who crash-landed near Romilly, wounded. JG2 is believed to have claimed Love too. Some time later came the news that Love was safe but a prisoner of war – so Gibraltar was out.

These two claims brought the Wing's claims to 98 and not unnaturally there was a sweepstake organised for the 100th. This was won by the airmen in the maintenance section on the 4th, as Johnnie Johnson and Squadron Leader Grant, OC 403, each bagged a German fighter. As befitting the 100th victory, the prize was £100. The downside to this was that Grant, after shooting down his victim, had himself been lost.

Johnnie Johnson made his last claim with his Wing on the 5th, a damaged, and Buck also claimed a damaged.

*Ramrod S33, 0745-0915 hrs*

| **A Flight** | | **B Flight** | |
|---|---|---|---|
| F/L N R Fowlow | MA592 | S/L R W McNair | MA831 |
| F/O D K Wilson | EN525 | F/L W S Quint | MA591 |
| P/O A E Fleming | BS398 | F/O W E Hasten | MA713 |
| F/O R W Nickerson | MA230 | P/O L R Thorne | LZ924 |
| P/O N B Dixon | BS200 | F/O K R Linton | MA417 |
| | | Sgt W Warfield | MA579 |

A total of 72 Marauders were heading for marshalling yards at Marlebeke, escorted by the Wing led by Johnnie Johnson at high cover. Just after bombing four Me109s were seen trailing behind the formation and were engaged at 0834 in the Deynze area by Johnnie and Buck.

Johnson was leading 421's Black Section, with Buck as Black 3. Johnson led the Section down on the four 109s, but their pilots half rolled before they could close, so the Spitfires half rolled after them, Buck opening fire at 400 yards on one from dead astern, closing to 300. He snapped off six bursts in all, the last four with just his starboard cannon as his port one had packed up.

He then broke off the attack, seeing tracer in front of his Spitfire which he later realised was his own! As he turned his windscreen became covered with a thick sticky liquid from the Messerschmitt, and his wingman, Flight Lieutenant Quint, saw black smoke coming from the German fighter. However, he could only put in a claim for a damaged, Johnson too not being able to claim more than this on his target.

As the Spitfires were reforming, two FW190s were seen south of Gravelines. They made a quick and ineffectual pass at 421 and then dived away. Flak from Ostend, Ghent and Dunkirk added to the fun, but everyone landed back safely at between 0915 and 0926.

There were three shows on 6 September. The first was Ramrod S35, a Sweep in support of 72 Marauders attacking Rouen. Then came Ramrod S35 Part II, escorting Forts back from Germany, and finally Ramrod S36 – high cover to 72 Marauders going for Abbeville. These Marauder attacks on German fighter fields was an attempt to hinder German fighters from attacking the American Fortresses and Liberators bombing German targets.

It was the second mission which produced the only positive action for the Red Indians (although Flight Lieutenant Phillip did damage a 190 on the evening show); the operation took place during the mid-day period.

*Ramrod S35 Part II, 1120-1320 hrs*

| A Flight | | B Flight | |
|---|---|---|---|
| F/L N R Fowlow | MA226 | F/L R W McNair | MA831 |
| F/O P A McLachlan | MA592 | P/O K R Linton | LZ924 |
| P/O A E Fleming | MA756 | F/L R D Phillip | MA591 |
| P/O N B Dixon | BS200 | F/L W S Quint | MA582 |
| F/L F J Sherlock | EN525 | F/O W E Harten | MA713 |
| | | F/O L R Thorne | MA379 |

On this operation Buck was leading the Wing. They made rendezvous with the bombers ten miles south of Bernay at 1204, orbited and picked up the first box of B17s at 1210, escorting them towards the French coast, where Spitfires from 122 Airfield (Wing) were due to take over.

Shortly after forming up over the Fortresses, at 25,000 feet, a lone, all-blue FW190 was seen following them, 7-8,000 feet below the Spitfires. Buck took his Black Section down to attack it. Closing, he opened fire from 300 yards, getting right in, finally having to break away to avoid a collision, but firing all the time. Strikes were seen on both its wings, ailerons and on the side of the fuselage. Pieces flew off the stricken fighter, hitting Buck's machine, damaging the spinner, but luckily missing the radiator, or he would have been in a similar position to his wingman Love, three days earlier.

The Focke Wulf went down very steeply as Buck pulled up, seemed to level off, but then crashed into some woods near a small village to the south-east of Beaumont-le-Roger airfield. Buck had found the 190 easy to follow owing to its blue colour. Reforming, the squadron tagged onto another box of B17s over the Channel and brought them back. Because of shortage of fuel, seven of the Spitfires landed away from Headcorn to refuel.

The German fighter may have been FW190 A-6 of 1/JG2 which crashed at Voué, in which Feldwebel Heinz Brendel had been wounded.

## Changes in Command

Norm Fowlow, who had just been awarded the DFC, left the squadron on the 7th. He went across to take command of 403 Squadron, where Squadron Leader Grant had been shot down and killed on the 4th by JG26. Flight Lieutenant R A Buckham DFC was posted in from 17 Wing Headquarters to replace Fowlow. Robert Buckham had been with Buck McNair in 416 Squadron the previous summer, now the two 'Bucks' were together again.

The next day Iron Bill MacBrien arrived to warn everyone of a big show on the 9th – Operation 'Starkey'. This was another scheme similar to the Dieppe Show the previous year only this time no troops would be put ashore, although a large convoy of landing ships would be sailed off the French coast under a massed fighter umbrella. Again it was hoped to entice the Luftwaffe into the air – and into combat – as well as testing everything and everyone for the future invasion of Europe.

In the event the Germans, and the Luftwaffe, soon saw through this elaborate scheme which produced no reaction at all and was, from a combat point of view, a complete flop. One hopes, that the planners got something out of it. No. 421 Squadron's diary noted: 'Despite good weather and four ops, enemy did not react to what might have seemed an invasion attempt.' In his logbook Buck, who flew on two of the shows, recorded them as Beach #1 and Beach #2 – patrolling Gris Nez-Boulogne.

However, this saw the end of Johnnie Johnson's term as Wing Leader and he was now rested from operations. His place was taken by Hugh Godefroy. With him Johnson took his famous call-sign 'Greycap'; from now on the Wing would be recognised by Godefroy's 'Darkwood'.

During Ramrod 216 in the late afternoon of the 11th, Flying Officer Andy MacKenzie's engine began cutting out on the way home and it seemed almost certain he would have to abandon his machine. However, Buck carefully coached him across the Channel and directed him to Ford emergency airfield where he landed safely.

If Buck McNair was reluctant to let anyone know of his eye problem, he was finding it increasingly difficult to see well in the air. He still carried some of the physical scars from the burns he'd received and so on the 15th, after escorting American B24s on Ramrod S77, he absented himself to hospital, but mainly – so he told everyone – to have his burns checked over. However, in his logbook he later recorded: 'Face and eyes too sensitive – will pack up for a few days.'

But he was back from Horley three days later in order to attend Johnnie Johnson's farewell party, with no less a visitor than the AOCinC Fighter Command. The party started with a dinner at 1930 followed by a talk by Air Vice-Marshal Dickson and a presentation of a gold watch by Bill MacBrien. Johnson left the Wing with a personal score of 26 destroyed. He would be back.

The next day Buck Buckham, temporarily in command of the Red Indians, shot down a Me109 on Ramrod 233 and Hank Zary damaged another. Meantime, the CO left for a week's leave and rest. After this it was going to have to be decided if he could carry on operational flying.

**Beurling Arrives**
One of the most amazing Canadian fighter pilots of WW2 was George
Frederick Beurling from Montreal, who Buck had met on Malta, and in
Canada during the bond drives. He had made a name for himself in the skies
over Malta in 1942, just as Buck McNair was leaving the island. Between
mid-June and mid-October he shot down 28 Axis aircraft and others
damaged. He possessed the most amazing eyesight too and could spot enemy
aircraft long before other pilots. As he ritually called everything and
everybody a damned screwball he soon became known as 'Screwball'
Beurling, otherwise, 'Buzz'.

On the island he had won the DFM & Bar, then after being commissioned
came the DFC and finally the DSO. Malta bred extraordinary men, not least
Adrian Warburton, the reconnaissance king who seemed to fight equally
against authority and blimpish commanders, as the enemy. But such men
seemed to get away with it on Malta, where results far outweighed spit,
polish and ceremony. Malta also suited Beurling's character and individual
way of fighting. He was an individual, not a team player, and was never
happier than when fighting alone. The results were impressive.

Back in England, after a rest, while his record had preceded him, so too
had his attitude to authority and discipline. Operating over France in 1943
left no room for the individual. Pilots who did not conform to rigid formation
flying and equally rigid discipline in the air, not to mention the ground, did
not last long.

Johnson had been asked if he would take Beurling into his Wing, and
although reluctant, felt he should be given his chance. It was decided to post
him to 403, a squadron in which he had briefly served prior to going to the
Med.

*　　*　　*

Despite Beurling being in the Wing, Buck took him out on a show on 1
October, in fact rather a special show. Buck was aware that if tamed, Beurling
could prove a good influence on his young pilots, and he was also keen to get
some experienced pilots on board. It would seem Buck was about to try
something different, recording this show as a 127 Airfield Rodeo. In fact it
was just four pilots – himself, John Sherlock, Beurling and Tommy Parks.
They took off at 1145 and were up for an hour and 35 minutes but it proved
uneventful, despite going almost to Paris.

He tried it again on the 2nd, taking Harten, Sherlock and Parks with him
for another 1.35 sortie, this time flying over Rouen-Amiens-Abbeville but all
they found was some accurate flak near Abbeville. In the afternoon Buck led
a normal Ramrod operation – No.255 – but still no fighter appeared. John
Sherlock remembers these two sorties:

> 'The four of us were sitting around complaining about the
> weather and someone mentioned that it certainly didn't
> compare with the weather over Malta where I don't think we
> saw a cloud in five months. Of course, we found, Beurling,
> Buck, Tommy Parks and myself, had all flown from Malta in

the summer of 1942.

'Someone also brought up the subject that flying in Wings of 24 or 36 aircraft on offensive sweeps was a waste of aircraft as usually only the wing leader of squadron leaders got a shot at any enemy aircraft, the rest of the fighters were just flying around covering the one or two chaps who were doing the shooting. Over Malta we did not have the luxury of large numbers of fighters and while sometimes we took off in groups of four, six or even eight, we almost immediately split up into pairs for greater mobility. I think it was George who said that it would be nice to fly like that again – four aircraft consisting of two pairs.

'Buck thought this was a good idea and, as the weather was poor, he arranged with Group to try this out as we had nothing better to do. On October 1, my logbook shows: "Rodeo 127 A/F – into Paris at 15,000 ft – saw two FW190s, they half rolled into 10/10ths cloud. With S/L McNair, Buzz Beurling and Tommy Parks. Blew a cylinder on way home – ruined engine. Dived on two FW190s but they disappeared in cloud." This sortie was timed at 1 hour, 35 minutes.

'On 2 October, my logbook shows: "Rodeo 127 A/F – into Paris, circled Abbeville and Amiens-Glisy. Duff engine again." The notation reads for this 1.35 sortie: "With S/L McNair, Tommy Parks and Webb Harten – bags of flak over Abbeville at 10,000 ft – 10/10ths cloud on way in and over Paris but clear in spots." I think the reason Beurling didn't fly on the second show was because he was actually in 403 Squadron while the rest of us were 421. It was not normal to mix up the pilots from different squadrons.

'I think we were hopeful that we would run into some enemy aircraft with successful results in order to prove that smaller groups, with experienced pilots, could range over a much larger area of enemy territory than we were doing with 24 or 36 Spitfires flying in a large group.

'The weather must have cleared up on the 5th as my logbook shows Ramrod 257, escorting 72 Marauders to Woensdrecht. Buck's engine packed up but he landed OK. My notation for this two hour mission reads: "Got up the tails of 14 190s, 500 yards. CO's engine blew and had to escort him home, but he fired at one." In the afternoon, Johnny Hicks, Packard and Linton each got a FW190, Coles got two! Cookie baled out and Barnes missing. Linton, Dixon and Packard all shot-up.'

This latter operation on 3 October was a day noted as the most successful for 421, during three operations. The first trip came mid-morning.

*Ramrod 257, 1025-1225 hrs*

| A Flight | | B Flight | |
|---|---|---|---|
| F/L R A Buckham | MA226 | S/L R W McNair | MA831 |

| P/O J Bamford | BS200 | F/L W E Harten | MA713 |
| F/L A E Fleming | MA592 | P/O A C Brandon | MA582 |
| F/L J N Paterson | MA794 | P/O K R Linton | EN525 |
| F/L F J Sherlock | BS398 | F/O P G Johnson | MA591 |
| F/O T Parks | BR978 | F/O L R Thorne | LZ924 |

Hugh Godefroy led the Wing as top cover to 72 Marauders bombing the airfield at Woensdrecht, Holland. They made rendezvous with the B26s and after the bombing run the formation was flying west of Neuzen, at which time a gaggle of aircraft were seen some distance to the rear of 421, at 23,000 feet. Buck turned to engage them and as the German aircraft backed off, gave chase, catching them at 20,000 feet near St Nicholas.

Buck closed in on the centre aircraft, actually putting himself ahead of six others off to his starboard side. He quickly ordered his starboard section to engage these as he concentrated on his victim. At 300 yards he thumbed down the gun button and after a 2-second burst his own engine seemed to explode and sheets of flame and smoke obscured all his forward vision. He immediately broke off, lost height and at 13,000 feet over Ostend, his engine picked up again and he flew home and made base safely.

As he spun down, his pilots broke off too and followed him down, anxious to see if he was alright and ready to protect him. Several pilots saw the German fighter hit and strikes caused smoke to pour from it, and then Buck Buckham saw it catch fire and go down in flames. Despite a problem with the recorded time of this action, it appears that this fighter was from 12/JG2 flown by Leutnant Johann Achenbach who was killed.

There were two further missions on this day, Ramrods 258 and 259. Altogether the Wing destroyed four aircraft during this busy afternoon. However, on Ramrod 259, came the big result although the squadron lost Flying Officer W F Cook, while 403 lost another. Crossing in at Hardelot they were at 22,000 feet as they reached the Béthune-Amiens area. Near the Roye airfield, which the Spitfires approached from the north-west, 15 Focke Wulfs passed underneath 421 while nearly 40 more 190s and Me109s passed over 403 – the high squadron – 500 feet above. A big air fight immediately ensued.

Buck kept his section above as cover, sending down Green Section (Karl Linton) and White Section. Linton and his No.2 opened fire on a diving 190 and it began to leave black smoke. Then something broke off the 190 and hit his elevator. Then four 190s made a head-on attack on the two Spitfires, both sides opening fire but observing no hits. This started a turning circle, each pilot trying to get behind an enemy, and Linton was just gaining nicely when they suddenly split up and went different ways.

At that moment Linton's engine cut out to he decided to head for home. As he did so, two more 190s came head-on at him. Both pilots fired, Linton from an inverted position which made it difficult to see if he had scored hits, but the 190 must have flown right through the burst. That moment he heard his wingman, Bill Cook, call to say he was baling out. Linton managed to get back to an emergency base and land, and later two pilots of White Section said they had seen a 190 he and Cook had fired at, go down and crash.

Green 3 – Hicks – also went down on the 15 190s and followed eight of them that broke away and half-rolled down. He went after one whose pilot pulled up sharply and in trying to follow, found another 190 behind him. As he pulled off, he spotted his 190 spinning down leaving white smoke and then looking down shortly afterwards saw an aircraft burning on the ground. Buck also saw a 190 crash and burn.

White Leader – Packard – made it three with an attack on another 190, but he was then hit in the wing and had to break from two other 190s. His wingman saw the 190 go straight in and blow up, and someone else saw a parachute appear.

Bill Cook baled out safely, landed and evaded capture. He was back in England six weeks later; he received the DFC in late 1944.

Next day came another Ramrod, and by mid-month he had flown three more. As he completed this page of his logbook Buck noted his score of combat victories as 16 destroyed, five probables and 11 damaged. This brought the reward of a second Bar to his DFC on the 7th. The Squadron also lost Flight Lieutenant Phillip, tour expired on the 4th, his place was taken by A E Fleming.

A story of this time concerned Buck's golden retriever, Peter. On the morning he heard of the award of a second Bar to his DFC, Peter had been missing for three days, but with the award came news that he had been found. He turned up in a farmer's barn, some 12 miles from the airfield, with a badly mangled tail. There was no clue as to how he had been injured, but Buck did not celebrate his latest 'gong' until after Peter had been returned and his tail successfully amputated.

**Wing Leader**
With effect from 15 October 1943, Buck McNair became Wing Leader of 126 Airfield, (commanded by Keith Hodson) consisting of 401, 411 and 412 Squadrons, which had just moved to Biggin Hill. He left 421 and headed off to his new command. No. 421 Squadron was taken over briefly by Charles Magwood, but before the end of October, Squadron Leader J F Lambert assumed command.

Jimmy Lambert had previously been with the Canadian Wing. He led the Red Indians until December and was married on 4 December, with Tommy Parks as his best man. On the 20th, only four days after his return from honeymoon, he was shot down and killed. His place was taken by Wally Conrad.

Buck's three squadrons were commanded respectively by Squadron Leaders E L 'Jeep' Neal DFC, Ian Ormston DFC and George Keefer DFC. Both Neal and Ormston had shared Buck's experience with a rescue from the sea.

At Biggin, Buck took over from his predecessor, B D Russel DFC. Dal Russel came from Toronto and had won his DFC during the Battle of Britain, and was about to receive a Bar to it. Buck took over his personal Spitfire as Russel was taken off operational flying and posted to RCAF Overseas HQ. It still carried the former Wing Leader's personal identification letters BDR.

Hugh Godefroy, again from his book *Lucky Thirteen*:

'With the relentless build-up of operational time among the

leaders in the Wing, some juggling had to be done. Johnnie had
not had a proper rest since 1940. The Canadian Government had
a ruling that no Canadian was allowed to do more than two
tours. Bill MacBrien approached me and asked if he sent me on
an extended leave, would I be willing to come back and take
Johnnie's place as Wing Leader. Deane MacDonald had secretly
married a girl from Wales and MacBrien wanted to send him
back to Canada for a month's leave and, on his return, put him
in command of one of the Squadrons of 126 Wing. Buck
McNair was fresh and would become Wing Leader of this unit
at Biggin Hill. With Bill MacBrien's powerful connections, the
whole thing was arranged with RCAF Headquarters.'

Buck's first op as Wing Leader came on 18 October. First a flight down to
Friston to refuel then the Wing took Marauders to Beauvais, but cloud forced
an abort at the French coast. A second attempt also failed later in the day. The
late autumn weather continued to play havoc and it wasn't until the 24th that
Ramrod 283 became Buck's first successful, if uneventful show, as
Marauders finally bombed Beauvais.

At the start of November Buck began flying a Spitfire with his own initials
on its sides – RWM. Whether this was Russel's BDR repainted is not known.
During that first week six operations were completed, but without opposition.
However, on the 9th Buck – and others – were off to Buckingham Palace,
where Buck was to be invested with the two Bars to his Distinguished Flying
Cross.

Others going along were Hugh Godefroy and Bob Buckham. Once at the
Palace, Hugh Godefroy recalled that they were briefed by an Admiral how to
act and what not to do and finally the doors to the investiture room were
opened. Hugh wrote in his book:

'A platform stretched the full length of one long side and in the
middle of it stood the King. On the flanks stood the Yeomen of
the Guard and clustered on either side of His Majesty, high-
ranking officers of the three Services. In front of the platform
row upon row of seated guests stretched from one end to the
other. While we waited, Buck and I passed the time searching
through the sea of faces for the girls [Hugh's guests]. We found
them well hidden behind women with large brimmed hats.

'"Wing Commander Godefroy – DFC and Bar." Suddenly my
heart was in my mouth and my knees weak as water. Overcome
with self-consciousness, I took two stealthy steps forward and
turned left. Thinking only of the long pace that I must take for
the convenience of the King, I forgot to bow, and took such a
long pace forward that I was but a few inches away from him. I
heard Buck say in a loud whisper, "My God!"

'For the first time I realised the King was very short. His nose
was about the same level as my second tunic button.
Determined to show respect, I bowed where I was and the King
obliged by bending gracefully backwards. To my great relief I

discovered he was smiling with considerable amusement. As he pinned on my medal, I thanked him, took one long pace to the rear, where I had space to give him a low bow.

'Just short of the double, I made my way down the ramp. At the bottom, an Attendant grabbed my medal from my breast, slapped it in a box and handed it to me. I was just in time to hear Buck's penetrating voice say:

'"Just fine, Sir, how's the Queen?"'

\* \* \*

Meantime, back in Canada, Buck's parents were about to receive another letter about their son. This one, dated 13 November 1943, came from the Minister of National Defence for Air, Mr Charles Power:

Dear Mr and Mrs McNair,
   Once again I would like to express the feeling of extreme pride with which all ranks of the Royal Canadian Air Force join with me in extending most sincere congratulations to you and your family on the additional honour and distinction earned by your son Squadron Leader Robert Wendell McNair DFC and Bar, through the award of the second Bar to the Distinguished Flying Cross.
                    [The minister then wrote out the citation]

   Your son's outstanding Service record is one of which we may all feel justly proud.

\* \* \*

Doug Matheson recalls Buck becoming Wing Leader, and a new arrival:

'Buck was given 126 Wing when Dal Russel was sent to HQ. Dal had been a super wing commander. Buck had a totally different style – tough as hell on anyone who was not prepared to shape up. Those guys were just gone in no time. I had been made flight commander of 411's B Flight during the summer, and when Buck arrived I was delighted that he placed his aircraft in my flight. You can be sure that it got the royal treatment; never did a Spitfire IXb so shine!

'George "Buzz" Beurling came to my flight in November. I went to Buck and said, "How in heck can I be Beurling's flight commander?" (what with a mere DSO DFC DFM & Bar). Buck understood and instead had him under his own direct command. Buzz was a good guy. It was too bad that he had not stayed in the RAF, they would know how to handle him. He wanted a Mustang to do his thing; the RAF would have given him one – like they did with all sorts of unusual types, but that was not the Canadian way. Everyone has to conform. Canadians are unable

to cope with extraordinary people who sometimes are called
heroes. Canadians can't stand heroes. Anyway Buck sent Buzz
to Kenley.'[1]

Don Laubman recalls Beurling at this time:

'The following story will act as a testament to Buck's skill as a
pilot. It happened one day during the winter of 1943-44 while
the Wing was at Biggin Hill and Buck was the WingCo Flying.
Because of the weather, we were grounded. The cloud base was
in the order of 300-400 feet and we, the pilots, were all hanging
around our dispersal huts. To our surprise two Spitfires started
up and became airborne. We later learned that they were being
flown by Buck and George Beurling who then proceeded to put
on the most amazing display of dog-fighting I had even seen.
For about fifteen minutes they performed for us, never leaving
the perimeter of the airfield and never going above 200 feet. It
was a fantastic performance.'

Rod Smith also recalls the time Buck took over the Wing:

'By this time the Canadian Wing had become known as 127
Airfield, then Wing, and when Johnnie left they appointed Hugh
Godefroy as wing leader instead of Buck. Buck didn't like that
very much. However, 126 Wing at Biggin Hill then needed a
wing leader so Buck was appointed. Keith Hodson was the
airfield commander – both being wing commanders.

'I met Buck one evening in the bar at Biggin. I had just
checked out in a Spitfire IXB and I said what a great aeroplane
it was. Buck replied that he thought it was a f . . . awful
aeroplane. He went on that Don Blakeslee, now with the US 8th
Air Force, with his long-range Mustangs had far better range
than our Spitfires and better long range ranks. I retorted that
compared to the old Spit Mark V, the IXs were much better. He
did agree, adding that now, if one got hurt, it was our own fault.'

For the rest of November, Ops came as weather permitted. Few Germans
were seen, and although a pilot in 401 bagged a FW190 on the 26th and two
more on the 29th, the Wing suffered five losses. On the 23rd Flight Sergeant
S M Kent had his engine cut while changing tanks and he crashed into the
Channel. Then on the 29th 412 lost two on Ramrod 339, despite
claims for two destroyed and two damaged: Flight Lieutenant A C Coles,

---

[1] Beurling had been in the RAF and had only transferred to the RCAF on 1 September
1943. By this date his score stood at around 30. He spent a short time with 403, then 411
and finally 412 before being shipped home to Canada, with a score of 32. With no suitable
job for him to do – incredibly – he was released from the RCAF in October 1944, mainly
due to his inability to conform to authority. He was killed in a plane crash in May 1948 on
his way to join the Israeli air force.

PoW, and Flying Officer J A Robertson, killed. Next day 401 lost two, both to engine trouble: Flight Lieutenants A E Studholme (PoW) and H D MacDonald DFC (killed).

Deane MacDonald, just back from his leave in Canada following his marriage, did not have his chance of command. Two pilots had stayed with him as he lost height but finally tried to bale out by pushing the stick forward. Unfortunately he fell astride the Spitfire and impaled himself on the radio mast and both went into the sea.

If all this was not enough, 411 Squadron lost two more on the first day of December. One was Doug Matheson on the first of two Ramrods:

> 'I was shot down on 1 December – a fairly big show – of about 120 Marauders and umpteen escorting Spits. We were to take the bombers to Cambrai, a Luftwaffe airfield. Just after crossing the coast on the way in I had spotted, from about 18,000 feet, several tiny specks moving across one of the many airfields on our route. I called Buck and went straight down. I shot down one FW190 and my No.3, Sid Mills, shot down another. We climbed up and re-joined the Wing.
>
> 'The bombers had done their thing and had turned around and were heading for home. I saw that two 190s were up at my 8 o'clock and when they came in I called the break and came head-on with the first 190. It seemed only a second or so when I did my tail check that this guy was on my tail – and close. I did a maximum slip and skid and chopped power, but I got hit in the rads. Glycol filled the cockpit, then this guy, trying to slow down, came right up off my port wing. I took one frantic poke with only machine guns (cannons empty) and then had to get out.
>
> 'It was not until the summer of 1999 that I was advised by a young reserve officer of the French air force historical section, that I had been about the 55th victim of Adolf Glunz, bearer of the Ritterkreuz mit Eichenlaub[1], so I didn't feel so bad!!'

Doug Matheson and Sid Mills had shot down the leader of JG26's 5th Staffel, Hauptmann Helmut Hoppe (24 victories) and his wingman, Feldwebel Rudi Wyrich (2 victories).

The weather continued to restrict operations and Buck was only able to lead five more shows during December. However, the losses stopped and a few German fighters were damaged. Beurling got one destroyed on the 30th.

---

[1] Oberfeldwebel Adolf Glunz of 5/JG26 knocked down both of 411's losses this day, Doug Matheson and Pilot Officer J A St Denis (killed), bringing his score to 49 of an eventual 71. His Knight's Cross was awarded 29 August 1943, the Oak Leaves on 24 June 1944. All but three of his kills were in the West, including 20 four-engined bombers and three Mosquitos. 'Addi' was never shot down or wounded during 574 combat missions and ended the war as an Oberleutnant.

# CHAPTER THIRTEEN

# WING LEADER

**Business as Usual**

January 1944 began with Ramrod 408, a Sweep on the 1st, but no enemy aircraft were seen. On the 4th the Wing was bounced by 20 or more German fighters but luckily sustained no losses. In fact only one Spitfire was hit. The previous day, the 3rd, Karl Linton had had a narrow escape. Weather prevented operations but by mid-morning it began to brighten up so Karl, now A Flight commander in 421, talked Tommy DeCourcy, Ralph Nickerson and Andy MacKenzie into flying a Ranger sortie, which in fact fitted in with a Sweep planned by 403 Squadron to Bernay, 70 miles east of Caen.

With nothing happening, the four 'Red Indian' pilots went down through cloud and met a 20-mm flak position hidden in a huge haystack, which opened up from close range as they flew by. DeCourcy's machine (MK907) was hit in the port aileron, making it difficult to manage. Karl's aircraft was also hit (MA592); a shell exploded in the cockpit, splattering his windscreen and knocking out his instruments. Calling the others, Karl ordered everyone to get home as soon as possible.

Despite a small problem with navigation, Karl got back over the Channel and rather than chance a few extra miles to get down at Kenley, landed at Biggin Hill. Of course, Buck McNair, his former CO, was now at Biggin, and he was the first one to meet Karl as he taxied up to the hangar. His clothes were white from small splinters of glass, but Buck helped him out and got him to the base hospital, suggesting he stay the night. As the wing padre was away on leave, and he normally shared a room with Buck, Karl had his bed. It was a chance to have a few beers and bring each other up to date with the news before Karl flew back to Kenley the next morning.

Buck's Wing bagged two 190s on the 6th (scored by Orr and Hamilton) but on the 9th they lost Flying Officer R M Davenport (401). Davenport was an American in the RCAF and was brought down by ground fire during a Rhubarb sortie. However, he evaded capture and was back in England in April. Hugh Godefroy wrote in his book the reason for all these recent engine problems:

'Buck's Wing was equipped with Spitfire IXAs which had the same Merlin engine as ours, except for the blower. Buck's aircraft had a blower that gave maximum performance between ten and twenty thousand [feet]. They were equipped with Stromberg carburettors made in the States that could handle 120 octane fuel. The bugs had not been worked out of this combination and a series of engine failures over enemy territory was the result.'

Two days later, the 8th, Buck and his pilots did their best to catch five Focke Wulfs on a Rodeo but failed. The Wing was still being troubled with engine problems. On the 24th Flight Lieutenant J Sheppard came down in the sea but was rescued, and on the 28th Flight Lieutenant D G McKay (412) had to bale out into the Channel but luckily he too was rescued quickly, by Walrus amphibian. On the 30th Buck had problems: his oxygen iced up on a Ramrod. Rod Smith:

'I was posted to 126 Wing at Biggin at the beginning of January 1944, so I found myself in Buck's Wing [401 Sqn]. I remember by this time he had two Bars to his DFC. When I was there Buck wasn't really flying very much due to medical reasons, so he never actually led me.'

Bob Middlemiss recalls Buck as Wing Leader:

'On one occasion when Buck was leading the Wing we had gone a fair distance into France where we ran into a number of 109s. Our 403 Squadron got milling about, and Buck, being a good leader, stayed above and directed the fighting. Then as I was turning and tossing about with a couple of 109s, Buck called on the R/T to reform and work our way out. I called, saying: "Give me a few minutes to get rid of these guys!" His reply was, "Hurry up and let's get out." So with much difficulty I did work my way out and arrived back safely. I point this out because some wing leaders would have led their squadrons into the battle, whereas Buck directed his forces to the best advantage.'

February '44 and it got busier. During the first two weeks Buck led nine Ramrod operations and while they only destroyed one enemy aeroplane, at least nobody was lost. Then on the 21st Buck was sent off on a three weeks army support course at RAF Milfield, Northumberland. According to 126 Wing's diary he did not return until 11 March but it will not be a surprise to see from Buck's own logbook that he managed to get in at least two operations by nipping back to Biggin while no one was looking! He also brought his total flying hours to over 1,000.

There was now an even more obvious build-up for the coming invasion of Europe. Air Vice-Marshal Harry Broadhurst DSO DFC AFC was now in command of 83 Group, 2nd Tactical Air Force, and Hugh Godefroy relates in his book a run-in 'Broady' had with Buck in the early part of 1944:

'As soon as his Field Headquarters was established, Broadhurst started weekly conferences for all the Wing Leaders under his command. Broady, as he was referred to, had led [the Hornchurch Wing earlier in the war] and subsequently made a name for himself as an efficient Staff Officer and a hard-nosed Field Commander [in North Africa]. He openly admitted at first that he had little use for Canadians and Buck McNair in particular. Buck had flown under him at Hornchurch before he had left for Malta. As far as Buck was concerned, the feeling was mutual.

'I distinctly remember the first Wing Commanders' conference that Broady called in his Headquarters. In desert tradition, the meeting was held in a long rectangular field-tent furnished with a mobile conference table, field maps and collapsible chairs. Broady chaired the meeting from one end of the table, and by chance Buck McNair occupied the chair at the other end. Through the meeting Buck sat with his chair pushed back, his arms folded, with a disgruntled frown on his face.

'The meeting had no particular purpose, except to give the Air Vice-Marshal an opportunity to tell us exactly what he expected of us. His remarks required no comment, and instead of asking if there were any questions, Broady hunched forward in his chair and, glaring at Buck, said:

'"McNair, I'm disappointed in you. This is the first time I have seen you sit there without opening your big mouth. Are you ill?" There was a long silence as Buck measured his gaze without blinking an eye. Finally he said with a smile:

'"These meetings of yours are interfering with my social life, Sir!"

'For a second Broady's jaw stiffened, and he glowered down the table at Buck. Just when the tension was getting unbearable, Broady suddenly threw his head back and laughed uncontrollably. Nervously the company followed his example.'

## Ops are Off

The last weeks of March saw Buck leading six further Wing shows, mostly escorting bombers on tactical targets such as marshalling yards. He watched as three Marauders were shot down by flak on the 23rd, also noted poor bombing on the 24th, but a lovely prang on some railyards west of Paris on the 27th.

Also on the 23rd Buck McNair flew down to Tangmere as it was proposed to move the Wing there in April. His reason for going was in order to stake an early claim to a favourable position on the airfield.

The last two ops of the month were a Sweep from Antwerp to St Quentin on the 28th and Ramrod 682 on the 30th, during which Flying Officer Don Laubman and Flight Lieutenant W B Needham of the Falcons (412 Squadron) found and shot down a Ju88 in the Griel area. This was only Laubman's second kill, but by the end of the year he would equal Buck McNair's tally of 16 victories.

At the end of the month Buck wrote a poignant few words in his logbook which signalled the end of his operational flying: 'Oh, the dreaded Docs have me now. Have had my chips!'

Buck was called for a medical inspection of his eyes. It was now no secret that he was having trouble, especially with that damaged left eye and he was sent off to hospital for tests. Under the orders of Squadron Leader Cam McArthur, the Wing MO, he spent some time in hospital, but also he had another important appointment, he was going to get married. Cam had been asked by Buck to help him because he often woke in the middle of the night, trying to bale out of an aircraft.

## Barbara

By this time, Buck McNair had met the girl whom he was to marry. Barbara Still lived in north London and was working at the American Embassy, working for James Foster Meyer, a former professor at Columbia University, New York. Several Americans had gone into the RCAF and a number had, of course, been at Columbia, so it was natural for some of them to keep in touch with Professor Meyer. Two of these had been Danny Browne and Hank Zary, both of whom were members of 126 Wing.

On one occasion they visited their old professor and, meeting the young, attractive Barbara Still, had invited her to a Wing party where they promised they would introduce her to their new, handsome, WingCo Flying, Buck McNair. They convinced her to come, and with James Meyer acting as a sort of chaperone, they duly arrived at the officers' mess at RAF Biggin Hill.

Towards the end of the evening Hank finally said it was about time he introduced her to the WingCo and immediately dragged her over to a room full of men and catching Buck's attention, made the introductions. It was nothing monumental at the time but the party was coming to an end so Buck asked if he could take her telephone number, saying he would give her a call. Barbara told him she could be found at the American Embassy but he insisted on her home number. Years later she discovered that he had put the number in a small black book he carried, with the annotation: 'Met Barbara Still – makes yer think!'

Barbara had the distinct feeling she was going to hear from him, so she decided to take some nice clothes to keep at the Embassy just in case she didn't have time to get home to change. Sure enough, although she had to wait four or five weeks, he did ring and asked her out to dinner. It became a foursome, with Keith Hodson and Edna, and they all met up at the Savoy Hotel. She noted that he had on what she thought were black leather carpet slippers, and so they proved to be, which he preferred to shoes. He also admitted that under his battledress he wore pyjamas! Perhaps he had merely pulled his uniform over his pyjamas when he got up that morning to fly, and had not had time to change.

During the meal Buck asked her if she would like a liqueur, but not knowing what one was, she merely said yes and it turned out to be a bright green *crème de menthe*. She had to be at the tube station by 10 pm and as he was on Ops the next morning they soon headed along the Strand for Charing Cross Station, but an air raid started. Barbara was shaking and Buck put his arm around her and ushered her down into the underground station. Not long after Barbara reached home he telephoned to make sure she had arrived safely.

Barbara's parents were both deaf, so during air-raids they would sleep in a Morrison indoor shelter downstairs and she naturally had the telephone next to her. She and Robert, as she preferred to call him, then began a telephonic romance over the next few months. They were unable to meet very often, in fact, as far as Barbara remembers, they only met about half a dozen times before they were married.

Buck popped the question in the early spring of 1944 and as he had two weeks' leave coming up, starting at Easter, and as he had yet to meet her parents, she put a hypothetical question to her father about marriage. Very sweetly he told her he would not give his permission, arguing that for a girl of 18 it was too young and that wartime might easily mean the loss of a husband. However, her mother, knowing the situation, took her to one side and said it would be alright with her.

Prior to the wedding, the couple arranged to spend a few days away; her father only agreed to it if they went to Aylesbury and stayed with friends of his. This they did and they had little time together, mostly going out for walks only returning for tea with the family, who had four young children. But it was this weekend they decided to marry despite the problems of only having one parent's permission.

Ba's mother came down to visit. The couple had already bought their 29s 6d utility wedding ring – all one was allowed in those days – with very little gold in it. They purchased it from a shop in Aylesbury. With the agreement of her mother, they arranged to get married by special licence on Easter Sunday, 2 April. They had to be at Biggin Hill on the Saturday evening for a big soirée, and Robert also had to ask permission to marry from Bill MacBrien. Later, Bill's second wife, Sonja, became a close friend of Ba's.

They had arranged to stay the night at the Waldorf Hotel in the Aldwych, and her mother was going to come down in readiness and would sleep there too, while Robert would sleep in an outer room. Mr Still was still being kept in the dark. In the event, Barbara and Robert didn't get up from Biggin Hill until about 5.30 on the Sunday morning.

During the evening, Ba had been talking with Cam McArthur, and Rob had sort of turned away to say something to someone else, as Cam had said, 'Say Buck, how's that baling out problem you had?' This was the first time Ba had heard of this and asked Cam what it was all about. It was just as well Cam told her, for during the first few months of their marriage, Buck suffered not only with his back, but also with severe migraine headaches which often had him waking up screaming in the night. Only hot towels over his forehead gave him any relief.

Meantime, the pre-wedding party had been in full swing and Barbara had gone off to catch a few winks, and finally waking in the early hours, had gone to look for her husband-to-be. She found him with about 20 pilots, plus the Group Captain, talking Spitfires and combats. Ba was a trifle upset at the hour but Robert finally disengaged himself, got a staff car and got away to town by about 4 am. Luckily they didn't wake Mrs Still when they arrived at the hotel.

During that Saturday evening at Biggin, Ba had danced with Norm

Fowlow, who was to be Buck's best man. He then confided that this night was one of the happiest nights of his life, which intrigued Barbara. He explained that he now felt ready to tell the WingCo that he had been secretly married some time ago, and in fact, they now had a four-month old baby son back in Nova Scotia, where mother and child were living with Norm's parents.

Barbara and Norman then walked over to Buck and she said that Norm had something to tell him. Norm was blushing as he blurted out the news. Buck cursed, but he was beaming from ear to ear, being totally thrilled for his friend.

*     *     *

Robert surfaced in the Waldorf only a few hours later with a terrific hangover and Mrs Still had to produce all sorts of potions from her hand-bag in order to get Robert in some sort of order before they could all get off to Caxton Hall for their 1030 appointment. As her father still hadn't been told, some slight of hand was needed with regard to signatures, but Ba's sister came – in uniform – and then Hank Zary arrived with the best man, Norm Fowlow. The ceremony went off without a hitch, having bribed the official £5 to come in on this Easter Sunday to perform the ceremony.

A lunch had been arranged at the Waldorf – just the six people – Ba, Robert, Mrs Still, sister Kathleen (known usually as Kaye), Hank and Norm. They had a magnum of champagne, and at about 3 pm Mrs Still senior left to give the news to her husband. Hank ordered another magnum – the second of an eventual three – and the next day the newly-weds travelled down to Devon.

They had their honeymoon at Coombe Martin but their week was suddenly cut short on the Wednesday or Thursday, with the arrival of a telegram from London, ordering Robert to report to RCAF Overseas HQ immediately. Robert probably knew that the medicos had finally made a decision, but he pretended that this was probably to do with the pending invasion.

They returned to London and Robert reported as ordered, where he learnt from Air Commodore Livingstone, a Canadian in the RAF, and chief eye specialist, that his operational flying days were over. It was the first time Barbara discovered Robert even had an eye problem. What had been discovered was that Robert had about three dozen tiny blood clots, known as a thrombosis, behind the left eye. This gave Robert vision something akin to looking down at a map of England from about 3,000 feet, with only tiny bits of daylight coming in.

The Air Commodore came out of his office to talk to Barbara, giving her the news too, which was a total shock for her, but Livingstone assured her that he was certain the clots would not go into the brain and that he'd be alright although his sight would be permanently affected. It had been hard for Robert to admit even to himself that this problem would stop him so equally, it had been impossible for him to admit it to anyone else, even his new bride. The only good thing was that away from operations he had a better chance of surviving the war, but Buck did not feel able to give her this assurance. No doubt at the back of his active mind, he was already scheming ways of getting round officialdom and to get back into the cockpit of a Spitfire. He had fought long and hard for this moment and did not want to miss out.

First thing however, he was going to have to relinquish his command of the Wing with effect from 12 April, and was told to report to 17 Wing Headquarters as Operations Officer working on 'Overlord' – code word for the invasion. His only consolations were the award of the Distinguished Service Order which was announced on 14 April 1944, and that Georgie Keefer was taking over the Wing.

The blow of losing the Wing became second place to the next bad news. Norm Fowlow was shot down. His secret marriage to Elsie Ogilvie, a Canadian nursing sister, on 22 April 1943 had just celebrated its first anniversary. On 19 May 1944, leading 403 Squadron over France he attacked a train on a railway crossing near Hazebrouck and was hit by ground fire. His Spitfire and the 500 lb bomb he was about to release exploded, killing Norm instantly. He was 22 years old. Almost exactly two years earlier, 18 May 1942, he had been shot down by a Me109 over Malta, surviving with wounds and a broken collar bone.

Elsie, Robert and Ba also became lifelong friends, as well as Norman junior.

## D-Day

By now the invasion plans were well advanced and the date all but agreed. Buck McNair got on with his new job as an operations officer and waited as keenly as anyone for the big day to arrive. It was no secret that the Allies were about to embark on this the greatest seaborne landing in history, only the actual date and place remained under close wraps.

Much to Barbara's and her mother's anxiety, Buck did not say specifically that he would not be an active participant, and it is probably true that he still expected to be able to get in on it somehow. If he had told them he would not be operational on D-Day, and he did manage to get on it, it would have been harder for them if he was shot down.

In the event he was unable to fix anything up, so many of his friends, some of whom he had flown with for many months, all took their part, but the country-boy hero had to fly nothing more hostile than a desk. He had fought so long for this moment and he was unable to be part of it. In truth, however, he had by anyone's measure, done more than his share already.

The nearest he got to the war was on 17 and 18 June – twelve days after the landings. In an Auster, a three seat communications aircraft, he flew from Tangmere to landing ground B.1 in France on the 17th, then back to Biggin. B.1 was the code number for the airfield at Carpiquet, just west of Caen and right in the battle area. And on the 18th Biggin-B.1-Tangmere took him again into the war zone. In his logbook he wrote: 'A bit smokey.' which undoubtedly it was over there, and then on the 18th: 'Hike to France. Beer, etc.' There was little to be said for bringing beer back from France, so this must refer to him taking beer to France in the Auster for the men on the ground. On one flight he also carried Bill MacBrien's dog over to his master. So, he *had* managed to get into the 'action' if not a combat mission, nor on the invasion date. And, of course, there was always a risk; and there was more to come.

Buck got himself back into a Spitfire at the beginning of July. On the 4th he flew a 412 Squadron aeroplane from his old Wing on a flight to B.1. He remained there for four days, only flying back to Heston on the 8th – for a bath! Next day he flew a Spit back to Carpiquet. On 15 and 16 he repeated the bath sortie, returned to France and on the 17th, flew back to England again, this time escorting an Anson because the cloud base was down to 100 feet.

However, that was that. His operational war was now well and truly at an end. By looking through his flying logbooks his total sorties and operational flying hours appear to be as follows.

1st Tour – 46 sorties   England, June 1941 to February 1942
2nd Tour ⎱– 39 sorties   Malta, March to June 1942
       ⎰– 37 sorties   England, July to September 1942
3rd Tour – 144 sorties   England, April 1943 to April 1944

Total sorties flown: 266 covering over 415 operational hours.

| | |
|---|---|
| Ramrods | 105 |
| Scrambles | 50 |
| Sector patrols | 32 |
| Rodeos | 24 |
| Convoy patrols | 21 |
| Sweeps | 15 |
| Escorts | 8 |
| Circuses | 5 |
| Rhubarbs | 3 |
| Air Sea Rescue | 2 |
| Roadstead | 1 |

\*   \*   \*

On 1 July he was posted to 'R' Depot, as President of Special Cases, RCAF, at Warrington, Cheshire. Cases which were brought before the committee of which he was president, dealt with airmen accused of LMF (Lack of Moral Fibre – cowardice), inefficiency or misconduct. The requirement for president was that it had to be someone of wing commander rank and with operational experience. Originally these cases were dealt with at No.1 RCAF Repatriation Depot at Rockcliffe, Ottawa, but in early 1944 it had been decided to establish a detachment of this board in England.

There is no need to go into the cases which came onto Wing Commander McNair's desk, but it would seem he had the right credentials. Being a no-nonsense man but knowing only too well the fallibilities of men under stress, he was probably fair in his assessments.

Buck was back at Buckingham Palace on 7 November, almost exactly a year since he and Hugh Godefroy had been there as related earlier. This time he was able to take Barbara with him. George Keefer was also receiving his DSO, and with no family in England, he took as his guest Barbara's mother. Barbara remembers the event, mainly because the King appeared to have a tickle in his throat as he pinned the medal onto her husband's chest, resulting in a few moments of hesitation, especially by one of HM's equerries who seemed unable to decide whether to slap his monarch on the back or hope it would clear itself.

Buck remained in this LMF job until the end of 1944, and was then sent to the RAF Staff College with effect from 1 January 1945. It was an extensive course and it was while here that he saw the end of World War Two. At least he was able to get back into an aeroplane while at the Staff College, although his flight in a Proctor on 1 March 1945 was his first trip since coming back from France the previous July. That month saw him making several flights, in Proctors and Magisters, and on the 26th he sat in the second pilot's seat in an American B17 Fortress for 70 minutes.

His next posting was as Commanding Officer of RAF Calvely, on 20 June but this did not last long, being then sent to RCAF Overseas HQ as a member of 'P' Staff at the end of July. During September Buck made a flying visit to Canada, travelling direct to Montreal by Coronado on the 15th, returning to the UK on the 29th in a Liberator of BOAC. Robert began flying Oxfords at the ECFS (Empire Central Flying School) on No.13 Course, at Hullavington, Wiltshire. In fact he was able to fly all manner of aeroplanes. These included his first jet, the new Meteor on 7 March 1946, Harvards, Oxfords, a Wellington, a Mitchell, and even a Spitfire again on 2 May for 80 minutes. On 24 May he had three trips in a four-engined Lancaster, which, after some dual, he flew from base to Boscombe Down, then to the Solent and back. By this time he had been posted to RAF Fakenham, Norfolk, and for a while he and Ba lived with Johnnie and Paula Johnson.

At the beginning of April Buck went for another eye check, and the report read:

> Since last seen vision has remained the same. [He] Has undertaken the duties of Station Commander and has completed the Staff College Course, without strain on his eyes and being inconvenienced in any way. No fatigue, no headaches after concentration, no trouble in flying course. Since eye trouble, 300 hours ten minutes with Spitfires, Oxfords and Harvards.
>
> There remains a small area of injury below and just affecting the lower edge of the left macula. It is the residue of an old haemorrhage and is past history, being part of the fluenal condition of the thrombosis/phlebitis of the central retinal vein from which he suffered.

At the end of May he received a certificate confirming he had successfully graduated from the ECFS course. At Fakenham he was able to fly Meteors, Spitfires and even a Seafire in June and July, not to mention another trip in a Wellington and a Lancaster. It was obviously a time to be able to add many types to his flight-log, for he had flights in a Mosquito, a Tempest II and an Anson as well. More Meteor flights in August and then a DH Vampire, a Mosquito XXXVI, and a DH Hornet, went into his logbook.

Johnnie Johnson was at CFE too, as OC Tactics Branch. He signed Buck's logbook at the end of August, as *late G/Capt, temp Wing Cmdr, S/Ldr any day now*. This in reference to loss of wartime ranks that most officers were having to contend with in the peacetime airforce. He was now told to prepare for a return to Canada and he arranged for Barbara to precede him, leaving at the beginning of August. Meantime. in September 1946 Buck flew Vampires with 247 Squadron based at RAF Odiham.

Meantime, Barbara had become pregnant but was having a rough time. With the imminent posting to Canada, she sailed on the *Queen Mary*, although it was uncertain exactly when her husband would be shipped over. Arriving in Canada on 18 August 1946, she initially stayed with Micky Sutherland, Robert's pilot friend from before the war, who lived with his wife in Winnipeg. A few days later she boarded a train for Saskatoon and on the journey she struck up in conversation with some businessmen, who all knew her husband's friend Ernest Buckerfield. Arriving at her destination, they got off with her and saw her safely into the hands of Robert's parents. She had half expected to meet Eileen, a nurse Robert had said he had installed to help his mother, but who, she discovered, had been the girl whom Robert had been engaged to back in 1942, although she had now departed the scene.

Hilda McNair was rather in awe of her new daughter-in-law. There was a world of difference between the country wife and mother, and the bright young woman used to London's Mayfair. There was a culture shock on both sides. One example was that the McNairs would, as a Sunday treat, go down to the local railway station just to see who was going on journeys and who was arriving!

Ba's pregnancy was not going well and there was still no firm news as to when Robert would be coming over. She had also developed a throat problem which eventually needed a tonsillectomy during her pregnancy. Her blood count was so low there was a high risk of losing the baby.

After a while Barbara managed to move in with the Buckerfield family, having discovered that Robert preferred she do so. In fact when their first son duly arrived, they named him Robert Bruce after Ernest Buckerfield's brother. Mary Buckerfield became the baby's godmother. (George Keefer was also a godfather.) They were wonderful and treated Barbara very well that winter and she feels strongly that the baby would not have survived had they both not been so well looked after in the Buckerfield home.

When Barbara moved in with them, she was met by Anna Buckerfield and Mrs Helen Major, née Buckerfield, who had been widowed in the war. In those months Anna Buckerfield became almost like a sister to her. Finally that Christmas Robert arrived but soon had to leave again. He had been posted to Airforce HQ, DOR/ORF (Operational Requirements Branch). Before he left Europe, the French Government had conferred on him the Croix de Guerre with Palm, and then made him a Chevalier of the Légion d'Honneur. Baby Bruce arrived on 19 January 1947 but it was not until March that Robert was able to visit.

Robert was posted to Ottawa in April 1947 but had to revert to flying Harvards for the most part. For over a year he was only able to keep his hand in by occasional flights in Harvards, or perhaps a Beechcraft. Just now and again he got his hands on a Vampire jet which the RCAF were starting to acquire.

On the home front things had not been going too well. Hilda McNair had used much of her hero son's money, sent to the family whilst he was fighting overseas, while he owed the Canadian Government $2,000 for his pension contributions. During the war, half a fighting man's salary was automatically sent home. Robert had wanted it to go into war bonds, but the McNairs had spent most of it. Father McNair had taken Ba aside one time and apologised, saying that they had incurred terrible medical bills, but it transpired the family had been trying to keep up with the 'Joneses', something which had begun after their hero son had returned home in 1942 and become a local celebrity.

Added to this he was now down to squadron leader rank – and salary. When considering whether he should go for a permanent commission in October 1946, Robert had been promised that he would retain his wing commander's rank. At almost the last minute the last two names on the list, Robert McNair and Bev Christmas (1 RCAF Sqn in 1940) had been struck off, both remaining squadron leaders. That had upset Robert terribly after the promises he had received.

He and Barbara had moved into sub-standard accommodation, without a refrigerator, washing machine, or carpets. When Ba's mother came to visit, she discovered rats in the kitchen. Ba then went down with an acute appendicitis, being taken into the Ottawa Générale Hospital, with Bruce just three months old and still being breast fed. That summer of 1947 became a nightmare. Alternative accommodation was not ready and Robert asked his old wartime buddy Bob Middlemiss if he could help. He recalls:

'I returned to Canada and married Hazel, my high-school sweetheart. In 1946, we bought our first house in the west end of Ottawa, a modest four room house with a small extension built on. It had two bedrooms, living room, kitchen, the small extension, and a basement. I had a call from Buck who brought his war bride, Barbara, and their son to Ottawa, and asked if they could possibly stay with us until they got quarters. Ba and Bruce stayed with us for three or four weeks. It was tight quarters; my wife, a two-year old son and a one-year old daughter, plus the two McNairs. Somehow it all worked out and I know that they were grateful to us during this time.'

Ba certainly was grateful for their kindness and hospitality. Rob managed to get into the mess in Gloucester Street, but would come along and visit for a few hours each evening. The families remained good friends, saddened only by Hazel's death in a plane crash some years later, but Bob's second wife Crystal also became friends of the McNairs. Bob Middlemiss further recalls:

'Both Buck and I worked in Air Force Headquarters, he in Operational Requirements Branch and I in Air Operations as Fighter Operations Officer. It was during this time that the RCAF had purchased Vampire aircraft from England and the Air Force was looking at the requirements that would be needed for this jet aeroplane. Buck and I were in the habit of discussing various operational and future requirements for the RCAF, and one of the items discussed was runway lengths for the new jets.

We agreed we would like to see 10,000-foot runways for these and future jet aircraft, with a minumum of 8,000 feet.

'He forwarded the suggested requirement to my Group Captain, who without discussing it with me, sent it back saying that the present 6,000 foot runways were sufficient. Buck was immediately on the telephone to me, saying that he thought we had agreed on 10,000 feet, with a minumum of 8,000. I quickly confirmed this to be so. He then said that the file had come back recommending only 6,000 feet. We certainly concurred that this would not do.

'It was at this time that a new Group Captain had come in and was double-banking the Groupie that he was soon to replace, the one who was shooting for 6,000 feet. Buck sent the file back with further comments and the new Group Captain called me into his office and asked me how long a runway was needed for our jets. I said 8,000 feet minimum but would like 10,000 feet. The old Group Captain in the background called out 'traitor' and with that the new man picked up the telephone and called the Chief of Operational Requirements and told him, Danny (that is what he used to call me) says we need 8,000 feet and would like to see 10,000, so that is what I agree. Of course, our runways were extended and proved a real necessity.

'Buck did an outstanding job both during the war years and post-war years.'

It was around this time that Buck, George Keefer and Rod Smith had a run-in with an old wartime pal, Jack Charles. Jack Charles had been a successful fighter pilot in England during the war, and with a DSO and DFC, had done well but his efforts had affected him badly. Back in Canada he began to show the first signs of schizophrenia. Rod Smith was flying with the auxiliaries while also attending McGill University and his squadron had followed Charles' unit at a base. Next time they met, Charles accused Rod's outfit of stealing his watch, at which Rod took umbrage and walked off. Not long afterwards, Charles tried to jump off a train.

A short time later, in Montreal, Rod and Rob went off with George Keefer on the Friday night to meet up with some old RCAF pals at St Hubert's and ran into Jack Charles again. Johnnie Johnson was over at the time, and they all met up in the mess. They didn't return until the next morning and when Ba opened the door she found Robert dishevelled, cut and bruised, and his uniform torn. All she could think was that he had become drunk and got into a fight, and Robert did nothing to contradict her suspicions. This too put a strain on things.

It wasn't until 43 years later that Rod Smith told Barbara (although he thought she knew, and was surprised to find she didn't) that Jack Charles[1] had attacked Rod over some stupid matter, and that Buck and George had intervened. There was a bloody fight between the two former fighter aces,

[1] Wing Commander E F J Charles DSO DFC, one time OC 611 Squadron and Wing Leader Middle Wallop Wing. He also equalled Buck McNair's score of victories.

ending with Charles being rolled up in a carpet in order to restrain him. Not long afterwards Jack Charles was taken into a mental institution where he remained for many years. This only came out in 1990 on the occasion of Charles' recent passing, during the time of Robert's induction into the Canadian Aviation Hall of Fame.

Jack Charles had undoubtedly been affected by the strain of combat flying during the war, and there is little doubt that at this time Robert too almost broke down. For some days he became very strange as far as Barbara was concerned, and she very nearly called in a doctor. She is certain that had she done so, things might have turned out very differently. That chink in Robert's armour, prised open on Malta, had nearly ripped him apart, but he overcame it once again, although from then on he seemed a very different Robert to that which she had known in England.

* * *

**More Jet Flying**
By the summer of 1948 Robert was flying Vampires, Harvards and C45s (Beech Expeditors) and during December went on to the P80C and then the F80 Shooting Star. These types, as well as a F86 Sabre jet, appeared in his logbook during 1949, plus a few more trips in Lancasters, all while still with Airforce HQ. In June 1950 he returned to England briefly, even flying a Meteor from his old Biggin Hill stamping ground. In August he was given command of Lachine, Montreal, within Training Command.

Wing Commander Campbell Mussels had been the previous CO of Lachine (a wartime bomber pilot who had won the DFC with 405 Squadron RCAF), and the McNairs found upon arrival that their quarter was not ready. However, Jean Mussels (formally of the Bonner family of Montreal) had a country house at Hudson Heights so let them live there for a few weeks, Robert commuting to and from the base, a journey of around 1½ hours. In due course the quarter was made ready and the family moved in.

No. 426 Squadron RCAF was the resident squadron at Lachine, a unit that would fly a good deal of air-lifting sorties to Korea and Japan during the conflict that had begun shortly before, in June 1950. It was a pretty dull time for Robert at Lachine, the only good thing about it was that he was not far from St Hubert where he could borrow aircraft to fly.

Not that he had very exciting aeroplanes to fly. Mostly it was a C54, Beech Expeditor. However, in October he managed a trip in a Vampire for an hour. Then in late October, and into November he was driven around in a four-engined North Star, including a tour of the Pacific in mid-month. Campbell Mussels gave him an air test and some duel before the trip and then, with Flight Lieutenant Bell as captain, they left on the 6th for Fairfield Suisen. The route then covered Hickam Field, Hawaii, Johnston Islands, Kwajelein, Guam in the Marianas, Okinawa, Haneda, Shemya, Naknek, Kodiak (Alaska) and back to base. In all, a two-week trip.

In December and January 1951 he was flying a North Star himself, while on other flights, Bell was again the pilot. One trip was over the Arctic Bay, another to Iceland and then across to England, landing at RAF Odiham. In the early months of 1951 he flew all over the place, once going as far as

Lagens in the Azores (as first pilot). In between times he flew C54s and the occasional Vampire.

Less than a year after taking up his post at Lachine, Robert became air attaché at the Canadian Embassy in Tokyo, and liaison officer to the UN Supreme Commander, a job he held for two years. Shortly before he left to take up this appointment in Japan, Air Commodore Len Birchall spent a weekend with the McNairs to advise them how to behave with the Japanese. It would be quite a change.

# CHAPTER FOURTEEN

# FINALS

## Tokyo

Robert's posting date was 16 July 1951. The Korean War had been raging for almost a year and Japan was the United Nation's main forward base. Everything flew into Japan before going on to Korea itself, troops, supplies, aircraft.

It was no secret that Robert had been going through a period of discontentment while at Lachine. This was nothing peculiar to him, for many former wartime flyers found it difficult to adjust to a peacetime airforce. However, in Japan, he was suddenly very near another war. He would see just how near he could get.

Robert went off at once, Barbara and the boys following in September. They had had a second son – Keith – in February 1949. By the time she arrived – via Wake Island, a trip that had taken three days – she found that Robert had no proper quarter, and had been living in a hotel. It seems that he had upset someone and things were being delayed. With his family now with him, they were moved into the Maranuchi Hotel for a few weeks, until they found a Japanese-style house to rent. The hotel was used as an R & R place, run by the Australians.

A Japanese house, of course, had no bath in the western sense. Water was heated, then ladled over oneself, the water draining away through a hole in the floor. All the doors were sliding panels and all the furniture was low-level. The two little boys thought everything great fun. However, after Barbara had collared someone with a bit of authority, they finally managed to move into a proper quarter, a four-bedroomed house with a garden. While in Tokyo the McNairs had to follow the usual embassies' circuit of cocktail parties and receptions, meeting and making many friends from other countries.

Meantime, Rob was being allowed to fly to bases in Korea, usually for periods of about ten days a month. This was in his official capacity as air attaché, as well as Far East Air Force Tokyo, under General O P Weyland (who with his wife Tinker also became firm friends of Robert and Ba), and as UN representative the latter entailing UN liaison duties. It was not long before Wing Commander McNair was getting himself truly involved.

While it is difficult to be exact as to what he became involved with, his logbook seems to indicate a sortie in a C54 Skymaster in September during a parachute drop, and two air evacuation missions over the next two days, one in a C119 and another in a C47. In October there was a more sober flight, and one more in keeping with his official job, taking Mr Menzies, the Australian Prime Minister, to the Korean base at K14.

In January 1952 he was hobnobbing with the Americans again, managing to talk himself onto flights in USAF B29 Superfortress bombers. From that vantage point it was an easy step to get himself onto a bombing mission, in fact in April he seems to have flown on two raids. From then on it was a mixture of flights to and from Korea and Japan, in a variety of aircraft. Then came a week-long trip in a C118 Fairchild Packet in February to Guam, Kwajelein, Hawaii, Wake and back, for which Robert checked out as second pilot. In April he flew to the Philippines. The first leg was in a wartime B17 Fortress to Clark air force base, then in a C47 to Luzon. The following month he flew in a Fortress to the Philippines again, landing at Clark and Anderson AFBs.

There was another Pacific tour in early July, again in a B17, this time to Wake, then down to Truk before visiting Hawaii. However, the fun stopped in July 1953; the Korean war came to an end just as he got back to Japan.

Meantime, Barbara had had several problems in Tokyo. Between Robert disappearing off to Korea, or wherever, she was soldiering on with a Japanese servant who had no English and having to cope with two small boys who were beginning a run of the usual childhood illnesses and ailments.

Bruce, the eldest, went down with mastoids. To cap this, Keith was involved in an accident at a hotel Ba had gone to with some friends while Robert was away. He had fallen onto a marble slab, which pushed his nose right into his face. This necessitated a period in hospital but he made a full recovery. Unbeknown to Barbara, the effects of mastoids often left a child with a form of deafness. Not knowing this, she was finding that Bruce's work at school was going downhill, and that the Japanese teacher, also oblivious of the problem, was starting to complain of his inattentive and seemingly disruptive attitude. Even Barbara was becoming concerned at Bruce's lack of response at home, especially to parental guidance. It was only much later that she learnt of the deafness problem, and suddenly all became clear. Then, when Keith came out of hospital, he went down with an attack of mumps.

Between times, Barbara worked with the Grey Ladies in 1952, part of the American Red Cross, helping with severe casualties from Korea – mostly head injuries, or those with multiple limb loss. Her help was not medical but dealing with the personal needs of the injured, contacting families, reading and writing letters for those unable to do this for themselves. It was a difficult time for her in many ways. It was forbidden to get too involved with the soldiers, many of whom, she knew, would not survive their ordeal, or if they did, would not survive long once sent home.

Head of this organisation in Tokyo was Margaret Ryan, an American from Ohio, who was held in high esteem, and someone who remained a friend of fellow Grey Ladies for many years after she retired and went to Washington DC as a member of the World Health Organisation. She travelled all over the world to meet up with old colleagues, visiting Barbara McNair in Montreal and later in England in 1969. A devout Roman Catholic, Margaret Ryan had the ability to calm any situation, being full of wisdom and charm. She was a most remarkable human being, a great character so full of life and fun.

## Back to Canada

According to one set of records, Robert McNair was posted back to Canada on 3 September 1953 to become sector commander of No.1 ADCC at Lac St Denis. However, a note in Robert's logbook indicated that his posting date was 13 October. Unless he missed some vital telegram or letter, the latter date seems more likely, because during September 1953 he was still flying around the Pacific.

In a Vickers Valetta he was flown from Japan to Okinawa, then to the Philippines, and then north to Hong Kong, stopping long enough to fly a Vampire at Kai Tak. Whilst at Hong Kong he got himself aboard an RAF Hastings aircraft to fly to Singapore and went on supply drops over Malaya in Valetta aircraft on 12, 13 and 14 September, for this was a period of unrest in this country, and British troops were 'in country'. The next day he was in an RAF Lincoln, bombing and machine-gunning communist guerrillas. It was becoming a case of: 'Is this a private war or can anyone join in?'

Posted back to Canada, Robert McNair decided to take the long route home, aboard ship. In the early evening of 17 September he boarded MS *Willem Kuys* and headed for Southampton, via stops at Colombo, passing through the Red Sea, Naples, Gibraltar, and England, arriving on 6 October. In England he took the opportunity of visiting Barbara's parents at Gerrards Cross and then on the 11th he climbed into a RCAF North Star at North Luffenham, flying via Prestwick to Iceland. Next day he headed for Goose Bay and Dorval.

\* \* \*

As it became clear that Robert was returning to Canada, Barbara set off at the start of September with the object of getting Bruce into a proper school. Once again Mary Buckerfield came to her aid (she had since married and become divorced) and gave Barbara the loan of her house at Kerrisdale, Vancouver. She was then not only able to put Bruce into a local school but Keith, now four, into a nearby nursery school run by a Mrs Wynn. Barbara was able to help Mrs Wynn half a day a week, which was a comfort for Keith and gave her a unique view of young children, since Mrs Wynn usually had two dozen youngsters at any one time.

Meantime, Robert had taken up his appointment at Lac St Denis. He was still able to get in some flying, mostly from St Hubert, flying aboard North Stars and C47s, whilst also piloting Expeditors and the odd Vampire.

It was no secret that Robert McNair was able to make friends readily, friendships that generally lasted. One such was with Moses Rothman who remembers:

> 'My friendship with Buck McNair came about in fortuitous circumstances. I am in the film business and my very good friend in those days was none other than Gary Cooper. I convinced 'Coop' that he should visit the RCAF Headquarters at Biggin Hill, where they had a rather large hospital to look

after the remnants of the RCAF still in England. This included a transport run by the RCAF to Montreal every day of the week. I promised the commander of the base that I would bring Gary for a personal visit, as he was filming in London and would stop by as a gesture of good cheer to the patients.

'The quid pro quo was a seat for me on the daily transport to Montreal – one way only – and so it was that I found myself for eight hours sitting opposite none other than Group Captain Robert McNair! The reason I use the exclamation mark is that for four and a half years I was in the lowest of ranks in the RCAF that could be possible, namely LAC, and here I was ensconced with a very famous group captain, with all the medals that he had earned and that his rank accorded him. Suffice to say that by the time we got off the plane in Montreal I was quite sold on this very handsome and charming man, who also turned out to be a great raconteur.

'My purpose in going to Montreal was to see my lady friend of the moment in New York and Buck and I later flew there together, which was in itself a very enjoyable pause away from my workaday chores. Our friendship continued in New York and I had the pleasure of introducing him to my lady friend and we became quite close. There was no question of my having to ask any favours from anybody at RCAF HQ in Montreal, because Buck volunteered and obtained a seat for me on my return trip.

'I cannot speak highly enough of a man who gave so generously of his time and his gesture of friendship was all encompassing. Of all the dozens of people I meet in my business, I cannot find anyone to compare with Buck McNair. That he later underwent such physical pain for so long a period of time was heart rending and I know from his wife how he withstood the anguish and the pain that he suffered. He will forever remain in my memory as the wonderful soul that he was.'

Mo Rothman had joined *United Artists* in 1952, and one of the films he was involved with at this time was the famous Cooper classic, *High Noon*.

\* \* \*

Robert missed the family Christmas that year, but managed to travel home just before New Year, but again, he had to miss these festivities as he had to return to base on 30 December. In the event, he never made it.

## The North Star Crash
It was an unexpected visit home and Barbara was taken by surprise. She was disappointed that Robert wouldn't be able to stay on a couple of days, and on the morning of the 30th he left for Vancouver Airport to pick up a 426 Squadron North Star aircraft.

For those not familiar with the Canadian name of North Star, this machine was basically a four-engined DC-4 transport aeroplane, but with Merlin engines. Thus it became the C54M, but known more familiarly as the North Star in Canada.

The aircraft – 17503 – took off at around 9.30 am, piloted by Flight Lieutenant John Evans. It was a scheduled flight from Vancouver to Montreal, via Edmonton. Service personnel and their families were either returning east after the Christmas break or going off on leave for New Year. Thirty-five minutes into the flight the number-four engine began to overheat and Evans decided to turn back. The aircraft had full fuel tanks and some freight so he knew he would be risking things to get over the Rockies on three engines. It was raining heavily and visibility was only marginal. Heavy icing added to the pilot's problems, increasing the stalling speed as he came back in; then the engine failed. The pilot had already called the tower to say he had a problem, and the fire and crash teams were alerted and ready.

Evans came in on instruments through the murk, and finally saw the airfield ahead. As he touched down at 1013 on the long east-west runway, first the nose-wheel and then the starboard wing hit the ground. The wheel buckled, the wing snapped off and the aircraft flipped right over onto its back, then proceeded to slide along the ground in a shower of sparks the length of the runway, finally going off the cement, before coming to a halt on the rain-soaked grass just short of the crash tenders. Petrol was streaming from ruptured tanks but while some passengers were quickly getting free and climbing out, others were suspended upside down in their seat belts. Despite the petrol, one fireman later recalled seeing some of those who'd got out, standing round, a little dazed, lighting up cigarettes!

Meantime, flames erupted from the problem engine, which had sheared off, but prompt action by the airfield fire crews, prevented the flames spreading to the spilled petrol. A second engine was also ripped off and lay several yards away.

All 52 people aboard the North Star found themselves upside down. Nearly all were servicemen, women and children. Releasing themselves with some difficulty they began escaping through broken windows and gaping holes in the fuselage.

Robert McNair was quick to aid his fellow passengers. Within seconds he was free and helping others not so familiar with aeroplanes, (especially one upside down, since the seats were now above them) out of the wrecked machine, through the broken sides by the bulkheads which had split. His clothes were soaked in aviation fuel, but he continually went back into the battered fuselage to help more people escape, despite the burning engine and the imminent danger of a fuselage fire. Fortunately there was no loss of life and only a few were injured. Most suffered cuts and bruises, but nothing very serious.

At home, Barbara had neither television nor radio and knew nothing of the drama being enacted a few miles away. Finally someone telephoned later in the day to say how proud she must be of her husband. Barbara, bemused, asked what on earth he was talking about. Only then did she hear of the crash.

Later still, Robert telephoned to confirm she still had a husband, although few details had emerged. When he eventually arrived home, smelling of petrol, she was still not totally aware of how serious the crash had been. Of course, Robert had once again come into his own. He was always at his best in an emergency, when courage and fortitude was needed. He had injured his own back, which was to give him some trouble for several months but for his heroism that December morning he later received the Queen's Commendation for Brave Conduct.

* * *

Life settled down once more. In the summer of 1954 Barbara finally joined Robert at Lac St Denis. She had been reluctant to expose the boys to the other youths on the base, and had wanted to get Bruce back on track, but eventually the move had had to come. Robert was also starting to complain about the shortness of money. With his family 'off base' in Vancouver he could not get family allowance from the RCAF. In addition, at St Denis he had, as Sector Commander, No.1 Sector, Air Defence Command, a four-bedroomed house, so couldn't move into the mess. The CO of the base had then turned the house into four single quarters as there was no family using it. So while Robert was not getting his full allowances he was still having to send money for the family in Vancouver.

Robert's back was better now and he began to take up skiing as the winter snows appeared. The family also had a boat too. All the family joined in skiing; Barbara did well, until she had an accident some time later, which damaged a knee and her confidence.

## Baden-Baden

Robert soldiered on at Lac St Denis for a further two and a half years. He was still able to keep his hand in flying, mostly North Stars plus Expeditors and T.33 jet trainers. In mid-1956 he began flying the CF-100 IVB (Canadair Silver Star), mainly with 423 (AW) F Squadron RCAF. At the end of October 1956, the squadron commander, Wing Commander J Lecomte, wrote in Robert's logbook: 'G/C McNair has shown outstanding qualities as a pilot and he has set a fine example to all aircrew in this squadron.'

He continued these qualites during 1957 too, mostly T.33s and CF100s, also adding an F86 Mark VI Sabre in April which he noted as a 'wonderful flying machine.' However in May he had a gall bladder problem resulting in an operation, and he did not get home until 9 June. Robert became desperately ill with this problem going into the Queen Mary Veterans' Hospital to have two operations. First a laparotomy then the gall bladder removal. He came to with tubes sticking out all over the place.

This naturally kept him out of the cockpit until mid-July. However, by August things were about to change. A note in his logbook simply says: 'Turned in all flying gear 12 August.' He'd been posted.

Group Captain McNair's new appointment was as commanding officer to No.4 Fighter Wing based at Baden-Baden, Sollingen, Germany. He sailed from Montreal aboard the *Homeric* on 21 August. Barbara had sailed into Southampton a couple of months earlier, not having visited home in 11 years, and then moved out to Germany as Robert was installed.

The Wing had been formed in September 1953, and Robert was its third

OC. Its base was in a superb setting, next to the River Rhine, with the Black Forest to the east. It had originally been built for the French Air Force, but taken over by the RCAF in 1953 for its contribution to NATO. By the time Robert took over, its three squadrons were Nos. 422, 444 and 419. The former two were day fighters with F86 Sabres, while 419 was an all-weather outfit, flying CF100s.

By the end of the month Robert had been in the air three times, once in a T.33 for a sector recco, and twice in Sabres on a visit to 2 Wing. From then on he flew whenever work allowed, paper work that is, and was in the air with whatever was available, T.33, F86 or CF100. In fact this was recorded in the station magazine:

> Our new CO, G/C R W McNair DSO DFC CD, did not waste time getting into harness. The day following his arrival at 4 Wing, he got his unit check out on the T.33 and shortly afterwards met 1/Lt Bill Pratt of the USAF who dropped into 4 Wing in the 4,000th visiting aircraft – the date was Friday, August 30th.

Al 'Red Lead' Brown was Robert's adjutant, and he was a little fearful upon meeting his new boss for the first time, especially with his superb flying record. Apparently they had no sooner met than Robert suggested they 'go fly'. Al Brown thought it meant that if he could give a good account of himself to the Group Captain, all would be well. Apparently he did!

Everyone knew, of course, of the Group Captain's dodgy eye, so the pilots who flew the target-towing aircraft during air gunnery exercises, became a trifle nervous on the occasion the Groupie was up to qualify. As Al Brown was to recall years later, he was never sure if Robert's practice of getting painfully near to the target banner before opening fire, was due to his Spitfire experience in WW2, or because of his bad eye! Whatever the reason, the result was always the same. A thoroughly tattered banner and a very agitated target-towing pilot!!

As it was a spa town it was very much a case of joining in with all the social events of the area, while Barbara busied herself with the ladies on the base. The four nearest houses to their own, which was called the White House, housed the three squadron commanders and the senior technical officer.

It was a good posting. He was able to fly a good deal, and in fact in September 1960 his flying hours topped the 4,000 mark. Mostly it was in the T.33, but he was no slouch on F86s and CF100s.

One of the 4 Wing pilots who recalls the McNairs is Serge Morin, of Montreal:

> 'I arrived at 4 Fighter Wing on 28 January 1959 as a bachelor flying officer, and started operational training the following day. Group Captain McNair was our CO.
>
> 'I was introduced to him at a TGIF reception the following week. G/C McNair was certainly the most notorious fighter pilot and the most highly appreciated Canadian Commanding

Officer of the Air Division in Europe. A few weeks later, I was introduced to his charming wife, Barbara. As I was to discover in the following months, both Barbara and Robert had a special consideration for young officers without family in Europe, and we were often invited to their home for dinner.

'Robert was also very sportive and I recall several weekends where he would join us to play tennis. We were on the court, and he would arrive, sometimes with his sons Bruce and Keith, and spend a few hours of pleasant competition.

'I also had the pleasure to fly one or two training missions on Sabres with him. It was said that during the war, he had been injured in an air fight over the Channel, and had lost part of his vision from one eye. If this was true, let me tell you that it was also a well known fact for all who flew Sabre missions with him, that his vision from the other eye was outstanding, for we were amazed how he could pick the most minute speck on the horizon and call its position. We could understand why he had achieved such an outstanding record on the Spitfire.

'Another anecdote I would like to mention is when the McNairs left 4 Wing to return to Canada in September 1961. The bachelors wanted to mark the special attentions we had received from them. At the gate of the base, those of us that were not on duty made a row of honour for their departure. While they stopped to bid us a last farewell, we hung on their back trailer a "just married" sign. I remember Barbara's laughter when she related how they finally discovered the prank.

'When I returned to Canada, Robert was SASO at St Hubert near Montreal. I had been posted to my old alma mater College Militaire Royal de St Jean. Again I recall several visits to their home. But I also had great pleasure to receive them one Saturday for an afternoon of skiing on the Richelieu River. I had a small outboard, which was equipped for this sport. Robert had never water-skied before and showed the same determination in learning that he had demonstrated in all his other endeavours. After several dives, he then emerged as a very good skier by the end of the afternoon.'

* * *

Much of Robert's time, of course, was spent running an important overseas base. But there were lots of other things happening, in what was comparable, really, to a small military town. No. 4 Wing's monthly magazine *Schwarzwald Flieger* (Black Forest Flyer) was full of pictures of Robert presenting a whole variety of trophies, ranging from hockey, curling, track and field events to tennis, golf and basketball, not to mention the flying ones. One of the latter was the Lloyd Chadburn Trophy, which 4 Wing won several times during the Sabre era. And there were not many men in 4 Wing who could say with pride that they had actually flown with the man in whose memory this trophy named. But McNair could!

There were also a plethora of visiting VIPs, big-wigs and dignatories. Among those who came during Robert's period in command were the Right Honourable George Drew, Canadian High Commissioner to the UK, the Chief of the Air Staff, Air Marshal Hugh Campbell, Air Chief Marshal (RAF) the Earl of Bandon, Doctor Adenauer, the German Chancellor, with minister Herr Kiesinger, and, in August 1957, just as he'd taken over the Wing, His Royal Highness the Duke of Windsor.

The McNairs also met the then Canadian Prime Minister, Mr John Deifenbaker, who made a visit to the Wing. He invited both Robert and Barbara to visit him at his official residence in Ottawa, which they did in 1963. Bruce went too and it was a great honour. Another of the McNair's favourite visitors was The Right Honorable Douglas Harkness who was Minister of National Defence, and Conservative MP for Calgary under John Deifenbaker. Douglas and his lovely wife Fran came for an official visit to Baden-Sollingen and a friendship was begun. Barbara was able to continue the friendship in Canada after Robert's death.

Douglas and Fran entertained Barbara in 1971 in the House of Commons at lunch and some years later she was a house guest in Calgary, where son Keith and family were living, Keith working with Shell. Douglas had an army background but Robert and he shared many similar views on military matters, defence in particular. A good deal of interesting exchanges of views took place in Germany and it was unfortunate that they could not have continued in Canada.

* * *

The following summer – 1958 – Robert was posted back home, to St Huberts. He was not over-happy with this move as he had wanted to go to the Imperial Defence College.

His new job was at NNR HQ, as D/Ops-DCC, a position he took up on 21 September 1961. This was a radar job and one of his first tasks was to go down to Syracuse, New York, for a crash course on the latest developments. The McNairs were here till the early summer of 1964, and Robert took another post at St Huberts on 1 June 1963, as Senior Air Staff Officer at Air Defence Centre HQ.

Finally, in July 1964, they left St Huberts to go down to Deluth, in the United States. Robert took a post at Sector HQ of NORAD, under Colonel Dowling, as Deputy Commander. Duluth, Minnesota, is at the south-western tip of Lake Superior, south of Grand Rapids, right next to the town of Superior, in neighbouring Wisconsin. Minnesota is known as the State of a Thousand Lakes, so it was a wonderful place for Robert and the two boys to hunt, shoot and fish, as they had done at Lac St Denis. They could also water-ski in the summer, and in the winter, snow-ski. Robert had taken up golf late in life but nevertheless enjoyed playing the game.

**Back to London**
Robert had been suffering more and more with his back for some time. Those bale-outs into the Channel, especially the one where he had dropped those

last feet into the water, landing on his back, had not been helped by the North Star crash at Sea Island, BC. The medics had diagnosed spinal damage which, if left untreated, would gradually produce a curvature of the spine. Given the choice of walking with a distinct and increasing stoop, or upright, Robert naturally chose the latter. As far back as 1955 he had been diagnosed as having Mariestrumpell, a calcifying of the spinal column. He had attended Doctor Bouchard at his neurological institute in Montreal, which eventually led to painful radiation and cobolt treatment in 1956.

This, in time, sadly produced a blood disorder, which in turn developed into leukaemia by November 1965. With this shattering news, especially in one so active and full of life, came the real blow; it was terminal and he could expect to survive only a further two and a half to three years.

There was never any question of Robert moping into a corner. He did not even want to retire. His life was the RCAF and within it he had his friends. Barbara, obviously bearing up under the severe shock, asked him if he would like to retire and do some of the things he had not yet done in life. However, he preferred to stay in harness, get on with the jobs in hand, and live what life remained with his family and friends. For her part, Barbara was determined to nurse Robert with all her strength, and it was as much to her love and care, as with the medical treatment he now began to undertake, that the period of life extended to five and a half years.

On 1 August 1968 they were posted to the Canadian High Commission in London. Robert in fact was offered two High Commission jobs, one in Bonn, Germany, the other in London. Robert chose London. He had met Barbara in London, and it seemed fitting that they should live the rest of their life together in the same locality. There were no illusions. He knew perfectly well there was no miracle cure. He was dying.

They flew to Ottawa, then took a plane from Rockcliffe to Gatwick. Quarters in the High Commission in Grosvenor Square were not yet ready for occupation, so they lived for several months in the RAF Club, thanks to the good offices of Sir Dermot Boyle, who managed to have the club rules bent slightly. Then they found a furnished flat at Eaton House, Grosvenor Street before they finally moved into the High Commission building, at No.1 Grosvenor Square, in May 1969, taking Flat 60.

Once in London, Robert came under the care of a team of specialists at the Post Graduate School of Medicine, Hammersmith. He continued with his High Commission work, as Senior Air Liasion Officer at CDLS, London, for the next two and a half years. Gradually his condition worsened but he never gave up. He was too much in love with life for that; ever the fighter. He even managed an official visit to Malta in September 1970, the first time he'd been back to the island since those traumatising days in 1942. His face was thinner but there was no difference in his smile. Son Keith accompanied him.

His illness at last forced him into the hospital on 3 January 1971. He died on the 15th, Barbara and Bruce close by. There was a memorial service in the RAF church of St Clement Danes, in the Strand, which Rod Smith flew over from Canada to attend. Tommy Parks was there too, the man who had helped rescue him from the Channel in 1943. Rod Smith:

'I arrived on the Sunday and that afternoon went to the flat in

Grosvenor Square. At about 4 o'clock Barbara asked me to go with her and Group Captain Rogers RAF, and his wife, to St Clement Danes to arrange with the Assistant Chaplain of the RAF details of the funeral.

'The four of us sat with the Padre and he made some suggestions on hymns etc. He asked what was Buck's main characteristic, and Barbara said bravery. I added that he was also a superb leader. The big thing about Buck was that he had the 'Nelson touch' as a leader. I have the happiest and finest memories of him. He certainly added a lot of inspiring and exciting times to my life and we all remember him that way.

'At the actual service lots of air attaché people, and others, attended, all in uniform. Mike Donnet made a superb speech, then we went out to Runnymede, the RAF Memorial. On our way we drove down the Strand by Trafalgar Square, under Admiralty Arch and along the Mall. As we did so I could see the back of the Duke of York monument in Lower Regent Street, which brought memories rushing back of Buck when he and I came out of the underground that day in 1941 and looked down Lower Regent Street to see our first view of war-time London; rather a sad moment.'

Robert was buried at Brookwood Cemetery with full military honours. As everyone gathered around the grave at the end of the interment, a lone aeroplane flew over their heads and waggled its wings. Barbara never discovered who arranged it, probably an RAF pal of Rob's. It was a very moving moment.

Robert 'Buck' McNair had lost his last fight, but one which he had fought and lost with dignity and with the same bravery and fortitude he had shown in wartime.

Valhalla is full of such men.

# HALL OF FAME

Canada's Aviation Hall of Fame was founded in 1973 by two famous Canadians, Punch Dickins (one of the first two flyers who had flown 4,300 km from Winnipeg into the sub-arctic in 1929) and Ray Munro. It is dedicated to documenting, preserving and publicising the achievements of Canadians whose contribution to aviation are or have been of benefit to the nation.

The Hall of Fame was situated in Edmonton's Convention Centre, which also housed the most extensive aviation reference library in western Canada. It later moved to the transport museum at Wetaskiwin, about 60 miles south of Edmonton.

It is not easy to be inducted. In fact it took two friends of Robert McNair 11 years to become so. These two were N J 'Buzz' Ogilvie[1], a former wartime RCAF fighter pilot, and Louis Leigh, who had been a pre-war Canadian bush pilot. Noel Ogilvie, in fact, had been on Malta with 185 Squadron, and was actually among the pilots led to Malta from Gib by Buck on 18 May 1942. Among the auguste list of the Hall of Fame inductees are such names as William Barker VC, Andrew Mynarski VC, Ian Bazelgette VC, David Hornell VC, Ray Collishaw, Russ Bannock and Robert's former CO, Stan Turner.

Once his name had proceeded through the various channels and committees, it was finally admitted to the list during an official ceremony at the Convention Centre on 8 June 1990. Barbara and Keith were invited over as guests of honour, an address of welcome being made by the National Board Chairman, Russ Bannock DSO DFC.

It was a proud moment for Barbara and his son Keith as they stood by the screen on which Robert's picture hung, and the citation of entry read:

**His leadership, courage, dedication and his indomitable will
to survive were manifestations of his contribution to
Canadian aviation.**

---

[1] Robert was godfather to Buzz Ogilvie's daughter Donna.

# RECORD OF SERVICE

| | |
|---|---|
| No.1 Manning Depot, Toronto | 28 Jun 1940 – 5 Jul 1940 |
| No.1 ITW, Toronto | 5 Jul 1940 – 5 Oct 1940 |
| No.7 EFTS, Windsor | 5 Oct 1940 – 1 Dec 1940 |
| No.31 SFTS, Kingston | 1 Dec 1940 – 21 Mar 1941 |
| Embarkation Depot, Debert | 21 Mar 1941 – 15 Apr 1941 |
| No.1 PRC, Uxbridge, UK | 2 May 1941 – 10 May 1941 |
| No.58 OTU, Grangemouth | 10 May 1941 – 21 Jun 1941 |
| No.411 Squadron, Digby | 21 Jun 1941 – 18 Feb 1942 |
| No.249 Squadron, Malta | 21 Feb 1942 – 27 Jun 1942 |
| No.411 Squadron, Digby | 1 Jul 1942 – 21 Sep 1942 |
| RAF Hospital, Rouceby | 21 Sep 1942 – Oct 1942 |
| Canada – bond tours | Oct 1942 – Nov 1942 |
| No.133 Squadron, Vancouver | 1 Dec 1942 – |
| No.403 Squadron, Kenley | Apr 1943 – May 1943 |
| No.416 Squadron, Wellingore | May 1943 – 18 Jun 1943 |
| No.421 Squadron, Kenley/Headcorn | 18 Jun 1943 – 15 Oct 1943 |
| OC 126 Wing, Biggin Hill | 15 Oct 1943 – 12 Apr 1944 |
| 17 Wing HQ, W/C Ops | 15 Apr 1944 – 1 Jul 1944 |
| R Depot, President Spec Cases | 1 Jul 1944 – 31 Dec 1944 |
| RAF Staff College | 1 Jan 1945 – 19 Jun 1945 |
| OC RAF Calvely | 20 Jun 1945 – 30 Jul 1945 |
| RCAF HQ, P Staff | 30 Jul 1945 – 1946 |
| WAC, Vancouver | 20 Aug 1946 – 2 Nov 1946 |
| AFHQ DOR/ORF, Ottawa | 2 Nov 1946 – 12 Aug 1950 |
| OC Lachine, Training Command | 13 Aug 1950 – 16 Jul 1951 |
| Air Attaché, Tokyo | 16 Jul 1951 – 3 Sep 1953 |
| 1 ADCC, Lac St Denis | 3 Sep 1953 – 20 Aug 1957 |
| OC No.4(F) Wing, Germany | 20 Aug 1957 – 14 Sep 1961 |
| NNR HQ, St Hubert. D/Ops DCC | 21 Sep 1961 – 1 Jun 1963 |
| ADC HQ & SASO | 1 Jun 1963 – 29 Jul 1964 |
| Duluth NORAD, Sector HQ | 29 Jul 1964 – Jul 1968 |
| Canadian High Commission, London | 2 Aug 1968 – 15 Jan 1971 |

APPENDIX B

# CITATIONS

**Distinguished Flying Cross**
*London Gazette: 11 May 1942*
This officer is a skilful and courageous pilot. He invariably presses home his attacks with the greatest determination irrespective of the odds. He has destroyed at least five and damaged seven enemy aircraft; four of these he damaged in one combat.

**Bar to Distinguished Flying Cross**
*London Gazette: 30 July 1943*
This officer is a skilful and determined fighter, whose record of achievement and personal example are worthy of high praise. Squadron Leader McNair has destroyed ten hostile aircraft (five of them whilst serving in the Middle East) and damaged a number of others.

**Second Bar to Distinguished Flying Cross**
*London Gazette: 26 October 1943*
Squadron Leader McNair is a tenacious and confident fighter, whose outstanding ability has proved an inspiration to the squadron he commands. He has completed a large number of sorties and has destroyed 15 and damaged many other enemy aircraft. His keenness has been outstanding.

**Distinguished Service Order**
*London Gazette: 14 April 1944*
Since being awarded a second Bar to the Distinguished Flying Cross, Wing Commander McNair has completed many further operational sorties and destroyed another enemy aircraft, bringing his total victories to at least 16 enemy aircraft destroyed and many others damaged. As officer commanding his Wing he has been responsible for supervising intensive training in tactics. The results achieved have been most satisfactory. The Wing under his leadership, destroyed at least thirteen enemy aircraft. Throughout, Wing Commander McNair has set a magnificent example by his fine fighting spirit, courage and devotion to duty both in the air and on the ground. He has inspired his pilots with confidence and enthusiasm.

**Croix de Guerre avec Palme (France)**
*Canada Gazette: 20 September 1947*

**Chevalier de la Légion d'Honneur (France)**
*Canada Gazette: 20 September 1947*

**Queen's Commendation for Brave Conduct**
*Canada Gazette: 7 August 1954*
Wing Commander McNair was flying as a crew member in one of the crew rest positions of North Star 17503 when it crashed at Vancouver, British Columbia, on 30 December 1953. The aircraft ended its crash landing run in an inverted position and as a result, all crew and passengers found themselves suspended in mid-air in an upside down position. Self-preservation was uppermost in the minds of practically everyone because of the imminent danger of fire or explosion but Wing Commander McNair, cognisant of the large number of passengers being carried and the state of turmoil that must be existing, threw caution to the winds, remained in the aircraft and fought his way to the passenger compartment. Here, he set to work, restored calm and through prodigious effort assisted all passengers in evacuating the aircraft as quickly as possible. Still not content, Wing Commander McNair remained in the aircraft and personally searched through the debris on the off chance that someone might have been overlooked. Only then did he abandon the aircraft. It is to be remembered that this officer was soaked in gasoline at the time of this incident from an overturned Herman Nelson heater, a condition which would immediately bring to mind the fact that he had been badly burned by fire in his aircraft during the war and therefore should have been acutely aware of his precarious position under the present set of circumstances. The fact that the aircraft did not explode or did not take fire should not be allowed to detract in any way from the magnitude of Wing Commander McNair's deeds, for it was only by an act of God that neither calamity occurred.

APPENDIX C

# AWARDS AND MEDALS

Distinguished Service Order

Distinguished Flying Cross and Two Bars

Queen's Commendation for Brave Conduct

Chevalier de la Légion d'Honneur

French Croix de Guerre avec Palme

1939-1945 Star

Air Crew Europe Star with France and Germany Clasp

Africa Star

Defence Medal

Canadian Voluntary Service Medal with Bar

(The silver bar with a maple leaf upon it denotes service outside Canada)

1939-45 War Medal

Korean War Medal with Oak Leaf

(The oak leaf denotes a Mention in Despatches)

United Nations Korean War Medal

Coronation Medal

Canadian Long Service Medal

(Generally presented after 12 or 15 years' service, although war service
counted double)

# VICTORIES

| Date | Type | Claim | Duty | Sqn | Spit | Loss |
|------|------|-------|------|-----|------|------|
| *1941* | | | | | | |
| 27 Sep | Me109F | damaged | Sweep | 411 | P8263/C | |
| 13 Oct | Me109F | **Destroyed** | Sweep | 411 | P7679/F | |
| ,, | Me109F | damaged | ,, | 411 | ,, | |
| *1942* | | | | | | |
| 18 Mar | Me109F | damaged | Scramble | 249 | GN-B | |
| 20 Mar | Me109F | **Destroyed** | Scramble | 249 | E | 7/JG53 |
| 26 Mar | Ju88A4 | **Destroyed** | Scramble | 249 | H | 3/KGr806 (6547) crash-landed, one crewman killed |
| ,, | Ju88 | probable | ,, | 249 | H | |
| ,, | Ju88 | damaged | ,, | 249 | H | |
| 20 Apr | Me109F | **Destroyed** | Scramble | 249 | K | I/JG53 |
| ,, | Me109F | probable | ,, | 249 | K | |
| ,, | Ju88 | damaged | ,, | 249 | K | |
| 22 Apr | Ju88A4 | **Destroyed** | Scramble | 249 | BP968/N | 6/KG77 |
| 25 Apr | Ju87 | damaged | Scramble | 249 | P | |
| ,, | Ju88 | damaged | ,, | 249 | P | |
| ,, | Me109F | damaged | ,, | 249 | P | |
| ,, | Me109F | damaged | ,, | 249 | P | |
| 22 May | Me109F | **Destroyed** | Scramble | 249 | BR176/C25 | |
| 25 May | Me109F | **Destroyed** | Scramble | 249 | BR109/C30 | |
| 10 Jun | Me109F4 | **Destroyed** | Scramble | 249 | BR107/C22 | 5/JG53 (7591) |
| 19 Jul | Do217E4 | damaged | Patrol | 411 | BL750 | II/KG40 (4278) |
| 19 Aug | Me109F | damaged | Patrol | 411 | BL735 | |
| ,, | FW190 | probable | Patrol | 411 | ,, | |
| 20 Aug | FW190 | damaged | Sweep | 411 | BL735 | |
| | | | | | | |
| *1943* | | | | | | |
| 20 Jun | FW190A4 | **Destroyed** | Circus 313 | 421 | EN398 | 4/JG26 (2372) |
| 24 Jun | FW190A5 | **Destroyed** | Ramrod 106 | 421 | BS152/P | I/JG2 damaged |
| 6 Jul | Me109G6 | **Destroyed** | Rodeo 240 | 421 | MA586/N | 3/JG27 |
| 9 Jul | Me109G | damaged | Rodeo 243 | 421 | ,, | |
| 10 Jul | Me109G6 | **Destroyed** | Ramrod 128 | 421 | ,, | 12/JG2 (15293) |
| 25 Aug | FW190 | damaged | Ramrod 15A | 421 | MA831/M | |

| 31 Aug | Me109G | **Destroyed** | Ramrod S17 | 421 | „ | |
| 3 Sep | Me109G6 | **Destroyed** | Ramrod S26 | 421 | „ | JG2 |
| 5 Sep | Me109G | damaged | Ramrod S33 | 421 | „ | |
| 6 Sep | FW190A6 | **Destroyed** | Ramrod S35 | 421 | „ | 1/JG2 (550536) |
| 3 Oct | FW190A5 | **Destroyed** | Ramrod 257 | 421 | „ | JG2 |

**16 destroyed**
10 Me109s
4 FW190s
2 Ju88s

**3 probables**
2 Ju88s
1 FW190

**15 damaged**
8 Me109s
3 Ju88s
2 FW190s
1 Ju87
1 Do217

APPENDIX E

# SPITFIRES FLOWN BY BUCK MCNAIR

MK II, DB-F, 411 SQ, P7679.

MK V, GN-N, 249 SQ, BP968.

MK V, DB-L, 411 SQ, BL735.

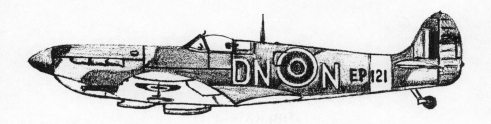

MK V, DN-N, 416 SQ, EP121.

MK IX, AU-M, 421 SQ, MA831.

MK IX, RWM.

# BIBLIOGRAPHY

*Spitfires over Malta*, by Paul Brennan and Ray Hesselyn, Jarrolds, 1943.
*Wing Leader*, by Johnnie Johnson, Chatto & Windus, 1956.
*Lucky Thirteen*, by Hugh Godefroy, Croom Helm, 1983.
*Malta, The Spitfire Year 1942*, by Chris Shores, Brian Cull and Nicola Malizia, Grub Street, 1991.
*Malta, The Thorn in Rommel's Side*, by Laddie Lucas, Stanley Paul, 1992.
*Flying Canucks II*, by Peter Pigott, Hounslow Press.
*RAF Fighter Command 1936-1968*, by Norman Franks, PSL, 1992.
*Aces High*, by Chris Shores and Clive Williams, Grub Street, 1994.

# INDEX OF PERSONNEL